Access to Justice

Harry M. Scoble
and
Laurie S. Wiseberg
(editors)

Access to Justice

Human Rights Struggles in

South East Asia

Edited for
Human Rights Internet
by
Harry M. Scoble
and
Laurie S. Wiseberg

Zed Books Ltd.

Access to Justice was first published by Zed Books Ltd., 57
Caledonian Road, London N1 9BU, in 1985

Copyright © Harry M. Scoble and Laurie S. Wiseberg, 1985

Cover design by Lee Robinson
Printed by The Pitman Press, Bath

British Library Cataloguing in Publication Data

Access to Justice: the struggle for human rights in South
East Asia.
  1. Civil rights — Asia, Southeastern
  I. Scoble, Harry M.
  II. Wiseberg, Laurie S.
  323.4'0959   JC599.A8

  ISBN 0-86232-292-8
      0-86232-293-6 Pbk

US Distributor
Biblio Distribution Center, 81 Adams Drive, Totowa, New
Jersey 07512

Contents

Tables

Notes on Contributors

(listed in the order of their contribution to this volume)

Harry M. Scoble and Laurie S. Wiseberg, editors, are both political scientists; they founded the Human Rights Internet in 1976 and have published research on human rights non-governmental organizations beginning in 1974.

Saneh Chamarik, a professor of political science, is Director of the Thai Khadi Research Institute located at Thammasat University, Bangkok, Thailand.

Remendra Nath Treverdi, practises law and is Director of the Human Rights Institute, Lucknow, India.

Buyung Nasution is Director of the Legal Aid Institute, Jakarta, Indonesia, and is also a professor of law at the University of Indonesia.

T. Mulya Lubis also teaches law at the University of Indonesia in Jakarta and serves on the legal staff of the Legal Aid Institute.

H. Johannes Cornelius Princen practises law in Indonesia and is Chairman of the Indonesian Institute for the Defence of Human Rights, in Jakarta.

Azmi Khalid is Dean of the Faculty of Law at the University of Malaya, Kuala Lumpur.

Viboon Engkagul is an attorney in private practice, Bangkok, Thailand, and a member of the Committee on Academic Affairs of the Lawyers Association of Thailand.

Jose B.L. Reyes is Professor of Constitutional Law (Emeritus), the University of the Philippines, Manila.

Chandra Muzaffar is a professor of political science in the School of Social Sciences, University of Malaysia, Penang, and also President of ALIRAN (a public affairs discussion group).

Abraham Sarmiento practises law in Manila, The Philippines.

Amarjit Kaur is a professor of history in the University of Malaya, Kuala Lumpur, Malaysia; her research publications have focused on the rights of women.

Sister Mary Soledad Perpinan (*"Sister Sol"*) is Director of IBON, a research group on issues concerning Third World development and human rights, and also of TW-MAE-W (Third World Movement Against the Exploitation of Women), both located in Manila.

Randolph S. David is professor of sociology and Director of the Third World Studies Center, University of the Philippines, Manila.

Wanee Bangprapha is a founding member of the Coordinating Group for Religion in Society, Bangkok, Thailand; her work has been directed primarily to the status of children.

Introduction

At the initiative of the Human Rights Internet (HRI), a workshop on 'Access to Justice' was held in Tagaytay, Philippines, from 14–19 February 1982. The workshop was co-sponsored by the International Human Rights Law Group, Washington, D.C., and the University of the Philippines College and Center of Law, with the co-operation of the Third World Studies Center of the University of the Philippines, the Indonesian Legal Aid Institute, and the Human Rights Institute of Lucknow, India. (Each of these organizations is more fully described at the end of this introduction.) The workshop brought together nearly 40 participants from the Philippines, Indonesia, Thailand, Malaysia (and a few from India and the United States) to discuss 'Procedures for the Implementation of Internationally-Recognized Human Rights in the ASEAN Region'. The participants included academics, lawyers, journalists, church people and other human rights advocates.

While Internet and the Law Group secured the funding and helped structure the workshop, the Asian participants prepared the working papers and defined the issues to be examined. These papers have been edited and organized, with headnotes, under three major themes: (1) Asian Perspectives on Human Rights; (2) the Present State of Human Rights in the ASEAN Nations; and (3) Particular Rights, Special Problems. The role of the non-Asian participants was largely that of resource people, particularly for information about international mechanisms and organizations that could be better exploited for rights protection.

Internet's interest in acting as a catalyst for this meeting derives from its commitment to networking as a logical complement to its information gathering and disseminating roles. In the early 1980s, it had become clear that the Asian countries were lagging behind both Africa (with its nascent Banjul Charter on Human and Peoples' Rights) and, especially, Latin America (with the Inter-American Commission and Court of Human Rights) in developing regional mechanisms for the protection of internationally-recognized human rights norms. Moreover, at the non-governmental level – given the size, the diversity and the poverty of the Asian region – opportunities for human rights advocates to meet face-to-face, to exchange information about common concerns and aspirations, had been inadequate.

Internet was in touch with many Asian human rights organizations and was aware of several indigenous Asian efforts to build regional non-governmental infrastructure. Internet hoped that this workshop might provide an opportunity for promoting NGO linkages and stimulating regional institution-building efforts: that is, it perceived its role largely as a facilitator.

It was, therefore, particularly gratifying that, during the Tagaytay workshop, a new regional human rights NGO was, indeed, created. Internet had nothing to do with its establishment. Those who proclaimed the Regional Council on Human Rights in Asia had begun to formulate their ideas several months earlier, when they had the occasion to meet during the seminar organized by the International Commission of Jurists (ICJ) and the Consumers' Association of Penang (CAP), in Malaysia, in December 1981. In this sense, the Tagaytay workshop merely facilitated another meeting of the founding members, this time in the Philippines. Thus, on 18 February 1982, the Regional Council on Human Rights in Asia was formally launched – a totally Asian effort. As its first task, the Council chose the preparation of a declaration that would emphasize the rights most relevant to the situation of the peoples of the Asian region. Nearly two years later, the Council met in Indonesia from 7 to 10 December 1983, to consider and adopt a 'Declaration of the Basic Duties of ASEAN Peoples and Governments'. Because of the importance both of this document and of the Regional Council of Human Rights in Asia, we reproduce the text of the Declaration in this volume.

Holding a human rights workshop in the Philippines in February 1982 – that is, during a period when, although martial law had been formally lifted in the Philippines, the country was still dictatorially ruled by President and Mrs Marcos – posed several problems. Related problems were posed by the fact that funding for the workshop was provided by U.S. Congressional funds, 116e money under the Foreign Assistance Act, appropriated and set aside to support the promotion of civil and political rights in the Third World. Most importantly, participants needed to be assured the seminar would not be exploited for political reasons by any government; and that the atmosphere would be conducive to a free and frank exchange of information and viewpoints.

For this reason, certain ground rules were set at the outset: that there would be no difficulties in obtaining visas for any invitees; that no government officials, from any country, would participate in the workshop; that the workshop would take place outside Manila and with no publicity; and that every effort would be made to keep the discussion free and pointed, and to focus discussion on concrete problems without, however, leading to any public resolutions castigating some, or praising other, governments.

Despite these ground rules, some whom we invited and had hoped would participate declined to come, either because the funding was provided by the U.S. government or because the meeting was co-sponsored by the University of the Philippines Law School and Center of Law, which are government institutions. Nonetheless, even those who felt they could not participate themselves encouraged us to go ahead with the workshop; and, on the whole, we feel that it was a very positive experience. Even so, it was not possible for the sponsoring agencies to agree to the joint publication of this volume of proceedings. The editors, therefore, assume sole responsibility for the editing and interpretation of the text which follows.

Sponsoring and Co-operating Institutions

Human Rights Internet (HRI), Washington, DC, USA

The Internet, founded in 1976, is an international communications network and clearinghouse on human rights, comprised of some 2,000 organizations and individuals worldwide. It publishes the *Human Rights Internet Reporter*, a series of human rights directories, and other reference works and resources. Internet is currently establishing a computerized data base on international human rights.

International Human Rights Law Group, Washington, DC, USA

The Law Group, established in 1978, provides legal services and educational programmes in the field of international human rights law. On a *pro bono* basis, the Law Group specializes in assisting and co-operating with non-governmental organizations in preparing complaints of human rights violations to be filed before international, regional and domestic legal fora.

University of the Philippines, Center and College of Law, Manila, The Philippines

The Center and College of Law of the University of the Philippines have been concerned with teaching, research and documentation in the area of international human rights. Since 1977, they have co-operated in developing a programme on 'popularizing the law' to develop functional legal literacy at the community level in the Philippines.

University of the Philippines, Third World Studies Center (TWSC), Manila, The Philippines

The Third World Studies Center of U.P. was established in 1977 in response to student and faculty articulation of the need for a programme of studies and research that critically analyses and confronts the problems of underdevelopment in the Third World in general and the Philippines in particular. In the human rights field, the basic aim of the TWSC is 'to document the consequences, the mechanisms and structures, of imperialist domination of the Philippines in all spheres of society'.

Human Rights Institute of Lucknow, India

The Human Rights Institute of Lucknow works for the promotion and protection of human rights as declared by the United Nations and embodied in the Constitution of India. It conducts research on Indian laws and proposed legislation to determine whether, and if so, to what extent, such laws violate human rights, and it supports measures for redress.

Lembaga Bantuan Hukum/Legal Aid Institute, Jakarta, Indonesia

The Legal Aid Institute was founded in 1971 by the Indonesian Advocates' Association for the purpose of promoting human rights, especially for the poor, in the Jakarta region. As well as handling thousands of cases a year, the Institute seeks to educate and conscientize the people about their rights.

Part I:
ASEAN Perspectives on Human Rights

1. ASEAN Perspectives on Human Rights

Within the ASEAN (Association of South East Asian Nations) region (as in the Third World generally), a claim that the concept of human rights is universally applicable is often rejected, in whole or in part, by three sorts of counter-claims.

The first is put forth by orthodox Communist Party members (but not necessarily by all Marxists). This counter-claim insists that human rights – defined as individual civil and political rights – are nothing more than a residual bourgeois contrivance, an individualistic and legalistic formula which permits, while it simultaneously conceals, the continued collective rule of the most wealthy and powerful class in society.

A second counter-claim, propagated equally by Western economistic developmentalists and vulgar Marxists (i.e. by two types of materialists), is that human rights are inherently incompatible with economic development. Here, the insistence is that there exists an ineluctable 'trade-off' between individual civil and political rights on the one hand, and collective economic, social and cultural rights on the other. To achieve the latter, the need for which is apparent and imperative in almost all the Third World, it is regrettably necessary to sacrifice the former.

Finally, the concept of human rights is rejected by a politically self-protective assertion made by Asian élites. (A similar assertion is repeated by Islamic and African élites but not, because of historical and cultural differences, by those of Latin America.) This is the claim that the entire concept of human rights, and indeed the concept of 'rights' generally, is alien to Asia. In this view, the bundle of individual rights associated with liberal democracy and that of collective economic, social and cultural rights enshrined in Marxist Socialism *both* evolved out of the historical crucible of European political and economic development. Further, in this view, the more recent concept of an international law on human rights, with the individual as a legitimate subject of this body of law, is in fact a localized by-product of Europe's dreadful experience with Nazism, World War II and genocide. For example, both the UN Charter (with its seven separate references to 'fundamental human rights', 'human rights', and 'fundamental freedoms') and the 1948 Universal Declaration of Human Rights were drafted and approved by a United Nations then

3

made up of only 50 member-states (i.e. less than a third of its present membership), and dominated by the Western allies, the United States in particular. The concept, in short, is seen as a peculiarly Western cultural artifact that is both alien and irrelevant to the ancient cultures of the East.

In the first paper presented in this section, Saneh Chamarik directly confronts and rejects these counter-claims. (Indeed, *all* of the papers prepared by the ASEAN conference participants at least implicitly and indirectly rejected them.) While under certain circumstances the establishment of civil and political rights *alone* might well be deemed a hollow victory, or the 'equal right to remain unequal' in Chamarik's words, there is hardly a clear and immediate danger that this possibility will materialize in the Third World any time soon. For within the Third World, once the initial goal of political self-determination was achieved, the goal of 'development' immediately succeeded to first place; and development clearly places the stress on economic, social and cultural rights – exclusively and dangerously so in some current formulations. Thus the two categories of rights, in both their positive and their negative conceptualizations, are essential and inseparable rather than incompatible. (Unfortunately, however, it is the case that the mindless projection of superpower competition into Third World arenas has made it appear as if these new nations were facing an unavoidable either–or choice, thus heightening a perception of inevitable conflict between the two broad types of rights.) In Chamarik's view, the contemporary struggle for human rights is simply the continuation of a world-wide historical process of human evolution: the quest for human freedom and dignity through the struggle for emancipation from both natural and human forces. Part of this evolutionary process has manifested itself in the struggle for constitutionalism. What is different in Asia (and in Africa and the Middle East as well) is that the struggle for constitutionalism has occurred later in time. Thus it confronts remnants of feudalism, and in particular an élite mentality of paternalism. At this point in time in the Third World generally, therefore, the successful resolution of this struggle for constitutionalism depends upon two institutional pre-conditions. The first is the establishment of a secure and procedurally regularized legal system. By this is meant due process of law (with rules of law, and courts to enforce them, and the legislature as their legitimate source), not mere 'law and order'. The second institutional pre-condition is the evolution of rules of the political game, initially requiring agreement among élites to resolve conflict through compromise.

The second paper, by R. N. Trevedi, addresses somewhat different questions, yet reaches conclusions similar to those of Chamarik, by tracing the history of the development of concern for the promotion and protection of human rights within the international community. Within this context of the gradual emergence of the individual as a valid subject of international public law, Trevedi additionally raises questions of particular import for the nations of the Third World: what is development? development of whom or what? is there a 'third-generation' right to development? and, if so, what is its logical basis and what are its legal components? In his answers to these questions, the author makes clear the mutually reinforcing interactions between and among human rights, law and development.

The second pair of papers with which this introductory section concludes was prepared by two leaders of the legal aid movement in Indonesia.

No one would contend, nor did any of these ASEAN conference participants contend, that there exists a 'one best way' by which to increase effective promotion and protection of international human rights. All participants agreed that there is no single, simple, sovereign solution; all agreed that the causes of human rights violations are complex, because numerous, interactive and often self-reinforcing. On the other hand, precisely because of this cycle of cumulative causation (as Gunnar Myrdal labelled the problem long ago in the landmark study of race relations in the United States, in his *An American Dilemma*), if one could effectively intervene at one point in the process, then this would in turn operate to open up new opportunities for remedial intervention at other points as well. And quite clearly one choice point in these complex processes entails intervention within the domestic legal system of the nation state. In this context, one may consider legal assistance directed towards bringing municipal law into conformity with international human rights standards as an agent of reform.

Both papers recognize that it is too simple to state, as a number of social scientists unfortunately have stated, that élites respond to the social participation and protest of non-élites with either 'reform' or 'repression'. In point of historical fact, in the face of perceived serious social protest, most élites have reacted with a combination of both repression and reform. But even this generalization is too simplistic. For one thing, reform remains too undifferentiated in this formulation. The generalization fails to distinguish between structural and institutional reform, on the one hand, and, on the other, a change in the implementation of the policies of *existing* structures and institutions to produce some amelioration of the conditions of everyday life of the masses – which is also commonly designated as reform. The first type of reform is fundamental in that it involves a redistribution of power, a broadening of participation and influence in the making of authoritative decisions, so as now to include some (if not all) of the formerly powerless sectors of the society. The second type of reform is more superficial in the long run (although in the short run it may indeed involve ending starvation, significantly reducing malnutrition in pre-school children, decreasing the length of the working day in the society, etc.). And this second type of reform is definitely contingent: it involves a sharing of the benefits of power holding, or the uses of power, in order to avoid the sharing of power itself. And since the locus of power remains unchanged, if and when conditions are perceived to have changed sufficiently favourably, the political élite will seek to revoke the concession(s) previously 'extorted' from it – Poland since 1981 being the most recent and widely recognized instance of such élite behaviour.

In addition to the need to discriminate between two importantly different meanings of reform, one must also note that there are different types or at least crudely measurable degrees of political repression. At one end of this continuum – at the level of least direct physical coercion – there is a form of political repression which might best be termed 'ideological repression' because the political élite seeks to control mass behaviour through its manipulation of official censorship and propaganda. At the other extreme, one finds extended periods of large-scale and severe sanctioning – loss of life, imprisonment, deprivation of livelihood – of designated categories of political dissidents among the mass citizenry. In some instances (e.g. Guatemala, El Salvador, Uruguay or Chile), the government has committed itself to something close to political genocide, seeking to eliminate an entire generation of those perceived as potential grass-roots leaders of all ideological hues.

Moreover, between these two categories of types of reform and repression, the political élite has available still other options for dealing with expressions of discontent among the mass base of society. Under the rubric of pseudo-reform, one finds two options combined. Both entail the élite's use of the technique of co-optation, but in the one case it is of persons and in the other of symbols. In the first instance, the élite may co-opt the spokesmen and apparent leaders of the discontented, offering them visible, often remunerative, yet powerless public titles or offices, and in this manner deprive the discontented mass of its effective leadership. In the second, the élite co-opts the slogans or other political symbols which represent the demands around which the discontented have coalesced; it thereby leaves the spokesmen and apparent leaders without their prior base of support in the mass public. Indeed, under certain conditions – such as non-violent protest by extremely marginalized groups – the élite may as an alternative engage in 'benign neglect', making no evident direct response to the discontented (i.e. neither reform nor repression in any of their varied aspects) but instead utilizing its monopoly over the sources of, and means for transmitting, social information to pretend that nothing untoward in fact has taken place.

It is within this frame of reference that the two papers on legal assistance in Indonesia by Adnan Buyung Nasution and T. Mulya Lubis should be considered. These papers together establish two broad points of general relevance.

The first point is that there exist two polar models of 'legal assistance'. The first of these is based on a traditional conceptualization which emphasizes that legal assistance is to be limited to conventional legal consultation and litigation within an individualistically-orientated case or controversy approach. The second, by contrast, may be viewed as a multi-disciplinary and multi-functional approach aiming at building up the legal and all other resources of the poor and powerless in the society (i.e. developing their community strength, their knowledge of and their collective capacity to make use of the law). It is multi-disciplinary in the sense that the lawyer must develop talents and techniques far beyond those of traditional litigation. For example, he must utilize existing social science research of relevance to the broad social categories his clients represent and, where none exists, he must stimulate such research or undertake it himself. In point of fact, this second conceptualization calls for the creation of an entirely new type of legal professional, one who will be:

1) an advocate of collective demands and group interests, both in courts and in legislative, administrative and all other institutions;
2) an educator, helping to develop community awareness and knowledge of relevant laws and helping to train community para-professionals;
3) a critic of existing or proposed legislation and administrative actions which impinge on the human rights of impoverished groups;
4) a law reformer, asserting claims for changes in legislation and in the structure and processes of government; and
5) a jurist, developing new jurisprudential concepts needed to realize the right to development of *all* individuals within the society (and not just the right to development of that society as an abstraction whose needs and desires are defined solely by a tiny, insulated, and self-perpetuating political élite).

The second broad point – which has already emerged in the Indonesian political context – is that the struggle for human rights in many developing nations will centre on a contest, between governing élites and parts of the legal profession (i.e. particularly law professors and younger lawyers), over the establishment and especially the control of legal assistance programmes. That is, the first (traditional) conceptualization of legal aid operates to defuse the potential political ramifications of social discontent by channelling disputes into formalized, existing judicial processes – as an alternative to increased participation by the powerless. Furthermore, within this approach, it matters little if a favoured occupational stratum – of lawyers – gives play to the natural tendency towards professional élitism and so acts independently of the interests of those to be served. (In fact, from the perspective of the political élite, such separatism is desirable and thus to be subtly encouraged.) Finally, since they function to preserve and reinforce the status quo, Third World governments can safely initiate legal aid programmes of this first type, even in the absence of any effective demands by lawyers or the mass public. Where, viewed in terms of social psychology, the first approach constitutes a process of reinforced adult socialization of clients towards acceptance of the existing socio-political system (and their powerless position within it), the newer legal assistance approach aims at nothing less than a fundamental *re-socialization* of clients away from their current status as passive victims of human rights violations.

2. Some Thoughts on Human Rights Promotion and Protection

Saneh Chamarik

Upon reflection, it is fairly safe to say that the growth and development of human rights have their roots in human nature itself. Whether or not human beings are born free and equal – a not unquestionable proposition, by the way – they all have aspirations one way or another depending on their own predicament. The difference is a matter of degree. Unfortunately, even this plain truth is not always sufficiently well recognized. Worse still, in the world of power politics – within or among nations – it is all too often dismissed as something so negative and destructive that it must be got rid of, by any means and at whatever cost. Human aspiration for freedom is part and parcel of social and political life processes, however. Thus it is only the question of how to respond to that aspiration that gives meaning to, and the measure of, a political system and its structure of authority. Perhaps a view drawn from Thai experience may help illustrate my point here:

> In this Reign, it is known for sure that His Majesty the King is highly *liberal*-minded. He used to be talking about the *form of government* even before coming to the throne. His Majesty is therefore fully aware of the fact that a good *form of government* is one that is most suitable for the country at the time. Although it is as yet necessary to maintain the *form of government* with absolute power, that absolute power needs to be very *liberal* in order to preserve itself. But as time has gone by, there will be increasing numbers of educated people. We have therefore to get prepared to cope with the (demand for) *emancipation* that will keep arising.[1]

That was the mode of thinking of His Royal Highness, the Minister of the Interior (and concurrently President of the Privy Council), one of the most powerful figures of his day, just five years before the 1932 Revolution that overthrew the absolute monarchy in Thailand. Compared to governmental reactions to the demand for political freedom elsewhere, the one cited above sounded very gentle and quite benevolent. It also showed insight into what was taking place outside the citadel of power. Nevertheless, its conservatism was typical enough, and this gave rise to all kinds of conflicts and complications on the issue of human rights and

9

freedom. The choice of the word 'emancipation' in this historical context was not entirely accidental, moreover, but in a significant sense was an instinctive reflection of the nature of things to come. For it vividly reminds one of Wertheim's theoretical observation concerning human evolution, which he phrased in terms of the innate tendency to strive for emancipation – not only from the forces of nature but also 'from domination by privileged individuals and groups' – which strivings together constitute human progress.[2]

Third World Predicaments

Human aspiration for freedom, then, is not just a matter of philosophical imagination or speculation but is actually an empirical phenomenon, a fact of life. While this is so, however, human progress in this evolutionary and qualitative sense has so often been looked upon, by reactionary Right and 'revolutionary' Left alike, with much misgiving. Even the so-called liberal West is no exception, as Ramsey Clark, the former US Attorney General, has pointed out in courageously speaking of a long-standing fact about the United States: 'We [the US] preached democracy at home and supported a despot abroad . . . we spoke of freedom and sat in silence while thousands were tortured and brutalized.'[3] It looks as though conflict and change, as motivating forces for social progress, have to be equated with and treated like alien and deadly sin, while the so-called Establishment seeks to remain in power despite proof that its own actions are exploitative and oppressive, unjust and inhumane, and likely to lead eventually to violence and suffering on all sides. In current academic jargon, one can also sense a certain conscious or unconscious sociological and psychological bias, where conflict and change tend to be fashionably conceptualized in terms of 'radical anti-thesis' as against 'conservative thesis' (a synonym for the status quo).[4] The point is that the reverse could in fact be equally true, at least from an evolutionary standpoint. For those concerned with education for peace and a new international order, something must be done about such a state of knowledge in the field of human conflict and social change.

  This brings us to the more practical question of how human rights could become the focal point of a system capable of their safeguard and protection. In this regard, attention will be focused, in a general way, on the problems of Third World countries. The reason is simple enough: they all seem to be facing the same dilemma of being torn between the two main streams of ideological confrontation represented by the First and Second Worlds, and yet, hopefully, there may still be room for more creative and relevant alternatives of their own. But first there is a real need for more objective understanding of the environmental factors involved in order to guard against either a tendency towards subjectivism about the issue or a temptation to offer ready-made solutions. Here it may be worth while to ponder for a moment the words of precaution of J. F. Lalive, then Secretary General of the International Commission of Jurists:

> It is only too easy to consider the concept of human rights and fundamental freedoms and the closely related problem of the Rule of Law as an abstract and theoretical conception or a mere political formula. In fact, we are dealing with practical and living notions charged with meaning and with positive reality and which, by their nature, do affect directly the future of societies as well as our every day life . . .[5]

What immediately comes to mind about this 'positive reality' is the historical and cultural background that gave rise to the 'practical and living notions' of human rights in the West, by contrast to the tradition-bound cultures of non-Western societies. This difference is easily recognized. But here again one must be careful not to allow this consideration to blind one's perception of the actual state of human affairs. For one thing, as shown by concrete historical experiences, the lack of a 'liberal' tradition does not prevent fellow beings, Western or non-Western, from being keenly aware of and struggling for their self-respect and dignity against both internal and external oppression. It certainly does not mean that without this cultural tradition there would remain no basis upon which human rights and freedom could be fostered and developed, although this negative view is still adhered to in many academic quarters. To be objective, one has to distinguish clearly between the concept and principle of human rights as universal values on the one hand, and as operative values on the other. As universal values, we all have been witness to a wide range of articulation and persistent struggle for rights and liberties, as represented, for instance, by Benigno Aquino in the Philippines or Alexander Solzhenitsyn and Andrei Sakharov in the USSR. While as operative values, the one adhered to and practised in the West (and externally by the West) has not been without serious short-comings, both conceptually and operationally.[6]

For all its limited applicability, however, the historical experience and cultural pattern of the West could still have a good deal to contribute to our understanding of the process of growth and development of human rights. It could serve as one way of learning something more about Third World conditions, albeit in reverse comparison. This point is succinctly emphasized by C. G. Weeramantry, former Justice of the Supreme Court of Sri Lanka, in noting the historical transformation of Western society following the Reformation and the Renaissance:

> The questioning of authority, however sacred or well-entrenched, the stimulus of sudden impact with ancient cultures, the opening up of new worlds which unleashed both mind and society from their traditional moorings – all these had in Europe broken up the ancient form of social

ordering, released the individual from the group and sent forth the concept of individual freedom and equality as the legacy of that age to all others.[7]

A spiritual and cultural break with feudalism thus paved the way for the philosophic and ideological revolution of the 17th and 18th centuries. In place of the divine right of kings came the new notions of natural law and natural rights, which put the sole emphasis on common men and individual freedom and consent as the sources and bases of political authority. The impact of this radical transformation of Western society needs no further elaboration here except to point to the consequent meaning and place of constitutionalism in the Western political system, as compared to that in the Third World context. A. V. Dicey's classic analysis of the English Constitution is quite instructive for he shrewdly observed that:

> The [English] constitution is pervaded by the rule of law on the ground that the general principles of the constitution (as for example the right to personal liberty, or the right of public meeting) are with us the result of judicial decisions determining the rights of private persons in particular cases brought before the courts; whereas under many foreign constitutions the security (such as it is) given to the rights of individuals results . . . from the general principles of the constitution.[8]

The implication of this distinction is clear concerning the status of human rights and freedom *vis-à-vis* state authority. Unlike in the liberal West where rights and liberties are held to be inherent in human nature and inalienable, and thus form the basis of the constitution and of governmental authority, rights and liberties in the non-Western states are things granted by the rulers to the ruled. In the West, ' . . . these rights and freedoms are indispensable to a dignified human existence and remain wholly intact from derogation upon ground of crisis . . . It can never be necessary to encroach upon these rights and freedoms, even in times of emergency . . .'[9] Outside the West, by contrast, these same rights are invariably subordinated to martial law and emergency rules, whatever the degrees of leniency in particular regimes.[10]

Issues of Negative and Positive Liberty

In practical terms, this means that constitutionalism in most – if not all – Third World countries is subject to arbitrary rule, precisely that ideology and operative system which concepts of human rights arose to challenge. The rationale today is substantially the same, although stated in different terminology: in place of the divine right of ancient times, the justification for more modern authoritarianism is asserted in the name of national sovereignty and unity. The main lines of argument sound familiar enough. They all point to the irrelevance and impracticality of the Western notion of human rights and liberties. This is, of course, true to a certain extent – but that extent demands a more critical scrutiny than it has received in the past.

One such justificatory argument focuses on the problem of nation-state building. The risks and danger of unrestrained political dissension are quite real in the initial stage after independence. The new states, especially the pluralistic ones, are indeed in great need of mobilizing all social forces available under one unifying banner so as to fight against the colonial past. Independence movements have for the most part been successful simply because they were widely believed to be serving the cause of human freedom and dignity. This is also true of political revolutions carried out in the name of freedom and democracy. But the irony is that these very movements, even after becoming long established, more often than not turn against freedom and democracy itself in their subsequent social and political arrangements. Hence all the demands on the part of ruling élites for one-party state systems[11] or, failing that, for emergency powers and corresponding suspension of rights and liberties. There is, of course, no lack of attempts to have all such expediencies built into the constitution and legal code and practices, some of which, paradoxically enough, are referred back to 'legal' precedents of the good old colonial days.[12] As far as the man in the street is concerned, this amounts to nothing much more than a shift from life under one type of colonial master to life under another. There comes a time, moreover, when such a state of affairs invites the question of what these élites and self-proclaimed national unity and interest actually stand for: for their own privilege of permanent rule, or for the freedom and benefit of the majority of the people? (This fundamental question also relates to the problem of institution building, which will be touched upon later.)

Another aspect of the argument is particularly relevant at this point, although it too is related to the problem of the élitist approach to politics mentioned above. This aspect is concerned, or rather is made out to be concerned, with the question of choice between civil and political rights on the one hand, and social and economic rights on the other. This writer's position is that the problem of choice here is actually more apparent than real, and that the two sets of human rights are in truth so interrelated as to form one and the same thing. It is indeed questionable how human freedom and dignity can be promoted and protected without both categories of rights. In taking this view, one is of course fully aware of the profound difference between the liberal Western and the Communist viewpoints. The inclusion of the two sets of rights, as a gesture of diplomatic compromise, in the 1948 Universal Declaration of Human Rights solved practically nothing.[13] Almost three decades had to elapse before the United Nations could manage to get through the 'second stage' in its Bill of Rights, not in integrated form but with the two separate instruments of 1976: the International Covenant on Economic, Social and Cultural Rights and the International Covenant on Civil and Political Rights. This is a matter of current international debate, however, and there is no logical reason to perceive this fact as indicating any incompatibility between these two sets of rights. The difference is, in fact, a legacy of the past failure of the ancient regimes as well as, in a large sense, that of the Western brand of liberalism which has been so ready to turn a blind eye to the bread-and-butter problems and hardship of common people.

It comes as no surprise, therefore, that serious doubts have now been raised as to the validity and practicality of the Western conception of human rights. C. G. Weeramantry, again, in his comparative study of the concepts of liberty and equality, stresses 'the inappropriateness of Western concepts' and takes the issue of inequality as most relevant to the Third World's problems and real needs. With the magnitude and political sensitivity of this problem, he notes the pressing need to 'seek a view of equality which means more than the perpetuation of inequality – a view of equality more substantial than one which means the equal right to remain unequal.'[14] In like manner, Fouad Ajami of Princeton University has questioned 'the "completeness" of the liberal conception of human rights, its vulnerability to charges of opportunism and self-righteousness, its capacity to speak to many forms of deprivations of human rights which are embedded in the contemporary global context.'[15]

In view of the chronic and widespread poverty and urban–rural disparities in the Third World, it is entirely natural that social and economic rights should be thought of as the first and even exclusive priority. By contrast, civil and political ones too often seem a luxury and an irrelevance in the face of stark inequality and starvation. This is, indeed, the harsh reality of our contemporary world. None the less, disillusion with Western liberalism ought not to blind us to a moral and political trap. It is imperative to view human nature and the problem of political relationships in a proper perspective, in order that we should not fall into either the extreme of unbridled *laissez-faire* or that of totalitarianism. For both are in the last analysis repressive of human freedom and dignity.

It is all very well, of course, for a government to promote the social and economic welfare of its own people. There is nothing wrong with that. After all, material well-being is not merely desirable, but is also as essential as positive liberty for human growth and betterment. But even for this seemingly simple matter, there is a vast difference between two divergent ways of viewing people. People may be seen as self-determining beings desirous and capable of living for their own purposes. Or they may be seen as mere dependants who must be taken care of and brought into line with the one 'true and only' way of living. The latter suggests a sort of teleological and architectonic vision of politics, which seems to fit only too well with the paternalistic mentality prevailing among Third World élites. It also fits in very well with their modernization and development goals which are understood primarily in terms of economic development. Hence all the fuss about development planning and administration – all dictated and controlled exclusively from the bureaucratic and technocratic centre. These objectives, to be sure, do not necessarily overlook the need to correct social inequalities and injustice. Yet, as Isaiah Berlin would remind us, we must ever be careful, in spite of all the obvious benefits claimed of altruism, of the real reasons that move us to do things for others as well as to protect them from social injustice.[16]

In a profound sense, then, the need for social and economic rights is concerned not just with the satisfaction of material needs, but also with the fundamental question of how a governing agency responsible for their implementation shall be set up. Governments could be expected to attempt to undertake many tasks; but the primary question, according to Berlin, is whether those tasks which relate to positive liberty are viewed as the means necessary for effectuating negative liberty or, alternatively, are prized as ends in themselves. That is, élitism, Platonic rulership, the Communist 'vanguard of the proletariat', are all imbued with an arrogance which proclaims that 'we know better than you what your true interests are'; each has a built-in tendency to subsume all people under one particular ideal, a single way of life. In this fashion, a doctrine of freedom is vulnerable to perversion into one of coercion and repression. In consequence:

> All of the diversity, color, and variety of politics would be lost, along with our human dignity, if the positive ideal of liberty were pursued too zealously. Pursuit of this, or any, ideal as the true good for all would depoliticize our world, reducing political questions to technical questions.[17]

This last consideration brings us back again to the question of the interrelationship between negative and positive liberty. The indispensability of civil and political rights certainly does not make of them the end of organized social life. Negative liberty, which is furthered to the extent that such rights are promoted and protected, essentially serves as 'a basal or foundation value' protective of a human freedom and dignity which is 'rooted in the capacity to choose one's goals for oneself . . .'[18] Though in constant need of social order, as purposive beings:

> we live for a variety of conflicting purposes, yet we must structure our societies so that we are protected in the choice of these purposes . . .
> . . . all that is needed for social life is agreement upon the requirements of civility which constitute the base.[19]

Problems of Institution Building

Therefore, given the exploitation, oppression, militarism, and consequent human suffering evident everywhere around us, it is now high time to embark on hard rethinking about the entire complex of human rights issues necessitated by our current global predicament. What is entailed is the search for a more comprehensive conceptualization and approach, a task to be kept uppermost in our minds during the course of this international dialogue. One could do well to look more closely, as Weeramantry has suggested, into the immediate problem of inequality and poverty among Third World populations who comprise the vast majority of mankind. But it certainly will not do to focus our attention exclusively on this problem, at the expense of civil and political rights – without which social and economic rights themselves can hardly be promoted and guaranteed. But nor should we simply aim our effort at answering the Third World's call for solutions, as if the West itself had nothing to do with the current state of affairs. The truth is that the traditional Western concept of rights is itself in great need of thorough re-examination and equally hard rethinking. It was the product of its own time and still remains largely so. Economic and social rights were practically unknown to the natural rights thinkers of the 18th century because the notion of rights was born, historically and philosophically, as the ideology of the haves and the affluent, that is, the rising middle class.[20] Thus the Western brand of liberalism needs to be overhauled, not just because of its original sin of self-aggrandizement in the past and present, but because of the global and interdependent nature of contemporary problems and solutions. These matters, again, should be dealt with in this distinguished forum.

What is to be briefly proposed here, as the final portion of this paper, is concerned with the way institutional mechanisms should be developed towards the goal of the promotion and effective protection of human rights. For this purpose, some of the constitutional and political experiences of the West will be brought up to serve as guidelines. Of course, political and constitutional practices cannot simply be imported. This is obvious to all. The writer's approach to the matter is, admittedly, partly due to his own limited resources yet partly also to a strong belief that certain institutional conditions are absolutely crucial and have to be fulfilled if human freedom and dignity are ever to be truly respected and lawfully enforced. As to the means to achieve these institutional ends, this certainly requires a most innovative effort on the part of everyone concerned, starting by looking into their own indigenous resources, real and potential. Religious values, like those of Buddhism under which this writer lives his life, provide a good example.[21] This is why the paths towards the common objective of human freedom and progress could vary according to differing historical, social and cultural contexts.

Aside from the historical and social background factors discussed thus far, there appear to be at least two main institutional requisites for the effective and peaceful development of human rights. Although, once again, these are drawn from the Western model of development, they nevertheless provide insight and understanding as to cause and effect.

The first is related to the legal system and law-making process. In this respect, Richard P. Claude's emphasis on a secure and procedurally regularized legal system is particularly instructive. In Claude's words:

> Preliminary to any movement towards human rights development, the framework of an operative legal system must be securely established. Where the security of the legal system does not exist, incipient or actual conditions of violence prevail in which *force majeure* capriciously and unpredictably sets up an equation between might and right . . . where law and the authority of its defenders end, neither security nor freedom is possible.[22]

Such is the operational basis for the rule of law as opposed to personal and arbitrary rule of all kinds. However, the security of the legal system does not simply mean 'law and order', as is so often asserted by some schools of jurists in the Third World countries. It means, in essence, due process of law, fair and impartial, as a safeguard against arbitrary use of power and favouritism. It is in this sense that it can be said that 'security' is prior to liberty. At the same time, security as such is not meant merely to preserve the status quo, for it must be flexible, must be capable of adapting to changing circumstances, be these economic, social, or political. This last point brings us to the second aspect of institution building.

The line of approach of this paper is drawn from Dicey's two guiding principles which, in turn, are closely connected in his analysis of English constitutionalism: the sovereignty, or supremacy, of the Parliament and the rule, or supremacy, of law.[23] Thus, related to the legal and judicial aspect is the political aspect, with the latter concerned with the question of who is the source of the law. The relationship between the legal and the political is not always agreed upon, however, a point made abundantly clear in the following statement by Joseph Raz:

> It is also to be insisted that the rule of law is just one of the virtues which a legal system may possess and by which it is to be judged. It is not to be confused with democracy, justice, equality (before the law or otherwise), human rights of any kind or respect for persons or for the dignity of man. A non-democratic legal system, based on the denial of human rights, on extensive poverty, on racial segregation, sexual inequalities and religious persecution may, in principle, conform to the requirements of the rule of law better than any of the legal systems of the more enlightened Western democracies. This does not mean that it will be better than those Western democracies. It will be an immeasurably worse legal system, but it will excel in one respect: in its conformity to the rule of law.[24]

The principle of the rule of law, evidently, is subject to variable – that is, broader or stricter – interpretation; but perhaps this sort of intellectual controversy is better left to professors of jurisprudence. In any event, so far as the problem of human rights promotion and protection is concerned, it is quite impossible to omit issues of democracy, justice and equality in our present discussion about the rule of law. For, in the last analysis, the security of the legal system and of the judicial process, which are the essence of the rule of law concept, must also depend upon a political process which is in harmony with it.

Furthermore, recent analysis of democratic development points suggestively to one critical phase in this historical process. Here, one particular point must be emphasized. That is, the problem of democracy has to be seen, not simply in terms of its comprehensive institutional definition as presently conceived in the West, but as a developmental process, for only in this way can one gain a clearer historical and empirical perspective. Specifically, what is termed, for instance, 'the decision phase' by Dankwart Rustow, or 'public contestation' by Robert Dahl, involves the settlement of conflicts among the élites whose compromise results in establishing a number of democratic rules of procedure.[25] In Rustow's analysis, his 'decision phase' is intermediate between a 'preparatory phase' in which opposing élites still engage in protracted and inconclusive struggle (a situation accurately characterizing Third World nations), and the 'habituation phase' in which rules of the game for political competition, established among and within the élites, are then extended to include a broader circle of citizen-participants. In this, Rustow's last stage is comparable to that which Dahl has labelled one of 'inclusiveness', by which he means extended participation, in that both of these political scientists' historico-logical analyses of the developmental process posit an earlier period of competitive politics among the élites themselves leading ultimately to system-wide toleration of organized opposition. Put differently, a democratic political culture develops first among the contending élites and then is projected – 'outward' and 'downward' – on to a successively larger mass public, with political democratization taking place concurrently with socio-economic change.

By contrast, the one characteristic commonly shared by the nations of the Third World is the lack of consensus on the rules of the game for political competition. (The possible exception to this generalization is India where the ongoing democratic experiment has exhibited ups and several brink-tottering downs.) It may be true that Third World countries are still undergoing the process of state building and therefore 'historically' cannot yet come up with – or 'be expected to come up with' – the kinds of compromise necessary for the peaceful settlement of political conflicts.[26] Perhaps; but this at best is only part of the story. For it is one which favours, by omitting the role of, non-Third World powers whose pressures, covert intervention and manipulation have considerable impact on internal political processes within the Third World. However, leaving both external and internal constraints aside, the point to be stressed here regarding the problem of institution building is that the prospect – at least at the present stage of political development of Third World nations – rests largely with the quality of their élites, and not with the populations-at-large, as so many academicians have seen fit to claim. To state this is not to contribute anything particularly constructive, of course. None the less, saying it may help to pinpoint where the main obstacles lie and what strategic points are to be tackled. Short of agreement on the fundamentals, that is to say, the legal-political rules, and the democratic spirit of agreeing to disagree, there can be no progress towards constitutionalism on which hinges the possibility of human rights development, in both their negative and positive aspects.

Concluding Comment

The promotion and protection of human rights indeed involve a wide range of problems. Here in the Third World one also finds a situation of human aspiration for freedom and dignity which is inexorable, although – unlike in the West – without the historical background of radical social transformation. The line of analysis taken in this paper is that democracy is necessary to serve as the basis for human rights and that, even from the more restricted standpoint of national unity and security, democracy within nations makes possible the integration of both leaders and their own people into one social and political entity. On the other hand, there remains a global dimension attached to the problems under discussion, as the world has become increasingly interdependent and practically all nations, large and small, have been drawn into one and the same arena of power politics.[27] In this light, it is all very well to visualize the problems of human rights, as suggested for example in the 1978 Copenhagen Resolution of the World Association of World Federalists, in terms of the broader issues of peace, security and social justice under a world authority.[28] Yet, as Lucille Mair, Secretary General of the United Nations Decade for Women, also reminds us:

> The international process has its limitations. It has tremendous value in that it can set standards, but a global strategy can be no more than a global strategy. It is not a substitute for a national strategy . . . Parallel to [this global plan of action] will be national plans of action. We cannot dictate to governments what should be done.[29]

That indeed poses a real challenge for each one of us to think about, though it need not and should not deter one from pursuing a global ideal of freedom, justice and peace.

Notes

1. Thai National Archive, R.7 RL 6/3, Minutes of the Privy Council Meeting, 11 April, B.E. 2470 (1927), translated by the author. Note also that italicized

words in this quotation indicate English language terms as they appeared in the original text.

2. W. F. Wertheim, *Evolution and Revolution: The Rising Wave of Emancipation* (London: Penguin Books, 1974), pp. 35–48.
3. *Newsweek* (30 June 1980), p. 52. For a similar criticism, see also C. G. Weeramantry, *Equality and Freedom: Some Third World Perspectives* (Colombo: Hansa Publishers Ltd, 1976), pp. 67–8.
4. Gerhard E. Lenski, *Power and Privilege: A Theory of Social Stratification* (New York: McGraw-Hill, 1966), pp. 5–14.
5. *The Rule of Law in a Free Society* (Geneva: International Commission of Jurists, 1959), p. 51. (This is the report of the ICJ on its 1959 New Delhi Conference on this same topic.)
6. Saneh Chamarik, 'Buddhism and Human Rights', paper delivered at the UNESCO Conference on 'The Place of Human Rights in Cultural and Religious Traditions', Bangkok, Thailand, 3–7 December 1979, pp. 7–9. On this point, see also Adamantia Pollis and Peter Schwab, 'Human Rights: A Western Construct with Limited Applicability', in Pollis and Schwab (eds), *Human Rights: Cultural and Ideological Perspectives* (London: Praeger, 1979), p. 15.
7. Weeramantry, op. cit., p. 13; also Pollis and Schwab, op. cit., pp. 2–3.
8. A. V. Dicey, *Law of the Constitution* (London: Macmillan, 9th edn, reprinted 1952), pp. 195–6.
9. Myres McDougal, H. D. Lasswell, and Lung-Chu Chen, 'Human Rights and World Public Order: A Framework for Policy Oriented Inquiry', *American Journal of International Law* (1969), p. 237.
10. Lawrence W. Beer (ed.), *Constitutionalism in Asia: Asian Views of the American Influence* (Berkeley: University of California Press, 1979), pp. 15–16.
11. For criticism of the one-party state system, see for example Conway W. Henderson, 'Underdevelopment and Political Rights: A Revisionist Challenge', *Government and Opposition*, Vol. 12, No. 3 (Summer 1977), pp. 276–92.
12. See, for example, Tun Mohamed Suffian bin Hashim, 'The Malaysian Constitution and the United States Constitution', and Enrique M. Fernando, 'The American Impact on the Philippine Legal System', in Beer, op. cit., pp. 128–39 and 140–78 respectively.
13. Maurice Cranston, *Human Rights Today* (London: Ampersand Books, 1962), pp. 36–42.
14. Weeramantry, op. cit., p. 10.
15. Fouad Ajami, *Human Rights and World Order Politics* (New York: Institute of World Order, 1978), p. 2. (This is Occasional Paper Number 4 of the IWO's World Order Model Project.)
16. Robert A. Kocis, 'Reason, Development, and the Conflicts of Human Ends: Sir Isaiah Berlin's Vision of Politics', *American Political Science Review*, Vol. 74, No. 1 (March 1980), p. 45.
17. Ibid., p. 41.
18. Ibid., p. 51.
19. Ibid.
20. Cranston, op. cit., p. 38; also Chamarik, op. cit., p. 7.
21. Ibid., for development of this point.
22. Richard P. Claude, 'The Classical Model of Human Rights Development', in

Claude (ed.), *Comparative Human Rights* (Baltimore: Johns Hopkins University Press, 1976), pp. 7–8.
23. Dicey, op. cit., p. 184.
24. Joseph Raz, 'The Rule of Law and Its Virtue', *The Law Quarterly Review*, Vol. 93 (April 1977), p. 196.
25. Dankwart A. Rustow, 'Transitions to Democracy', *Comparative Politics*, No. 2 (April 1970), pp. 337–64, and Robert A. Dahl, *Polyarchy: Participation and Opposition* (New Haven: Yale University Press, 1970), pp. 33–47.
26. Pollis and Schwab, op. cit., p. 16.
27. J. E. Goldthorpe, *The Sociology of the Third World: Disparity and Involvement* (Cambridge: Cambridge University Press, 1975), p. 1.
28. World Association of World Federalists, 'Declaration from the WAWF Conference on Human Rights', Copenhagen, 17–18 February 1978.
29. *Newsweek* (14 July 1980), p. 60.

3. Overview of International Human Rights Law in Theory and Practice: Its Linkages to Access to Justice at the Domestic Level

R. N. Treverdi

Human rights, rights of man, or fundamental rights, are names given to those elementary rights which are considered to be indispensable for the development of the individual. What people essentially need for an existence worthy of human dignity is, in the first instance, guidelines or touchstones for the formation of positive law. Only when incorporated into positive law itself do human rights acquire legal status in the conservative sense of the term.

The purpose of human rights is, above all, to provide a set of rules for the relationship between the individual and government, bearing in mind the fundamental inequality of power between those two poles. This inequality is inherent in the state system.

Human rights have thus been considered to be primarily a matter between the state and the individual. Inasmuch as the protection, preservation, promotion or violation of human rights were considered to fall within the domestic jurisdiction of states, and be subject to the jurisdiction of municipal courts alone, they did not come within the purview of international law.

Early Efforts

Gradually, however, the international community became concerned with gross violations of human rights and it became conscious of the need to create a just order. As states recognized their obligations, several treaties were entered into in the early 19th and 20th centuries, e.g. the 1885 Treaty on Slavery and the Slave Trade, which was described as the General Act of the Berlin Conference and forbade trading in slaves in conformity with the principles of international law. This was followed by the 1889 Brussels Conference, which provided remedies against the slave trade and slavery. The ravages of war resulted in the development of humanitarian law to permit relief to the sick, the wounded and prisoners of war. With the establishment of the League of Nations, another step was taken towards the embodiment of human rights into law. Article 22 of the League Covenant created the Mandate system, placing

> those colonies and territories which as a consequence of the late war have ceased to be under the sovereignty of the States which formerly governed them and which are inhabited by peoples not yet able to stand by themselves under the strenuous conditions of the modern world

under the tutelage of 'advanced' nations. They were to be governed in accordance with 'the principle that the well-being and development of such peoples form a sacred trust of civilisation'; the Mandatory Powers were expected to guarantee, among other things, freedom of conscience and religion and the prohibition of such abuses as the slave trade.

The Individual as a Subject of International Law

The atrocities and genocide perpetrated during World War II shook the faith people had in the adequacy of the existent system of international law. In their dealings with each other, states had ignored the rights of the individual. Thus, in the Preamble to the United Nations Charter, there is a resolve to create a new order.

> We the *peoples* of the United Nations determined to save succeeding generations from the scourge of war, which twice in our lifetime has brought untold sorrow to mankind, and to reaffirm faith in fundamental human rights, in the dignity and worth of the human person, in the equal rights of men and women and of nations large and small . . . and to promote social progress and better standards of life in larger freedom, and for these ends . . . to employ international machinery for the promotion of the economic and social advancement of all peoples, have resolved to combine our efforts to accomplish these aims . . .

Article 76 provided that the basic objectives of the Trusteeship system, in accordance with the purpose of the United Nations laid down in Article 1 of the Charter, would be to encourage respect for human rights and fundamental freedoms for all, without distinction as to race, sex, or religion, and to encourage recognition of the interdependence of the people of the world. Although the provisions relating to non-self-governing territories were phrased in general, rather than specific, terms, the General Assembly invited the Administering Powers to transmit information, under Article 73(c), about the extent to which the Universal Declaration of Human Rights was being implemented in the non-self-governing territories. (At present, there is only one Trust Territory – the Pacific Islands, otherwise known as Micronesia – which remains under the surveillance of the Trusteeship Council.)

The Universal Declaration of Human Rights, the Covenants on

Economic, Social and Cultural Rights and on Civil and Political Rights, and various other instruments sought to protect the individual from the arbitrary actions of the state. The International Labour Organization has adopted over 100 conventions relevant to human rights, many of them with a reporting system to ensure implementation. The provisions of Article 55 of the UN Charter oblige states to promote higher standards of living, to establish optimum conditions for economic and social progress and development, and to promote a universal respect for, and observance of, human rights and fundamental freedoms for all. Article 56 requires all member-states of the United Nations to take joint and separate action in co-operation with the Organization for achievement of the purposes set forth in Article 55. The International Court of Justice, while interpreting Articles 55 and 56, was of the view that the obligation to take joint and separate action binds member-states to observe and respect human rights.

Gross violations of human rights are no longer protected by the domestic jurisdiction theory. The provisions of the Universal Declaration of Human Rights are now binding as part of customary law and have great moral and political authority, not only in theory, but in the practice of law making at both the international and national levels. The constitutions of Libya and Eritrea, drafted in co-operation with the United Nations, and the constitutions of the Federal Republic of Germany and of France include many of the guarantees provided for in the Universal Declaration. Indeed, the Charter and the Universal Declaration were considered basic to the formulation of many post-World War II democratic constitutions. Part IV of the Constitution of India substantially incorporates all the guarantees elaborated in the Universal Declaration of Human Rights.

Implementation
Article 68 of the UN Charter provides for the establishment of a Commission on Human Rights to ensure the protection of the individual against arbitrary actions by the state. The Commission on Human Rights completed its work on the two human rights Covenants in 1954, but they were approved by the General Assembly only in 1966. India has ratified both Covenants but with two notable reservations: one relating to self-determination and the other to the non-payment of compensation to persons who are arbitrarily detained. While the guarantees provided in the Covenants are reflected in the Constitution of India, the courts in India initially took an extremely conservative stand with respect to these provisions. The courts held that the goals or the aspirations set forth in Part IV of the Indian Constitution, namely, the Directive Principles of State Policy, were matters which were not enforceable through the courts. However, the Supreme Court of India has been gradually invoking the provisions of the Directive Principles of State Policy while interpreting the Indian Constitution or the laws. This invocation of the Directive Principles of State Policy indirectly amounts to the invocation

of the United Nations Covenants and the Universal Declaration of Human Rights. Increasingly, the courts have come to the aid of citizens who have been deprived of their economic and social rights.

The Forums

International human rights law further finds embodiment in a number of regional arrangements. It is heartening that a large number of European countries who are members of the European Community permit individual citizens to invoke the jurisdiction of the European Court of Human Rights, after they have exhausted domestic remedies. An Inter-American Court of Human Rights has also been established. Recently, African nations have come together to draft an African Charter of Human Rights and the Rights of Peoples, which will establish an African Human Rights Commission when it is ratified by the requisite number of states. It is unfortunate that no effective steps have yet been taken for drawing up an Asian Charter or for setting up an Asian Commission or Court of Human Rights.

Rule of Law and Rule of Justice

Despite the elaboration of international human rights law, in all countries of the world individuals are deprived of their human rights by inequitable and arbitrary laws and by their enforcement through the executive. Although decisions of the courts may be in conformity with enacted domestic legislation, often such laws do not conform to the minimal standards of internationally accepted human rights. Individuals thus deprived of their rights have no recourse to effective remedies for enforcing internationally recognized human rights. It is imperative that there should be accountability for the laws made by states in order to determine whether or not they conform to international norms and standards. Perhaps the most efficacious method lies in charters and codes at a regional or sub-regional level.

It would seem, therefore, that even under a rule of law people may be deprived of their human rights. We must mature from the state of the rule of law to rule of justice. The Preamble of the Charter states that the peoples of the United Nations were determined to establish conditions under which *justice* and respect for obligations arising from treaties and other sources of international law can be maintained and to promote social progress and better standards of life in larger freedom. Article 1(1) again talks about the maintenance of international peace and security in conformity with the principles of *justice* and international law. Article 2(3) provides that all members shall settle their international disputes by peaceful means in such a manner that international peace and security and *justice* are not endangered. Article 73(a) provides for a *just* treatment of people in territories which have not attained full self-government.

International Human Rights Law in Practice

Although international human rights law in theory has developed to ensure peace and security and the conditions under which the dignity of the human personality can be protected, in practice, and in the name of maintaining peace, over a hundred battles and small wars have been fought since the United Nations was established, many of them on the Asian sub-continents. Again in the name of peace, we, the people of the United Nations, have amassed an arsenal of weapons which can wipe out the entire planet, including nuclear weapons and chemical weapons.

Practice does not conform to theory. Those who are the most vocal exponents of freedom of speech and of expression have yet to ratify the International Covenant on Civil and Political Rights; meanwhile they give open support to regimes which suppress the freedom of speech and expression of their citizens. Although the prevention of arbitrary arrest and detention is the accepted norm throughout the world, it is so hedged by restrictions such as considerations of internal security or sovereignty, that states have licence to subjugate their people. In theory, equality is proclaimed and racial discrimination is proscribed. Yet we witness the crying shame of South Africa. Although the right to life is theoretically protected, it is still treated as a gift of the constitution and the laws. Over 700 years have elapsed since the Magna Carta, but one still witnesses detention without trial. While there is freedom to profess one's faith and religion, any number of killings are justified in the name of religion. And, although affluent nations strive to provide far more than minimal economic standards for their citizens, they resist the application of those same norms by underprivileged nations.

Access to justice at the domestic level is beset with difficulties similar to those experienced at the international level. There are four major sources of violations of human rights:

> 1) Human rights are universally violated by legislatures when they enact laws which are in violation of the United Nations Charter, the Universal Declaration, other human rights covenants and instruments, and even their own constitutions. Legislative accountability is, thus, of primary concern.
>
> 2) A second source of violations is the executive branch of government. Even if the laws conform both to the national constitution and to internationally accepted minimal standards, the executive is often unaccountable in implementing the law. This non-accountability of the executive may be due to its obsequiousness to self-seeking politicians or to its pursuit of personal power or gain.
>
> 3) The third source of violations is sometimes the judiciary itself. A person who has been rebuffed by politicians and who has not had a hearing from the executive may turn to the courts to vindicate his grievances. The judicial system, however, may subordinate itself to the so-called expectations of the government in power. In that case, the judiciary may interpret the law in a manner which does not appear reasonable, just or fair to the common man

and which, with the passage of time, will prove to be arbitrary.

4) The fourth source of violations is the structural violence which is a result of various pressures in society, often caused by economic disparities, religious and ethnic tension, and a lack of understanding between individuals.

Thus, when we talk of access to justice, we must understand the concept in terms of legislative, executive and judicial accountability and structural change. In India, great strides have been made in the use of the courts to secure justice for the victims of human rights violations. By and large, the Supreme Court of India has been responsive to the aspirations of the downtrodden and underprivileged.

To ensure access to justice also requires that people know their rights. Unfortunately, neither those rights which are guaranteed under international law, nor those guaranteed under domestic law, are widely publicized, with the result that people are generally unaware of their rights. It is, therefore, imperative that there not only be machinery for monitoring human rights violations, and access to appropriate remedial forums, but also that information on human rights law be widely disseminated.

Towards a New International Human Rights Law

During the past decades, there has been a gradual expansion in the concept of human rights. There are some who suggest a three-tier generation of human rights: 1) civil and political; 2) economic, social and cultural; and 3) the right to development. It is now well accepted that there can be no 'trade-off' of human rights. One cannot say that it is necessary to curb civil and political rights in order to realize economic goals, even though some reasonable restrictions may have to be placed on them. When we talk about a right, some take a conservative, legalistic approach and argue that all rights have corresponding duties or obligations. My effort, here, is to demonstrate that there is a right to development recognized by international human rights law.

Within the body of international law already elaborated, the right to development is already implicit. Reference may be made to Articles 55 and 56 of the United Nations Charter and to Articles 22 and 27 of the Universal Declaration of Human Rights. Also relevant are the provisions contained in Articles 2 and 11 of the International Covenant on Economic, Social and Cultural Rights. Various other covenants, especially those of the International Labour Organization, can be cited in support of the view that the international community has resolved to co-operate in improving the standard of living of all of the peoples of the world.

In June 1979, the Commission on Human Rights of the UN resolved that the right to development is a human right. Others, however, are of the view that the right to development is a third-generation right (after

27

civil and political rights and economic, social and cultural rights), or that it is of an instrumental nature. Here, however, it is submitted that the right to development is neither third generation nor instrumental but that it is a *resultant* or *consequential* right. That is, if the guarantees provided under the Charter, UN declarations, and other instruments are faithfully observed, then human development in totality would be the result.

It is unfortunate that some of the more affluent nations do not concede any right to development although they do not deny the need for faithful observance of civil and political rights, or even of economic, social and cultural rights. It is odd, indeed, to suggest that the ingredients of development (i.e. civil and political rights, and economic, social and cultural rights) must be conservatively understood – as involving corresponding obligations – and not acknowledge the consequences or results that are inherent in the exercise of those same rights. In this sense, the right to development is a derivative right.

This still leaves a question unanswered: whose development? Is it the development of the state or of the individual? There are countless examples of states indulging in grandiose, unrealistic and unproductive spending while, at the same time, they suppress the civil and political rights of their citizens, and their economic, social and cultural rights as well. In other instances, governments proclaim development goals; yet the people are so far removed from the decision-making processes that there is no real popular political participation. A clear example is that of Brazil which, in spite of tremendous increase in Gross National Product (GNP), has done little to improve the lot of the poorest of the poor. Coupled with this is executive non-accountability. Do the developed countries have an obligation to assist in this pattern of 'development'?

Economic assistance is, of course, often used as an instrument of extending political power, even if it is accompanied by development rhetoric. In these cases, the two superpowers expect adherence to their systems of government and their economic policies, rather than any development criteria. If the peasants of El Salvador raise their voices in favour of agrarian reform, they are perceived as a security risk for the United States. Likewise, if the Polish trade unions call for freedom of speech and freedom to organize, they are considered a security risk for the Soviet Union. In the context of human development, what is important is not freedom *of* speech but freedom *after* speech.

The developed countries, which are in a position to assist the developing countries, ask why they should be obliged to support a state which either does not have a similar political or economic system, or is unfriendly. Similarly, the citizens of developed nations may ask why they should provide development assistance to others when they have their own problems of food, housing, medical care and social welfare at home. From a global perspective, it is extremely difficult to find optimal denominators for a wholesome co-operation between the developed and the developing countries. Yet, I submit that if development is considered in relation to the individual, then all the afore-mentioned objections can be met. If the obligation to provide for development is interpreted as development for the individual, the underprivileged of both the developed and the developing world would be addressed. It is worth while to recall that the Preamble to the United Nations Charter reiterates the need for improving the lot of the individual.

Development and Justice

A careful reading of international documents suggests that development is envisaged not as mere economic growth but as the total development of the human person. While some states argue that the suppression of civil and political rights is necessary to achieve economic growth, it is now well-established that there can be no trade-off between civil and political rights on the one hand, and economic, social and cultural rights on the other. The conceptualization of rights in terms of generations is misleading. Human rights constitute a holistic concept and the demand is for the total development of the individual. That there may be circumstances which require marginal adjustments between rights does not alter this fact. It is coincidental, perhaps, that it is the countries of the First World which lay emphasis on the so-called first-generation rights (civil and political), those of the Second World which give primacy to so-called second-generation rights (economic, social and cultural), and the countries of the Third World which underline the third-generation (development) rights. However, if rights adhere to people and not states, there cannot be any generation gap. If all human beings are to be treated equally as human persons, the division of rights on a geographical basis, or in terms of economic constraints, is not a viable proposition.

Various international instruments provide for the formal equality of nations by providing that each sovereign state should have one vote and that all states should be treated as equals. In an unequal world – where power is unequally distributed – this kind of equality is illusory. Formal equality is, however, a negative concept. The need of the hour is to bring about substantive equality, which necessarily requires affirmative action by states. Unequal cases have to be treated unequally in proportion to their degree of inequality; for otherwise, any system or order will only result in maintaining the status quo and perpetual inequality.

Developed nations often argue that there is no right to development because, if such a right were conceded, one would at the same time be conceding to duties or obligations. Such a conservative approach requires the identification of the donor of the right, the recipient of the right, and sanctions for enforcement. There is, however, another view. The existence of need, the assertion of a need, the acceptance of the necessity or the expediency to fill a need by those with the resources to do so, and the maturity of the sense of obligation all act to convert a need into a right. The mechanism for the enforcement of such rights is built into the process of maturation.

Want of sanction cannot, by itself, determine whether a particular need is a right or not. The right to life, in its broadest interpretation, is not a gift of a constitution or of law makers. Even though sanctions against South Africa have proved ineffective, this does not undermine the right of South African blacks to equality. Can it be said that the starving millions of the Third World have no right to life because of the non-availability of resources, or because of the lack of enforcement sanctions even where resources are available? Can it be said that the Directive Principles of State Policy, written into Part IV of the Indian Constitution, do not contain rights because the Principles are not strictly enforceable in the courts and because there are no sanctions for non-enforcement? Are the guarantees for adequate food, clothing, shelter, education, medical care or social welfare mere empty formalisms in the absence of sanctions? The incapacity of a system to fulfil all the rights that are proclaimed, or the lack of enforcement mechanisms for non-compliance, are not the determining factors. A new jurisprudence must be developed for determining when needs are transformed into rights.

To quote Mr Shridha S. Ramphal:

> In terms of hunger, wretchedness, deprivation and death, intimations of the 'Third World War' have already claimed thousands of casualties; a toll that increases daily and which those who argue that the nuclear race has maintained a balance of peace conveniently ignore. The field of carnage may have been shifted from Europe; but the consequences to humanity remain the same.

In this war, our alignments should not be between Left or Right but between right and wrong.

4. The Legal Aid Movement in Indonesia: Towards the Implementation of the Structural Legal Aid Concept

Buyung Nasution

The Development of Legal Aid Organizations in Indonesia

The decade of the 1970s and the beginning of the 1980s have been marked by a prolific growth of new legal aid organizations in Indonesia. At least 70% of all existing legal aid organizations, including the Jakarta Legal Aid Institute (of which this author is the head), were established during that period.

Irrespective of whether this trend is merely a phenomenal yet isolated growth or a reflection of more basic changes in the interrelationship between law and society in Indonesia, it is evident that the development of the legal aid movement is an established reality among other socio-political realities of the nation.

The models of legal aid carried out, the form of legal assistance rendered, the political attitude and orientation, the tactical and strategic alternatives of legal aid organizations, their potentials, capabilities and limitations, differ from one legal aid organization to another, depending upon both internal and external factors which influence them.

A theoretical study by Berney and Pierce has suggested, *inter alia*, that the various legal aid models in fact reflect different stages of development and signify the extent of the professional response within the given country to these stages; likewise, the social powers and conditions, the political institutions, and the personalities of the persons who extend legal aid greatly determine what model a particular country will utilize for its legal services to the poor.[1]

Legal aid organizations in Indonesia at present number more than 80, of which 20 are located in Jakarta (the national capital, with approximately 3% of the total population of the country). With reference to the organizational base (or sponsoring group), this total number may be subdivided into five main groupings:

1) Legal aid organizations established by the Indonesian Bar Association and at present further co-ordinated by the Indonesian Legal Aid Institutes

31

Foundation, such as the Jakarta Institute of Legal Aid, the Medan Institute of Legal Aid, the Surabaya Institute of Legal Aid, and similar ones created in the principal cities of major island-provinces;
2) Legal aid organizations operating under the auspices of the law faculties of state universities;
3) Legal aid organizations operating under the aegis of the law faculties of private universities;
4) Legal aid organizations operating under the patronage of socio-political organizations, such as the Institute for Legal Services and Information of the Working Group, and such others;
5) And, finally, legal aid organizations with orientations towards particular interest groups in Indonesian society, such as the Legal Consultants for Marine Law, the Institute of Legal Aid for Women and Family Relations, and legal aid organizations which are not (or not yet) affiliated, such as the Indonesian Lawyers' Association, the Legal Aid and Study Group, and several other legal aid groups domiciled in Jakarta.

The above development is to be noted merely as a quantitative increase in the relevant institutions, because qualitatively it still remains to be seen how far they have in fact extended in geographical distribution, or been diffused throughout the national territory, so as to improve the face of justice in the country.

Nevertheless, the said development has brought forth certain tendencies favourable to indigenous efforts to realize the ideals of a state based on the rule of law and also to efforts for structural changes aimed at the goal of a more just society, for several reasons. First, with the spread of legal aid organizations, more possibilities have been opened up for the target groups of legal aid – namely, the poor who are ignorant of the law – to obtain legal services and thus the opportunity to receive justice. Second, there has been a subsequent effect on governmental authorities and legal practitioners alike, both having been rendered more sensitive and responsive to the legal needs of the poor. And, third, the growth of these legal aid organizations has provided increased opportunities for making the laws more effective and for institutionalizing all forms of participation in this process; simultaneously, this growth has also intensified efforts towards law reform in Indonesia.

Factors Affecting the Growth and Role of Legal Aid Organizations
Although a legal basis for legal aid activities was already provided in Indonesian law regulations prior to the 1970s (for example, in the *Herziene Inlandsche Reglement* [Code of Criminal Procedure]), a firm legal basis for organized legal aid which is in the interests of the poor who are ignorant of the law and which is orientated towards servicing the lower strata in Indonesian society has never been expressly provided. Even with the passage of the new Basic Law on Judicial Powers (No. 14/1970), while the 'right' to obtain legal aid is mentioned in the articles of that law,

it is only 'in passing': no mechanism is provided to assure the substance of the right, nor any remedies for its denial.

At the conceptual level, the original idea for the establishment of legal aid with a clear orientation towards the interests of the people was brought to the fore only recently, for it was at its 1969 annual Congress that PERADIN (the Association of Indonesian Lawyers) approved a resolution for the setting up of a legal aid institute for the poor in Indonesia. This later came to be known as the *Lembaga Bantuan Hukum* Jakarta (LBH Jakarta, or Jakarta Institute of Legal Aid).

The establishment of the LBH Jakarta and, indeed, the expansion in numbers of other legal aid organizations (most of which has occurred since 1978) ought not to be viewed in isolation. That is, these developments definitely cannot be separated from broader political, economic and social changes taking place throughout the country over the past two decades of development. One can sum up these broader changes in terms of three parallel trends (which seem evident, in greater or lesser degree, in all Third World nations). First has come an explosion in the need of the people, especially the poor, to obtain justice based upon regularized, institutionalized settlements. In Jakarta, for instance, the process of implementing the national plan of development has generated a number of side-effects, perhaps foremost among which has been the forcible eviction of people from the lands they had traditionally occupied and worked simply because the policy of town development so decreed. Meanwhile, in other regions of the nation, the problems which the people face in the legal field are tremendous: inhuman treatment in a biased judicial process, the negation of the most basic rights, and other legal and social problems which definitely require legal solution and effective protection.

Secondly, the process of development, as it actually takes place, has led to a heightened political struggle which has also become broadened, incorporating the goals of a state based on the rule of law and of a system in which international human rights norms are promoted and protected. For example, as Daniel Lev has pointed out, the concrete steps to establish legal aid organizations in Indonesia began as a strong reaction, initiated in 1967–68 by some intellectuals, journalists and human rights activists, against a new wave of preventive detentions, arrests and other forms of repression launched by insecure, politically suspicious local authorities. The significance of this intensified struggle for the rule of law was put in the following terms by Lev:

> For the others, amongst them professional lawyers, intellectuals and other people committed to further change, a state based on the rule of law means a more over-all re-arrangement of the Indonesian state to expand the benefits in the form of security, orderliness, protection of personal rights and procedural equality through the prosperous people in the cities to the poor in cities and villages. Due to this liberal perspective, but in a moderate

radical context, there emerged new legal aid programs, pressures on traditional legal doctrines, and the kind of demands for reform which [however, in fact] were defeated in Law No. 14/1970.[2]

It is true, as implied, that the movement for organized legal aid in Indonesia grew out of the earlier and more encompassing struggle for constitutionalism and the rule of law: almost all of those involved in developing the idea of legal aid had themselves been active supporters of constitutionalism.[3]

Parallel to the above two trends, in part stimulated by them, a third trend may be noted in Indonesia. Somewhat paradoxically, there has been a controlled opening towards political freedom by the New Order government of General Suharto, undertaken for its own political reasons within the context of the desire to achieve the manifest goals of its overall development policy.

As mentioned earlier in this paper, the development of legal aid models cannot logically be separated from the particular stage of development in which a country finds itself.[4] From this perspective, the growth of the Indonesian legal aid movement is an integral part of the types and amount of political development now being attempted by the New Order government. In the past decade, the government has promulgated a development strategy of 'equitable distribution'. The fullest expression of this strategy was reached with the publication of the State Policy Guidelines of 1978, in which the New Order government asserted that its policy included the effort 'to open the main path of equitable distribution of opportunity to obtain justice'. If this is the operational goal, then of course it made sense, given the underdeveloped nature of both the judiciary as an administrative structure and of the legal profession in Indonesia, to enlarge political freedom sufficiently to permit the establishment of legal aid organizations. Just this has happened, especially since 1978.

However, from a different perspective, this extant freedom to organize legal aid ought properly to be viewed as closely intertwined with the calculated and sophisticated adjustment of political repression, which is of a complex and universal nature. That is, both more vigilant administration and greater tolerance for more independent organizing within the middle classes are indeed characteristics of a certain stage of development in what may be termed 'developmentalist repressive regimes'.[5] A kind of limited freedom for establishing organizations of the legal aid type often forms part of the policy of such a country.[6] This stage of development, and type of regime, may be marked by the difference between permitting the citizenry a limited capacity to fight against certain kinds of injustice, and allowing it unhindered freedom to participate peacefully in the search and struggle for justice.

Meanwhile, quite apart from the three above-mentioned conditioning factors, theoreticians and practitioners of legal aid in developing countries view it as a humanitarian response to a demand for help, an essential prerequisite to the functioning and integrity of the system of justice.[7] In particular, these advocates see four specific social objectives being furthered by legal aid: 1) the establishment of a unified, nation-wide legal system; 2) the development of a larger sense of responsibility to the public on the part of government officials and bureaucrats; 3) the stimulation of greater participation by the public in the process of governing; and 4) the strengthening of the legal profession itself.[8] Thus, from the point of view of law development, a third and still different perspective, legal aid is in general a legal institution to reach participative objectives in a responsive legal system.[9]

To summarize the main points of this section of my paper, legal aid organizations have potentials and limitations in the performance of their roles. The realization of the above objectives (or hopes), the fulfilment of the public's legal needs, and the orientation of the legal profession itself – these, however, are not the most decisive factors determining the role of the legal aid organizations. This is so because there still remain many factors obstructing legal aid,[10] factors which are both cultural, such as the values existing in the society, and structural, in the form of unequal command and control of the resources available in that society – including legal resources.

Differing Perspectives Towards the Development of the Concept and Implementation of Structural Legal Aid

Within Indonesia, the initial extension of legal aid activities did not emerge from a single perspective concerning the concept of legal aid, and especially concerning the types of operations to be undertaken.

Even today, some practitioners and legal aid activists still hold to 'legalistic' guiding principles. Thus their legal aid activities are steered to hold faithfully to conventional judicial procedures in the legal field. And within this traditional frame of reference, the main activity of legal aid is limited to litigation activities involving vague and poorly co-ordinated target groups.

The official perspective emanating from the New Order government, meanwhile, indicated that it envisaged legal aid activities limited to consultative activities and traditional litigation. In short, the legal aid organizations are to keep away from any and all activities of a 'political' nature.[11]

Nonetheless, more and more of those involved in the legal aid movement have been brought to a more critical understanding of the meaning and function of legal aid. This critical perspective evolved in reaction to, and from reflection on, the political, economic and social realities unfolding in the Indonesian mode of development and in particular the new injustices seen as accompanying the workings of a legal system responsive only to the needs and wants of the upper levels of the Indonesian social structure. In this enlarged perspective, the aim of legal aid must be to assist the massive numbers of poor in the society who are ignorant of the law; and the scope of activities of legal aid must not be limited to conventional litigation, but must instead have a wider scope, permitting the co-ordination and consolidation of litigation with non-litigating activities.[12]

While for political reasons and economic considerations many legal aid activists *in practice* still adhere to a traditionalist approach, the broader, more progressive concept – which had been pioneered by the LBH Jakarta – has now been widely accepted. In 1978, for example, a Legal Aid Workshop was held for practitioners throughout Indonesia and, in fact, was attended by participants representing most of the legal aid organizations in the country. The main achievement of the workshop was the acceptance of what we term 'the structural legal aid concept' as the guiding principle for the work of all participating legal aid groups.

This concept of structural legal aid emerged as the consequence of our comprehension of the law, its sources and functions. The legal reality confronting us is a product of social processes which occur in a certain pattern of relationships among the existing infrastructures of Indonesian society. Consequently, in our view, law is actually an ever-changing superstructure, the resultant of the interactions between and among the infrastructures of the social system. It follows that, so long as the pattern of relationships between and among these infrastructures tends to be unbalanced, the realization of a law which is just will be difficult. In that case, the injustices and oppressions which we so often perceive in our society actually do not come solely from the behaviour of an individual who consciously abuses human rights, but mainly have their sources in the unbalanced patterns of social relationships. Violations of human rights are structurally determined and, in this sense, are largely 'thoughtless'.[13]

As such, this means that structural legal aid shall consist of a series of programmes, aimed at bringing about changes, both through legal means and in other lawful ways, in the relationships which form the bases of social life, towards more parallel and balanced patterns. This is the essential pre-condition for the development of laws which provide justice for the majority of the poor in Indonesia.

At the operational level, structural legal aid must reach out to rural as well as urban areas; it must actively search out those cases to defend or initiate which most involve the public's collective interest, and those cases, undertaken in the interests of the poor, which create the opportunity for providing legal education to that broad public of labourers, peasants and fishermen.

On the societal level, therefore, structural legal aid is a growing power by means of which legal aid activities can positively influence and create conditions for law development fitting the people's needs. For this objective to be met, two conditions have to be fulfilled: 1) legal aid activists must consciously guard themselves against the professional élitism of so many lawyers; and 2) their organizations must not be separate, or insulated, from the clients they are intended to serve.

The concept of structural legal aid is neither dogmatic nor static; we are still in the process of developing the concept and fully understanding its implications for the specific activities that can and should be carried out. Thus a second, national Legal Aid Workshop was held at Prapat, Medan, in November 1980 by the Indonesian Legal Aid Institutes Foundation. At that workshop, a formulation was agreed which states that the main objective of structural legal aid is 'conscientization' as a means to gradually change the unjust social structure. Clearly, conscientization must be accompanied by organizational efforts as well.

The Jakarta Institute of Legal Aid is currently in the process of incorporating that reformulation of structural legal aid within its programme and operations, still within the framework stipulated earlier of co-ordinating and consolidating litigation with non-litigating activities. The litigation activities conducted by the LBH Jakarta are definitely not limited to technical and juridical activities only. Cases are selected which involve various kinds of conscientization efforts such as widespread publicity for those which reflect structural injustice and/or which illustrate what would be necessary to make law effective in the interests of the poor. Non-litigation activities mainly consist of research and publication from a point of view other than that of the law on the actual condition of various occupations and categories in Indonesian society, including the consequences of the implementation of the development functions assumed by the New Order government, of efforts to seek effective alternatives in rendering legal aid, and of efforts to comprehend the process of enabling people to become law-conscious. The latter, of course, is co-ordinated with organizational efforts to publicize information about and promote international human rights standards.

Closing Note

The quantitative growth in legal aid organizations in Indonesia and their qualitative development at the conceptual level are related to a number of factors, both within the legal system itself and as a consequence of major changes being wrought in the broader society.

Structural legal aid is a concept which is considered to be capable of becoming the guiding principle for organized legal aid activities in the country – and indeed elsewhere in the Third World. The concept is being implemented through a variety of programmes and actions which, hopefully, will be able to raise various forms of active participation by the masses – imprisoned as they are by structures of poverty and injustice – in the search for a more just social life.

Notes

(NB: The *Lembaga Penelitian, Pendikan dan Penerangan Ekonomi dan Sosial* (Institute for Economic and Social Research, Education and Information) in Jakarta conventionally refers to itself, and is referred to by Indonesians, as 'LP3ES' – which abbreviation will be employed here as well. Also, LP3ES publishes *Prisma*, a journal of social science and public affairs. However, to avoid confusion, the issues of *Prisma* cited below are of the monthly Indonesian-language versions (i.e. *not* the English-language version which comes out quarterly, of which the most recent issue available at the time of writing is No. 26 for September 1982).)

1. See, for example, Arthur L. Berney and Harry A. Pierce, 'An Evaluative Framework of Legal Aid Models', *Washington University Law Quarterly*, No. 1 (Spring 1975), pp. 5–44.
2. Daniel S. Lev, 'Kekuasaan Kehakiman dan Perjuangan untuk suatu Negara Hukum' ('Judicial Power and the Struggle for a Nation of Laws'), *Prisma*, Vol. X, No. 1 (January 1981).
3. See Adnan Buyung Nasution, *Bantuan Hukum di Indonesia/Legal Aid in Indonesia* (Jakarta: LP3ES, 1981), especially p. 118.
4. Berney and Pierce, op. cit.
5. The theoretical framework for understanding 'developmentalist repressive regimes' in Asia has been provided by Herbert Feith, 'Rezim-rezim Developmentalis Represif di Asia: Kekuasaan Lama, Kerawanan Baru' ('Developmentalist Repressive Regimes in Asia: The Old Ruling Powers and the New Upheavals'), *Prisma*, Vol. IX, No. 11 (November 1980), pp. 69–84 (also reprinted as a pamphlet entitled 'Escape from Domination' by the International Affairs Division of the Christian Churches of Asia, Singapore, 1980).
6. For additional understanding of the mixed motives of Asian regimes in their 'controlled opening of political freedom', see Jan Breman, 'Rezim Baru di Asia Negara Lembek dalum peralihan menjadi Negara Kuat' ('The New Weak Regimes of Asia which Transform Weak Nations'), *Prisma*, Vol. X, No. 3 (March 1981), p. 72.
7. On this point, see Barry Metzger, 'Legal Services to the Poor and National Development Objectives', in Barry Metzger (ed.), *Legal Aid and World Poverty* (New York: Praeger, 1974).
8. Metzger's analysis has been applied with regard to the cultural and structural factors conditioning the development of legal aid activities in Indonesia in Nasution, op. cit.
9. See Philippe Nonet and Philip Selznick, *Law and Society in Transition: Toward Responsive Law* (London: Harper & Row, 1978). In that volume, the authors have developed a threefold typology to describe the nature of law in society: *repressive law*, which is the slave and instrument solely of the repressive powers in the system; *autonomous law*, which is capable of taming executive repression and protecting its own institutional integrity; and *responsive law*, which is a means to respond to social needs and aspirations. Responsive law is thus characterized by the increase of various forms of citizen participation through legal institutions in the given legal system.
10. Nasution, op. cit., p. 23, is an attempt to discuss a number of factors – specifically, culture, political concepts and economic development plans – which obstruct legal aid activities in Indonesia.

11. At the time of writing, this official perspective is still adhered to. Recently, several important officials of the New Order government have issued public statements criticizing the 'politicization' and 'commercialization' of legal aid activities as 'beyond the [boundary] line'. In various ways, the government is trying to contract the activities of legal aid organizations back to the safe areas of traditional legal consultation and conventional litigation. These pressures have been felt most by those organizations operating under the auspices of the law faculties of the state universities – which were effectively 'depoliticized' as a consequence of the repressive attack by the Suharto government in the late 1970s.

12. *Buta hukum* (or 'being in the dark concerning law') was the term employed by the author, in his presentation at the 1969 Congress of the Indonesian Bar Association, to define those large numbers of Indonesians who are ignorant of the law, who are so lacking in education as to be unaware of their rights as legal subjects, or who, because of their lowly socio-economic position (and as a result of pressures, intimidation and harassment by those who are stronger), have no courage to defend and fight for their rights.

13. See Nasution, op. cit., especially p. 126 for elaboration of a theory of structural legal aid.

5. Legal Aid: Some Reflections

T. Mulya Lubis

In Delanggu (Klaten), a little town in Central Java, there is a legal aid unit. There is one in Imogiri, near Jogyakarta. Some villages near Surabaya have access to a legal aid unit. It seems that there are also such units in villages near Bandung, in West Java, and perhaps in other places too. None of these have signs up outside so only people who live nearby are aware of their existence.

Under the Programme for the Legal Aid Movement (PPBHI), data have been collected which show that there are approximately 100 organizations active in the field of legal aid, some professional and others amateur.[1] However, PPBHI has counted only organizations which use signs. We therefore do not know exactly how many legal aid institutions actually exist in Indonesia.

Several questions are raised by the tendency not to use signs. Is this a symptom of distrust of formalities? Are the formalities suspected of having a negative effect? Or is this a movement of conscientization that must involve the local population? Has a legal aid movement been created by the masses? It is too soon to answer these questions. At the moment, legal aid is still in its preliminary stages of development even in the cities, and even more so in the rural areas. As a term, 'legal aid' is no longer a strange one. However, it is not yet commonplace in the lives of ordinary people or perceived by them as a need.

The term 'movement' must be interpreted in qualitative, rather than in quantitative, terms, and as more than a surface phenomenon. The principal questions here are whether the 'movement' is strong enough to challenge apathy and the status quo, and whether it is becoming rooted in society. The contrast between a surface or horizontal phenomenon and a deep-rooted or vertical one is of absolute importance to the promotion of structural legal aid.[2] One must not exaggerate the importance of legal aid merely because it has been written into the Basic Outline of State Policy and Indonesia's Five-Year Plans.[3] As with Indonesia's co-operative movement, so with the legal aid 'movement', one must ask whether it has become rooted in fundamental societal needs.

Limitations of the Legal Aid Movement

At this time, no one can claim that there is a fundamental need for legal aid in Indonesia for the following reasons.

First, not many people understand what legal aid is. Even though the number of legal aid organizations exceeds 100, this is a very small number for a country whose population is 147 million. The Institute of Legal Aid (LBH) must conduct research on a national scale and must promote an understanding of legal aid. At the present time, the LBH's impact is still peripheral to society and it is largely dependent on the mass media to channel information to the people.

Second and very significantly, we do not know how important law is in the minds of the people, and hence the importance legal aid can assume. In the government's conceptualization of the 'Development Trilogy', law comes *after* the distribution of economic growth and stability.[4] While legal aid should be integral to the first element of the trilogy (economic distribution), both law and justice have been placed at the very end of the 'Eightfold Path of Distribution' in the government's formulation. And, in fact, in everyday life, it is 'stability' which receives the greatest emphasis.[5] What we must determine is the degree of importance that the law and legal aid have for the population.[6] What we do know is that there are large sectors of the population who are poor and have no time for law – sectors who are described as 'law ignorant' by educated Indonesians.[7]

Thirdly, there are boundaries which demarcate the areas in which legal aid can operate from consciously guarded areas in which legal aid is prohibited. It is very difficult to push beyond these limits. None the less, the Institute of Legal Aid has been steadily pushing, using what support it can get from the mass media. The effectiveness of this tactic and the fact that legal aid has become an embryonic movement worry the government. For this reason, legal aid – and the Institute of Legal Aid (LBH) – have been criticized by the authorities as commercial and political.[8] The concern of the government is that an unopposed legal aid movement can become an alternative power base. For this reason, it has attempted to co-opt the movement, taking the initiative to unify all legal aid organizations under one umbrella organization. Similar tactics have been used to control farmers' and workers' unions.[9] Centralization simplifies control.

A fourth and final factor to note is the limited funding and manpower available to legal aid. Even where there are openings which permit the extension of legal assistance, the limitation of resources prevents movement into these openings.

These four limitations can be charted in their internal and external dimensions:

Internal	*External*
1. Insight	1. Insight
2. Organization	2. Social conditions

3. Manpower   3. Political conditions
4. Funds   4. Ignorance

Taken together, these limitations make it impossible to call legal aid a 'movement'. Legal aid is growing into a movement but has not yet become one. At most, there are a number of institutes, or bodies, or centres of legal aid 'power resources' that worry the Establishment.[10]

The Dilemma of Legal Aid

The legal aid 'movement' is also hampered by the fact that there is still a lack of agreement over the *concept* of legal aid.[11] Divergent conceptualizations can be grouped under two main headings, although there are many variations within each: 1) individualistic or traditional legal aid; and 2) structural legal aid.[12]

The individualistic conceptualization of legal aid is one which is basically in line with the existing legal system. Here the concept implies legal aid in any individual case where a defence is justified in the eyes of the law. The main emphasis is on the *law* itself, and the law is always regarded as neutral or egalitarian. Often, however, law is not justice. In these instances, to view the law as neutral is to benefit those who have wealth and power at the cost of the poor masses.[13] From this perspective, legal aid has no power to achieve justice. 'Justice' is caught in its own orbit and becomes static; in fact, it turns into injustice.

The concept of structural legal aid is tied to the destruction of injustices in the social system. It is directed not merely towards aiding individuals in specific cases, but towards an emphasis on cases which have a structural impact. Legal aid becomes the power to move in the direction of restructuring social order so that a more just pattern of relationships can be established. Law, in and of itself, cannot address the question of injustice. Indeed, it often strengthens the status quo because it is obliged to be neutral. Once one accepts that society is neither just nor egalitarian, then one must reject neutrality in favour of supporting the weak in their confrontation with the strong. Structural legal aid, therefore, places itself on the side of the weak who form the majority of the population. The legal struggle must be orientated towards creating a law that is supportive of the weak.

The legal aid 'movement' must, therefore, reach some consensus about the meaning of 'justice', 'social justice' and 'structural justice'. One must go beyond appearance and get to essentials.[14] One must not remain at the level of formality but reach for the substance. This is particularly important because conscious and deliberate efforts are being made from some directions to blur the distinction between 'appearance' and 'essence'. If labourers realized how much of their labour is underpaid, they might stop working for their employers. Most labourers, however, are not aware of this fact and are kept in the dark so that the socio-economic gap between them and the wealthy can be maintained. In a capitalist society, there necessarily exists a difference between appearance and essence.

All the above-mentioned elements – the continued predominance of the individualistic conceptualization of legal aid, the formalistic view of justice, and a dependence on legal means – pose a dilemma. Often the commitment to the law means surrender to the system in existence. Legal aid activists are forced to stop at the boundaries created by law itself, even if they believe that the real function of legal aid is to break out of these limits.

This dilemma can be illustrated by the case of villagers who traditionally collected wood, rattan and other forest products and sold them in the city. One day, this forest (state property) was claimed by a commercial firm and the villagers were forbidden to collect forest products from that land. As this was both a traditional activity and their only means of livelihood, the villagers ignored the prohibition. They were arrested and brought to court as thieves. From the perspective of formal legality, the firm was indeed the legal owner of the land and the villagers had engaged in theft. But from the perspective of justice (the essence of the law), the questions are different. Is it fair to charge these villagers with theft when they carry on their traditional activities? Is it not they who have been robbed by the commercial firm?[15] Is the search for livelihood theft? In this case, we see both the favouritism of the law and the limits of legal aid. If legal aid activists limit themselves to legal means, their activities are in vain; if they use extra-legal means, they tread on difficult ground.

It is these difficulties, faced in case after case, that produce ambivalence among legal aid activists. On the one hand, they must push beyond the boundaries of the law. On the other hand, they are aware that they are hostages in the hands of the law. In a state where the law is unjust and does not work as it should, it is impossible to avoid such ambivalence unless the legal aid activists are consciously aware that their objective is the restructuring of an unequal social system.

The Role of Democracy

Moreover, even when the activists adopt a structural legal aid approach, in the final analysis, legal aid frequently reinforces the system. When a case with implications for structural change comes to the forefront, legal aid becomes one resource in the struggle for change.[16] Yet its emphasis is generally on diffusing a conflict, not on solving it. As a consequence, the existence of the Institute of Legal Aid is useful for the government, as long as it does not cross the boundaries of law. Hence, the answer to the question – 'Why does the government tolerate the Institute of Legal Aid?' – is that it has become an effective instrument for dissolving conflict. In this regard, the Institute is not so much a threat as an establishment within the Establishment.[17] This can be clarified by reference to the following facts.

First, in Indonesia anti-subversion laws are still applied which reduce the effectiveness of the New Code of Criminal Procedures (HAP). In subversion cases, there is little role for legal aid. The activists from the Jakarta Institute of Legal Aid have often been informed by interrogators that they cannot take on criminal law cases if subversion charges have been brought against the defendants.[18] This illustrates how the government prevents the Institute from crossing set boundaries. Political cases are insulated from legal aid.

Secondly, and with reference again to the New Code of Criminal Procedure, there are difficulties in ensuring that the suspect is aided by the defender in the initial interrogation. HAP states that legal advisers and legal aid activists *may observe* the course of interrogation, but they cannot be present at the interrogation.[19] In many police stations, interrogation rooms have a glass partition which permits legal counsel to *see* what is happening but not to *hear*. This is another means of maintaining existing boundaries and preventing legal aid from becoming a movement. If HAP seems to provide a door through which legal aid can be rendered, it remains a closed door, even if it is a transparent one.

Thirdly, beyond the court room, legal aid activists encounter difficulties in their conscientization programmes, their research and their teaching. The government frequently denies them permission to engage in research which would bring them into close touch with the masses. Research into labour cases can be carried out only informally because union bosses threaten labourers who co-operate with legal aid activists. District Heads around Jakarta constantly, on orders from higher authorities, deny permission for the establishment of legal aid posts. Thus, efforts to create a legal aid structure are hampered by government obstruction.[20]

A fourth and final fact to note is one that has already been referred to: namely, the government's power to unify legal aid organizations under one body. The government has already established umbrella organizations for groups including workers (FBSI), farmers (HKTI), journalists (PWI) and youth (KNPI). The motivation behind this centralization is greater government control over legal aid. Legal aid activists rightly fear co-optation, a danger that is particularly real when one considers the centrist bureaucratic strains of legal aid.

All these factors work to prevent legal aid from becoming more than a surface phenomenon. Even though the legal aid 'movement' often seems fiercely critical of injustice, it rarely reaches below the surface. Yet, unless it does so, the advantages to the government will outweigh the capacity to effect justice. It will be window-dressing on the dynamics of state policy. At best, it will be a minor annoyance to the Establishment without disturbing the social system. At worst, it will reinforce injustice and add to the misery of the poor. The Institute of Legal Aid is forced to confront this challenge.

Legal aid activists have become aware of both the internal and external limitations described above and are, consequently, attempting to assess realistically the goals of the legal aid strategy. For the time being, there is little hope that legal aid can transform itself into a real movement, or that legal aid can produce fundamental structural change. These are inflated and misleading expectations. Nonetheless, legal aid activists must, at the same time, free themselves from ambivalence and support structural, not individualistic, legal aid. Perhaps those involved in developing a legal aid strategy should think in terms of small-scale and simple legal assistance organizations. They should work towards conscientization and a strengthening of fundamental human rights so that they can hasten the process of change in the social system.

Notes

1. See *Bahana*, Vol. III, No. 3 (May–June 1981). Here the number of legal aid organizations is stated as 70; but our latest data show that the number has now exceeded 100.
2. It is necessary to note that we must be careful in using the term 'movement' because there is a tendency in the Third World to think of a movement as merely a surface phenomenon. On the contrary, we conceive of a movement as something more deeply embedded in society, in the minds and actions of the masses of citizens.
3. See T. Mulya Lubis, 'Bantuum Hukum Struktural: Redistribusi Kekuasaan Dan Partisipasi Dari Bawah' ('Structural Legal Aid: Redistribution of Power to the Lower Level'), in *Prisma*, No. 5 (May 1981).
4. See No. IV/MPR/1978 regarding the 'Basic Outline of State Policy' (abbreviated, GBHN). In the section on law in the GBHN, one finds the following statement: 'The development of legal aid for under-developed sections of the society' (i.e. as one of the official goals).
5. If one examines the Indonesian mass media, it cannot be denied that the Institute of Legal Aid (LBH) has received considerable coverage. (In one recent period, for example, the LBH got into the news every day for a month.) However, reporting of the government's stress on 'stability', within the context of 'development first', clearly overwhelms any references to law and justice associated with the LBH.
6. See President Suharto's Address to the Nation in Parliament, 16 August 1978, as published by the Department of Information of the Republic of Indonesia.
7. On the problems involved with being 'law ignorant', see T. Mulya Lubis, 'Pembangunan & Hak-Hak Asasi Manusia' ('Development and Basic Human Rights'), in *Prisma*, No. 12 (December 1979), pp. 11–20.
8. See the 1979 report of LBH Jakarta on the need for legal aid among the urban poor in the country (unpublished).
9. See Adnan Buyung Nasution, *Bantuan Hukum di Indonesia* (Legal Aid in

Indonesia) (Jakarta: Institute for Economic and Social Research, Education and Information, 1981).

10. See, for example, *Tempo*, Vol. XI, No. 15 (13 June 1981), which quotes the Indonesian Minister of Information, Ali Murtopo, as criticizing the Institute of Legal Aid for 'deviating' from its initial goals – without, however, clarifying what these goals are supposed to be. Therefore, our understanding of this situation is simply that the government is afraid of the Institute's possibilities of growth.

11. See, for instance, the effect of the industrial workers' union (FBSI) on urban workers or that of peasant unions (HKTI) on peasants, as a result of the centrist nature of these government-decreed 'umbrella-organization' unions and the ease with which they may be controlled.

12. If each existing legal assistance organization has ten workers, then we now have a total of some 1,000 legal aid workers. This is clearly a very small number in a population approaching 150 million.

13. In the 1981–82 national budget, the government provided a sum of Rp. 800 million. At current exchange rates, this is approximately US$1.25 million. We feel this sum is insufficient.

14. Lubis, 1981, op. cit.

15. The debate over legal aid continues. An interesting discussion of it is included in Nasution, op. cit. Also see Abdurachman's *Beberapa Aspek Tentang Bantuan Hukumdi Indonesia* (*Some Aspects of Legal Aid in Indonesia*) (Jakarta: PPBHI – Institute of Criminology, 1980) and his *Beberapa Pemikiran Tentang Bantuan Hukum: Ke Arah Bantuan Hukum Struktural* (*Some Ideas About Legal Aid: Towards Structural Legal Aid*) (Bandung: Alumni, 1981).

16. Lubis, 1981, op. cit.

17. See C. J. M. Schuyt, 'Keadilan & Efektifitas dalam Pembangunan Kesempatan Hidup' ('Justice and Effectiveness in the Development of Life's Opportunities'), an address translated (into Indonesian) by Paul Mudigdo (unpublished). See also the UNESCO/ESCAP publication, *Social Problems of Low Income Groups*, Report of the Bangkok Workshop, 17–23 February 1981.

18. A useful discussion of this problem may be found in Marshall Cohen *et al.* (eds), *Marx, Justice and History* (Princeton: Princeton University Press, 1980).

19. Ibid.

20. Basically, projects that would open the doors for approaching the people are almost entirely closed to the Institute of Legal Aid. Permission for certain proposed LBH activities has never been given and probably never will be given.

Part II:
The Present State of Human Rights in the ASEAN Nations

6. Human Rights in the ASEAN Nations

Introduction

The following seven chapters have been grouped together as Part II because each paper focuses on the writer's own country, describing the present state of human rights in that country and also presenting an assessment of the types and causes of human rights violations there.

It should be noted, however, that this Part – as was true of the conference and its entire proceedings – treats only Indonesia, Malaysia, Thailand and the Philippines within the Association of South East Asian Nations (formed in 1967 to provide for political and economic co-operation among five non-Communist nations of the region). It does not cover Singapore, the fifth ASEAN country, which can be dealt with briefly in these introductory notes.

Singapore was a British Crown Colony from its founding in 1819 until 1959, at which point it became autonomous within the Commonwealth. In 1963, Singapore joined – briefly – with Malaya (and the Sarawak and Sabah portions of Borneo) to create the Federation of Malaysia; but 'communal tensions' – ethnic conflict between Malays (who dominate Malaysia) and Chinese (74% of Singapore's population) – led Singapore to withdraw and become a separate nation, a highly urbanized island republic, in 1965.

Concerning politics and human rights in Singapore, most observers agree in generalizing that the ruling People's Action Party (PAP) and the government of Prime Minister Lee Kuan Yew have maintained a very tight rein on the 2.4 million population. For example, it was only in 1982, after some 18 years of independence, that the first (and thus far only) opposition party member was elected to Singapore's 75-member Parliament. In general, the permitted range of political expression and action is quite narrow, the penalties for political deviance very harsh. In fact, Singapore is an apparently deviant case, when contrasted with the other four ASEAN nations (and with much of the Third World), only to the extent that it has effectively combined political repression with what has generally been regarded as corruption-free government.

More specifically, those who have been outspoken in public criticism of the People's Action Party and Singapore's policies – opposition party leaders and candidates, journalists, union leaders, defence attorneys – have been arrested under the Internal Security (preventive detention) Act and held for long periods without charges or trial, a significant number in excess of ten years. Amnesty International, for one, has investigated reports – which the human rights organization judged as credible – that prolonged interrogations were accompanied by both physical and psychological torture: around-the-clock sessions and sleep-deprivation; prisoners being stripped naked, doused with ice-cold water, and interrogated in rooms with air-conditioners set for the extreme; severe beatings. Such arbitrary, indefinite detentions can be ended if the prisoner confesses to 'Communist activities' and/or 'pro-Communist sympathies', usually with relation to the outlawed Communist Party of Malaysia. There is no public record to demonstrate that any one of these confessions has ever been tested in an open court trial held according to commonly recognized, due process standards. The confessions, however, have proved useful to the regime of Prime Minister Lee. It has frequently publicly televised such political recantation sessions, keeping a fearful sense of 'the enemy within' alive in the public mind. Furthermore, on the basis of such dubious confessions *alone*, the Internal Security Department of the Singapore government has often then arrested those individuals named by a prisoner who has confessed, and they in turn have been indefinitely detained without formal charges.

In at least one documented case, when a prisoner refused to confess, his wife was also imprisoned, to increase the pressure on him. Additionally, other political prisoners, with or without public recantation, have been summarily stripped of their citizenship under the Banishment Act, but then have remained indefinitely imprisoned – because they refused to accept 'deportation to a country of their choice', under the terms of that legislation, which the Singapore government had arbitrarily specified as the People's Republic of China.

Such actions, and the documentation on them assembled by international human rights non-governmental organizations, caused the Dutch Labour Party to demand the expulsion from the Socialist International of Singapore's ruling PAP. In mid-1976, just prior to the London meeting of the Socialist International which was to examine the evidence in support of the expulsion demand, the PAP withdrew from that organization. The withdrawal was immediately followed by a new wave of arrests and detentions to 'prove' that the prisoners had intentionally disseminated 'distorted' information about Singapore, which 'Euro-Communists' had then brought to the Socialist International in order to discredit the People's Action Party. Another victim in this wave of repression was a newly-formed Human Rights Committee for Singapore. Three former members were arrested; their confessions dutifully alleged that the real, and sole, purpose of this committee was to discredit the government and to aid the activities of the 'Communist united front' within Singapore by forcing the release of 'hard core Communist detainees'. (However, two other members, a medical doctor and a Roman Catholic priest, also named in these publicized confessions refuted the government's allegations, insisting that they believed it was legitimate and proper for Singapore's citizens to concern themselves with promoting and protecting human rights and civil liberties.)

In view of the above, it was not surprising that, in a 1981 pre-conference trip to each of the five ASEAN nations by the Executive Director of the Human Rights Internet to enlist participants in the 1982 Access to Justice workshop, no Singaporean volunteer could be identified. The government had successfully equated human rights activity and domestic Communist subversion with severe sanctions attaching.

This Part begins with two chapters on Indonesia. The first, a second contribution by T. Mulya Lubis, examines Indonesian law with regard to basic human rights (BHR) of the poor and powerless. Taking parliamentary legislation enacted in the 1969–79 decade (which encompasses the government's first two Five-Year Plans), the author analyses both the law and actual practices with regard to: wages; land reform; equality in education and health services; and the rights of assembly and participation. In all subject areas, Lubis points out serious discrepancies. And these he attributes to two primary causes: a deliberate governmental 'policy of non-enforcement', with the government immediately cancelling out the effect of apparently landmark social legislation by indefinitely postponing the issuance of the requisite Implementation Regulation; and a 'trickle-down' national development strategy designed by technocrats utterly unconcerned with either the non-economic causes or consequences of development. The second, shorter paper by H. J. C. Princen takes a broader view, perceiving the problem of human rights violations in the context of the common dependence of the South East Asian nations upon a global economic system which favours the strong. Within this region, irresponsible governing élites permit and encourage the exploitation of natural (and human) resources by the West, especially by the United States and Japan. In response, Princen proposes self-organization and self-defence as the logical strategy for genuine emancipation.

Malaysia is the subject of the next two chapters. In the first, Azmi Khalid documents the historical and legal steps by which, since independence in 1957, a Western parliamentary system and dedication to the concept of the rule of law have degenerated into a closed system of unfettered executive discretion. He finds that rule *by* law – a command for 'law and order' backed by superior force – has brought about the measurably significant decline, if not actual extinction, of individual freedom in this former British colony. The analysis presented by Khalid is grimly confirmed by the unsigned legal memorandum, 'Notes on the Domestic Legal Remedies Available in Malaysia to Protect Human

Rights', provided by an individual who has been engaged in domestic litigation and other lawful activities in defence of human rights there. (To protect the human rights organizations and associates with whom this individual works, a request for anonymity has been honoured.) Addressed to practising private attorneys, this memorandum underscores the extremely constricted role defence counsel can hope to play within the legal system when attempting to assist those individuals whose personal liberties have been violated by the government of Malaysia.

Viboon Engkagul, also a practising lawyer, provides the fifth paper which treats the situation in Thailand. The institutions of government and their apparent functions are seen to be Western in form only. Thus, for example, the judiciary will not exercise its admitted power of judicial review as a remedy for governmental violations of individuals' rights, instead deferring to the long Thai history of absolute monarchy. There is a written Thai Constitution which provides a detailed enumeration of the rights and liberties of the individual, and it substantially conforms to the enumeration in the Universal Declaration of Human Rights and the codifications in the two International Covenants; yet they are immediately made subject to vague prohibitions against exercising any of them against the nation, religions, or the king and the constitution. And they are further negated by the ambiguous provision that none can be exercised except in accordance with 'the provisions of the law'.

Chapters 12 and 13 focus on the Philippines. The first paper is by a distinguished professor (emeritus) of constitutional law of the College of Law at the University of the Philippines. In it, J. B. L. Reyes initially treats with brevity the reasons given by the Marcos government for refusing to ratify the International Covenant on Civil and Political Rights: the financial implications of the right to compensation, granted in the Covenant, for unlawful arrest or imprisonment; and the fear that the mechanisms established by this Covenant (i.e. the new Human Rights Committee of the UN and state-to-state complaint procedures) might constitute a derogation of national sovereignty and allow the superpowers to interfere in the domestic affairs of less developed countries. (The first reason may be dismissed as involving an insignificant fiscal burden for any government to assume. The second appears to be a shallow demagogic appeal for 'Third World solidarity' via the new nationalisms alive in the Third World generally, including the Philippines, and also an attempt to project an image of 'non-aligned' independence for a nation historically and deeply enmeshed in diplomatic, military and economic relationships with the United States.) Reyes's paper next provides a succinct catalogue of specific human rights violations that occurred in the nine years of Marcos's martial-law rule. This is followed by a close analysis of what did – and what did not – occur with the decree, promulgated by President Marcos on the day after his 1981 re-election, 'lifting' martial law. The analysis concludes that the process was entirely cosmetic, changing only the appearance of the form of rule in the Philippines. The Reyes paper is followed by a concluding one in this section, which focuses on the government's employment of 'strategic hamletting' and thus amplifies the final paragraph of his paper. (The authors of the paper on 'strategic hamletting' desired anonymity, which we here respect, for fear of further reprisals to the hapless victims who were the sources of the information in the paper and for fear of reprisals to themselves, their families and associates. We add, however, that the major factual findings and conclusions of the anonymous paper have subsequently been confirmed by an independent investigation undertaken by the duly constituted human rights committee of the Integrated Bar of the Philippines, i.e. the national bar association.) 'Grouping' – an official euphemism for the strategic hamlet policy – is an application of counter-insurgency doctrines with the objective of rural pacification. It has entailed the uprooting of peasant families from their homes and fields and their forced migration to and concentration in more densely populated centres; the mandated destruction of their former homes and the construction of new ones (but without the provision of any supporting services by the military or civilian departments of government); strictly enforced curfews from sunset to sunrise, which drastically limit the time – and energy – available for work on subsistence crops; and, during curfew hours, 'free-fire zones' wherein government security forces are instructed to fire at any human-appearing targets. 'Salvaging' – another Filipino euphemism, this time for the kidnap, torture and murder of 'disappeareds' at the hands of government agents – has also been documented in the Laac region. Whether, as rumoured, 'grouping' is merely the first step towards land grabs by high military officers and/or transnational agri-business corporations, one would assume that enough damage has already been done in turning the victims against the central government. And in this regard, the Filipino situation, at least locally, is similar to that which has been much more widely reported concerning Guatemala and El Salvador.

If these seven chapters are analysed as if they were dealing with a single composite country of 'Aseana', then certain recurrent features would appear with regard to constitutionalism and the legal system, to governmental structure and politics, and to the economy. Identification of such recurrent features also directs attention to human rights problems common in the Third World.

There is, first, a weak tradition of constitutionalism. Written constitutions are ignored, simply deemed to be non-self-executing or otherwise have any operative clauses. This seems an appropriate description of the Indonesian experience. Elsewhere, constitutions are readily replaced: Thailand had ten separate constitutions between 1932 and 1982, with an average life of five years each. Alternatively, the procedures for the formal amendment of existing constitutions have been established as no more difficult than the passage of ordinary legislation; thus, recently ratified constitutions have been easily and multiply amended, as the situation in Malaysia reveals (since independence, the Malaysian Constitution of 1957 has been formally amended 23 times, or an average of almost once per year). Or, as has occurred in the Philippines, the declaration of a state of exception – imposition of martial law, in this case – provides the occasion for subverting the former Constitution (in 1972–73 President Marcos rigged the process – by handpicking the membership of the constitutional convention and manipulating a plebiscite for ratification – in order to rewrite and replace the 1935 Constitution). Apparently it is more important simply to have a written constitution, articles of which can be defensively quoted verbatim by governmental representatives, than it is to concern oneself with fundamental social, political and legal principles that ought to be embedded in a constitution; indeed, in this sense, it is evidently sufficient – to meet the demands of one's citizens and the expectations of most of the international community – just to have a written constitution. Meanwhile, if the fundamental political compact of a society can be so quickly and drastically changed, then it should be evident that the idea of self-limitation that comes from adherence to certain substantive and procedural rules previously agreed upon – the essence, that is, of the concepts of due process and the rule of law – is weakly established in that society at best.

The weakness of the tradition of constitutionalism, if indeed it should be dignified by terming it a 'tradition', is especially evident in the matter of individual rights and liberties. Third World constitutions read and sound most modern, for they – like the United Nations' Human Rights Declaration and Covenants of this same post-World War II era – enumerate the full panoply of civil and political rights incorporated in the earlier Western liberal democratic tradition, while at the same time they also specify significant collective economic and social rights from the more recent Communist/Socialist tradition. But the apparent dedication of most Third World governments to individual *and* collective rights is rendered illusory by two counter-traditions which came into existence almost simultaneously.

The first of these is the widespread use of what international lawyers refer to as 'clawback clauses'. That is, after the right has been verbally identified, the clawback clause immediately follows and states that the individual right being 'guaranteed' can in fact be taken away by some governmental body, usually the legislature. There need be no special circumstances (e.g. an emergency such as imminent external invasion which is deemed threatening to the life of the nation) to justify the restriction or extinction of the right. Whatever ordinary legislation is passed – meaning essentially whatever the executive can cause the legislature to enact – is constitutionally valid by virtue of its mere existence. (The effect of these clawback clauses is not greatly different from that resulting from the principle of constitutionalism utilized in the Soviet Union and its East European satellites. There, the individual's rights – to free speech or to free association, for example – are granted subject only to the condition that they be exercised in fulfilment of the citizen's 'duty to construct Socialism'. This, history has recorded, is a proviso placing essentially unbounded discretion in the hands of the authorities.)

The second counter-tradition is that governing the process of 'derogation'. Derogation, as a principle of international public law, allows for the temporary suspension or breach of certain nation-state obligations (e.g. on the part of a government to preserve the civil liberties of its citizens) under circumstances of war or public emergency; and the principle is based on the logic that the state – as the organized political expression of the nation – has the right and duty to maintain its own existence. But wartime or a serious public emergency constitute periods of high negative emotions, of uncertainty, fear and anger, which greatly increase the probability that a government will abuse its own citizens. (The forced 'relocation' into concentration camps of some 120,000 Japanese-American citizens, most of whom were American born, by the United States government during World War II – apology and compensation for which are finally being officially debated – is a regrettable example.) Thus, an effective respect for human rights places two kinds of restrictions on the process of derogation: it limits the circumstances and specifies the procedures under which derogation may be legitimately invoked; and it also identifies and reserves certain core rights – the individual's rights to life, freedom from torture, and freedom from *ex post facto* laws are the most vital from a political science perspective – as absolutely *non-*derogable. At the time of the independence of many Third World nations, particularly those which became independent earliest, their constitutions evidenced respect for human rights by prescribing both procedural and substantive limits on the process of invoking a state of exception (whether martial law, siege, or emergency). More recently, however, a tendency – the second counter-tradition – has appeared to make the process easier and easier. (The 1981 amendment to the Malaysian Constitution is apposite here.) Thus, one now finds Third World constitutions in which: the executive alone can declare an emergency whether the legislature is sitting or not; the highest court is denied the authority to review the decision in any way; the proclamation need specify no time-limit for this extraordinary suspension of civilian government; military decrees issued during a state of exception continue indefinitely in existence unless specifically terminated by the legislature; and so on. And therefore one also finds in the Third World governments which have continuously (Taiwan and Syria) or almost continuously (Malaysia) or for long periods (the Philippines) functioned with extraordinary powers. When the exception becomes the operative rule, as it clearly has in so many Third World nations, human rights of all forms, including economic, social and cultural rights, become the subject of systematic violation.

There is a new trend in constitutionalism which has recently appeared in the Third World. It is ironic that it has been created by precisely those governmental leaders who have demonstrated least respect for the written constitutions of their own countries, who have utilized the laws to make a mockery out of the concept of the rule of law. As the Reyes paper points out, President Marcos prudently had the 1973 Constitution amended in 1981 in order to provide permanent and total immunity to himself and his subordinates for any actions taken during his tenure. Any possible criminal prosecution, civil action for damages, or other remedial legal proceeding is absolutely barred. Nor is this Marcos effort at self-immunization unique: Generals Videla, Viola, Galtieri and their military successors have been similarly demanding an absolute bar on any future governmental inquiry into the cases of some 20,000 'disappearances' before the military retires from Argentine politics. Those who have used government to commit most monstrous crimes against their fellow citizens now seek to encourage respect for constitutionalism in the event of their retiring from, or losing, power and yet remaining alive!

Under the above conditions, it should be clear, the structure of governmental institutions and their ostensible functions become atrophied, deformed. The legislature is necessary – but primarily symbolically, for domestic and external propaganda purposes. A minority-party representation within the legislative membership may even be carefully preserved to demonstrate the robust political life of the nation. (But the laws defining and regulating political parties, trade unions and other associations, and those defining the system of representation and providing for electoral administration are variously employed to ensure that such a demonstration project does not get out of hand.) In fact, the functions of the legislature dwindle down to a few: dutifully to pass the annual budget, to ratify constitutional amendments devised by the executive, and to enact formal legislation making broad, increasingly vague, delegations of legislative power to the executive branch.

In like manner, the judiciary must be harnessed to the purposes and will of the executive. Government contracts may occasion disputes, commercial life goes on, ordinary crimes continue to be committed. Therefore, civilian courts remain necessary, functional – so long as potentially politically 'unreliable' judges have first been removed, forced to retire, reassigned to remote provincial benches, and so forth. However, since ordinary political activity threatens the stability of the regime, new categories of political crime have to be created or reacted to. These are best handled by special (i.e. military) tribunals. In these, the 'right to counsel' becomes the right to a military-appointed military counsel, usually meaning one not versed in the law and always meaning a careerist whose occupational success depends upon conforming to the perceived wishes of his military superiors. Other 'simplified procedures' – on 'openness', confronting and cross-examining accusers, or presenting evidence of torture or confession under duress – also limit the individual's right of defence, permitting speedy and harsh conclusions. In short, all effective power becomes concentrated in, and at the very top of, the executive branch of the government. At its discretion alone, decisions are made concerning what the law is and should be.

To justify such changes, an official state ideology is promulgated proclaiming the 'New Order'. The interminable 'talk-talk', delays, compromises and corruption of the former civilian governmental institutions are relegated to the dustbin of history. Development is both the overriding goal and the means to that desired end. For its achievement, national unity is imperative. Any activity detracting from national unity is subversive. Symbols, or slogans, of both democracy and Socialism are richly incorporated into the new state ideology; yet at the same time the ideology stresses the uniquely national (or indigenous) path being taken to democracy and Socialism. The latter feature has multiple advantages. It has the effect of stressing cultural continuity and consistency as both process and goal; this in turn obviates the necessity of defining either democracy or Socialism in institutionally or procedurally specific terms; and, finally, it elevates the existing political élite to the indispensable position of final arbiter and interpreter of what does or does not contribute to the preservation of cultural integrity. Given these features, the state ideology is inherently ambiguous, quite deliberately and functionally so from the perspective of the power holders. Meanwhile, the state ideology provides the substantive content for political socialization into the system. The élite assumes and tightens its control over the institutions of public education, the electronic media and newspapers, even film, theatre and other 'public manifestations', to ensure that the citizenry is properly socialized. The unarticulated goal is individuals who think of themselves as active, autonomous citizens but who act as passive subjects.

For those who remain imperfectly socialized, for those who think and act in politically deviant ways (in the view of those with the power to define and sanction such deviance), political repression is the necessary response. Therefore, the positive side of the state ideology must be complemented negatively by an official doctrine of 'national security' (which has attained its fullest elaboration – within the Third World at least – in the recent military regimes of Latin America, particularly those of Chile and Argentina).

The importance of a national security doctrine is to be found in its two major attributes. Its manifest function is to be found in the designation of who 'the enemy' is; and it accomplishes this, first, in terms of an external, alien and threatening system and, then, in terms of domestic adherents of that system, individuals who have placed themselves beyond the pale and therefore have caused whatever political repression must necessarily take place. (In the ASEAN region, since all five countries can be characterized as having dependent-capitalist economies, those citizens who are democrats, nationalists, economic nationalists, and/or Socialists are commonly stigmatized as being Communists, meaning that they – along with native and genuine Communist Party members – are the subversive agents of Moscow or Beijing as the particular case, and current foreign policy, demands.)

The second feature of the doctrine is that the concept of national security is intrinsically vague and therefore inherently expansible. Practically any human behaviour can be, and historically has been, rationalized as threatening to damage the security of the nation – especially where, as is common among political élites, incumbent power holders psychologically conceive of themselves as if they were the nation itself. (After all, Europeans, Anglo-Americans included, are not so distant in time from the day when it was a crime, punishable by death, to 'encompass the death of the King'.) For these reasons, the alleged external threat identified by the doctrine justifies a substantial military establishment, particularly a standing army, for which the alarming internal threat justifies further increases in budget, personnel and functions. But since an army is an exceedingly blunt instrument for domestic governance, and since the sophistication and conspiratorial secretiveness of subversives make them very difficult to detect, an internal 'secret' – meaning non-secret and political – police is also necessitated. Furthermore, these twin instruments of suspicion, surveillance and repression, so essential to effective socio-political control, must be rewarded so that they will continue to sustain the incumbency of the existing executive. In turn, this means that budgets must be increased, privileges and perquisites extended, corruption tolerated. In sum, the preservation of the loyalty of these two institutions to the leader requires increased lawlessness. A system is created whose maintenance depends on continuing, widespread and visible-but-'inevitable' violations of the full range of international human rights.

In turning to the economic and social features observable in a generalized 'Aseana', and to the consequences of these for human rights, we note that they have already been adumbrated. Here it will suffice to examine briefly the factors of land, natural resources, and labour which a Third World nation has to offer for development and integration into the global capitalist system.

Productive land is taken out of subsistence farming and from the cultivation of staples for domestic consumption, and is now devoted to agri-industrial production of export crops. Large tracts of unused arable land are also consumed, not for farming but for large-scale infrastructural development projects such as hydroelectric generating systems. These changes in turn have multiple consequences. Intensive monoculture, pursued long enough, degrades the soil's productive capacity. Meanwhile, no provision is made for the populations displaced: they are simply left to their own meagre resources. Initially, most remain in the neighbouring area, landless and part of a growing potential pool of agricultural day- or seasonal-labourers most of whose members are, at best, vastly underemployed. In time, these conditions push first the breadwinners and able-bodied males, then whole families, into the shanty towns surrounding the dominant urban centres of the country where they are free to construct their own shelters from the scrap materials they can purchase, steal, or simply discover. Here, too, they stand in line to wait, grossly underemployed when not totally unemployed. Urban industry's child labour force is recruited from the families of those so displaced and marginalized, assisted by the brokerage services of middlemen whom a Charles Dickens would immediately recognize. So also for the workforce of young, single, untrained women needed in many light-assembly manufacturing processes. In Asia, if there is an American military base or a Japanese tourist hotel nearby, prostitution may offer gainful employment for some of the women, perhaps some of the young males as well.

Where self-sufficiency in domestic food production formerly existed, it now disappears. A food deficit requires importation of basic foodstuffs and establishes a new need for foreign-exchange earnings through exports. If genuine rural development figures at all in the multi-year national development plan (and usually it does not, if only because the burgeoning urban concentrations are perceived as more immediately threatening politically), the programmes and projects prove – intentionally or otherwise – to be biased, disproportionately benefiting the absentee and/or largest landowners and their economic allies (e.g. suppliers, money-lenders, etc.). There are some few instances of reform of land tenure systems which vest titles in co-operatives and formerly landless individuals or squatters; and which also provide access to credit (for improved seeds, fertilizers and pesticides, and machinery), to the scientific knowledge of agricultural extension services, and to the market. But these are almost without exception small-scale demonstration projects stimulated by externally-based private development agencies and funding – those, for example, of Oxfam or Western Churches. No government of the four relevant ASEAN nations, for Singapore is the urbanized exception here, can claim any significant credit for such achievements. Meanwhile, however, the government must control the prices that domestic peasants and farmers receive for their produce. If theirs is a significant cash crop intended for the export market, the government usually creates a monopolistic buyer (e.g. a government marketing board) to which all domestic producers must by law sell at prices set by that buyer – so that the profit margin on resale contributes to the general revenues of the central government. Or, if the produce is for domestic consumption, prices must still be controlled by the government, directly through ceilings and/or indirectly through consumer subsidies, in order to provide a minimum adequate diet for – and thus control over – a potentially explosive urban population. Therefore, for most of the rural populace, who constitute most of the populations of these Third World countries, the national capital is no less alien than the metropolitan centre of a former colonizing power. The government provides no services in the Western sense to these rural people; it merely sends forth soldiers to maintain order.

Concerning the development of natural resources, domestic ('nationalistic') opponents of authoritarian Third World regimes charge that the latter have voluntarily surrendered, or lost, control over the national patrimony. In many instances, the claim is correct, for most such resource-exploitation projects are highly capital intensive. (And even where not, such as in one-time-only 'clear cutting' of virgin stands of timber or strip-mining for minerals, the wasting asset is exchanged in a transaction leaving long-term environmental damage.) Thus, even without evidence of bribery/extortion, multiple sets of corporate books, or other forms of white-collar corruption on which Watergate briefly opened a window of vulnerability, Third World governments have entered unequal exchanges, trading sovereignty over natural resources for an increase of a few thousand (lower-paid) jobs for their nationals. For example, mineral extraction projects – such as the opening up of a new copper or bauxite mine – exhibit three dominant characteristics: they are very large-sum investments; there is a long lead-time before pay-back production begins; and they are necessarily intended for long-term production. Prior to the 1970s, that is, from the Cuban Revolution up to the military overthrow of Allende in Chile, these projects were undertaken by *individual* American or European corporations which necessarily faced real risks of expropriation or nationalization of their assets if an unfriendly nationalistic or leftist Third World government came to power. Now, however, the lawyers and bankers serving the multinational corporations have invented new legal concepts of property ownership and new home-country policies which have the effect of drastically raising the costs for any Third World government contemplating expropriation to regain control over its natural resources. For example, equity ownership of a new mineral extraction project in Indonesia is syndicated, parcelled out among the multinational corporate members of a consortium drawn from the United States, West Europe, and Japan; partial World Bank and/or regional development bank funding is carefully folded into the project; *and* the direct private investments of the multinationals are proportionately insured against 'political risks' by their respective home-country governments. Consequently, the counter-risks that a Third World government contemplating nationalization now faces have been dramatically escalated: it would face a coalition of the most powerful Western governments, their most powerful corporations and commercial banks, and also the international financial institutions (in which these same Western governments have effective control through their combined voting power). In short, the combined economic sanctions which the Trilateralists can now impose are far greater than those the United States alone brought to bear on Allende's Chile. They make it highly unlikely that a Third World government, once its natural resources have been developed to the point of being integrated into the existing international economic order, could by itself re-establish political control over those resources.

Finally, development implies a modernized sector of the economy – heavy industry, manufacturing centres serving as export-platforms, and the like. Within a broad region, Third World governments scramble to compete for the direct foreign investments that will make these a reality. Tax deferrals, customs-duty exemptions, unlimited profit margins, unlimited repatriation of profits, unlimited access to the host-country's credit market, absence of requirements for technology transfers, for minimum domestic equity ownership, or for 'indigenization' of corporate managerial positions – these are some of the incentives competitively offered. (To the extent that these all operate to reduce available host-country governmental revenues, they constitute a 'voluntary' limitation of collective self-determination.) Other inducements, depending on the manufacturing processes involved, may lie in the absence of any occupational health and safety codes or any pollution regulations. (These are externalities, unquantified and apparently abstract social costs which, however, are borne by identifiable individuals within the work-force and population of the host-country.) However, the chief attraction is a large and reliable pool of cheap labour. In the urban sector, the workers remain largely ununionized. And where unions are permitted, they usually function as bureaucratic appendages of the government, their elected leadership subject to certification by a government department, their assets subject to control by a governmental agency, forbidden to associate with or to contribute funds to political parties (even where these are permitted). Most important, however, is that Third World labour is denied its most basic weapon – the right to strike. Labour-code legislation is drawn up, often with the helpful assistance of Western commercial attachés and foreign legal experts, so as to render it almost impossible to engage in a legal strike. Thus, lock-outs, wholesale firings, and black-listing of union organizers and activists are permitted if not actively encouraged. Spying on labour is engaged in by both host-government and foreign employers alike. Indeed, the full array of brutal anti-union employer tactics prevalent in the United States prior to World War II is in evidence. In effect, the host-country government assumes the surrogate role of company foreman, employing its police and military to enforce labour discipline. In such a context, where the rural population has simply been written off, it should surprise no one that the urban labour force experiences both a relative and absolute decline in real income. The end product of development in 'Aseana' approaches that of 'Belgeria', a term coined with reference to Brazil in the 1970s to call attention to the existence of a modernized, technologically sophisticated economic enclave the size of Belgium superimposed on a mass base of poverty, illiteracy and traditionalism the size of Nigeria. It is a political economy, functioning as part of a much more extensive system, whose maintenance depends upon fairly widespread and certainly continuing violations of all relevant individual human rights.

The above composite description and projection of trends are appalling in terms of the goal of human dignity. It is not argued that this composite fully applies in each particular detail to all ASEAN countries. After all, an opposition drawn from the most highly educated stratum of the populace is grudgingly tolerated in Marcos's Philippines and, as previously noted, Singapore seems remarkably free from governmental corruption. But the description does seem to capture most of the dominant characteristics of these five countries and, in fact, of the largest modal category – probably constituting the overwhelming numerical majority – of nation states within the approximately 130 countries lumped together as the Third World. And the compelling tragedy is that, in reality, the alleged 'trade-offs', employed to justify political repression as a necessary (if not causally self-sufficient) pre-condition to economic development, have not taken place. In the isolated instances of 'economic miracles', such as Taiwan, South Korea, or Brazil, the material gains have proved tenuous and fragile and the regimes are most unstable politically. That 'future' for which the post-1945 generation has already been sacrificed recedes further and further beyond grasp. There seems small rational basis for expectation or hope that the lives of their children or even grandchildren will be substantially different.

7. The Law and Basic Human Rights in Indonesia

T. Mulya Lubis

When we discuss basic human rights (BHR), we are forced to talk about the law as if BHR were concerned only with the law. BHR are certainly an inherent part of the law.[1] However, such a statement is misleading because basic human rights are in fact related to every aspect of our life, from the insignificant to the substantial: social, economic, political, legal and cultural aspects of life.[2] Investigating BHR, therefore, really requires a total dissection of social life; very broadly, one must ask how far our world provides a fitting place for humanity.

Because basic human rights cover all aspects of life, we are actually involved in discussing our social situation. Our quèstions then become: how far does Indonesian development, currently being implemented, share in expediting the upholding of BHR? how far does our legislative programme guarantee BHR? and how far does our socio-political situation support citizens in realizing their BHR? Other questions, certainly, could be added; but the above three should show that the problem of BHR is very extensive and has also broken through the legal barrier which has been holding us hostage thus far.[3]

Considering how extensive the orb of BHR is, we are faced with the question: basic human rights for what and for whom? This question sounds foolish because, when we talk of BHR, we in fact mean the BHR of every citizen without exception.[4] The fundamental assumption of the above view is that each citizen has the same status or standing before the law. But is it true that all citizens have the same status and standing before the law? Schuyt, a Dutch sociologist of law, has stated that 'equality before the law' is only a dream of legal experts.[5] There is no basis, he explains, for expecting equality in situations that are unequal – let alone if we are speaking of a country like Indonesia where the ravine separating the rich from the poor is so wide.[6]

According to Schuyt, equality is our Utopia; and to this end we endeavour to eradicate poverty, to overthrow oppressive patron–client relationships, to join with all the people in the formulation of their wishes, and to give them all the tools of production.[7]

It is within this context that we discuss the situation of BHR in Indonesia. And the question, 'BHR for what and for whom?' should have been answered by the brief analysis above, since it places fundamental stress on the basic human rights of the poor and oppressed, and the need to liberate them from the pattern of relationships which renders them powerless.

The Law and BHR

Among the colonial legacies which still apply in our lives are categories of regulations (i.e. laws) in almost every field of activity. These colonial laws have been firmly retained in order to avoid legal vacuums, so long as they do not contradict the spirit of our independence. It is by no means an easy task to draft legislation; besides, it consumes much time before proposed legislation is successfully enacted.[8] Political forces both inside and outside Parliament usually struggle over various amendments; this often takes much time, if not substance.[9]

There has not yet been a systematic comparison of the extent of inherited colonial law still in existence, and national law drawn up since our independence. Without specifying the number and content of extant colonial laws, we may be certain that many important colonial laws remain dominant in everyday Indonesian life. As an example, we could cite the Penal Code which deals with all types of criminal activities. There are also both the Civil and the Commercial Codes, dealing with family law, the rules of evidence, all matters of property, contracts, the business world, and so on. Even the laws of Indonesian court procedure are still colonial laws which have been in force for a considerable period and which are only now about to be replaced by new legislation.[10]

The question, therefore, which should be asked here is, how far do these dominant colonial laws protect the basic human rights of the poor? Clearly, the answer is that many of the colonial laws, including those just mentioned, encroach upon and indeed violate the BHR of the poor.[11] This is so particularly because colonial laws were characteristically individualistic and discriminatory – despite the claim occasionally made that they guaranteed 'equality before the law'.[12] Colonial laws favoured the upper classes of society who are rich, not the lower classes who are poor.

However, laws enacted since the time of independence have brought us no closer to upholding basic human rights. Even though there have been improvements, they have been merely partial, often cosmetic, not fundamental, improvements. And if we look further, to the stage of implementing laws, then we see more and more bias within the law towards the upper strata, for example in the Act on Foreign Capital Investment[13] and in the Act Concerning Political Parties and Functional Groups, allegedly for 'the simplification of the party system'.[14] We could certainly add to this list, up to and including the proposed Act of Criminal Law Procedure currently being debated in the Parliament (in *Dewan*

Perwakilan Rakyat, the People's Representative Council), which is considered by a large number of legal experts to be a gross retrogression from the *Herziene Inlandsche Reglement* (i.e. colonial-era Indonesian Criminal Law Procedures).[15]

As long as the law sides with the upper classes, it will not uphold the BHR of the poor. Even if we assume that the law is not biased at all, in a country where the gap between the rich and poor is large, basic human rights are necessarily violated. It is complete nonsense to speak of 'equality before the law' in a socio-economic system of inequality.[16]

During the first two Five-Year Plans (from 1969 to 1979), the Indonesian government promulgated many laws in the form of Acts, Government Regulations, Presidential Decrees, and Presidential Instructions. Their numbers have progressively increased, and we are going to see many more laws promulgated by both the central government and the regional governments. It is as if we were in an endless jungle of laws.[17] These increases are shown in Table 7.1 following.

Table 7.1
Total of Legislation Promulgated, 1969–79

Year	Acts	Government Regulations	Presidential Decrees	Presidential Instructions
1969	16	33	99	14
1970	14	56	78	19
1971	13	75	85	6
1972	6	37	75	8
1973	7	48	50	14
1974	11	46	56	17
1975	5	29	47	17
1976	11	26	52	16
1977	2	36	65	12
1978	8	34	44	13
1979	5	36	59	22
Totals:	*98*	*456*	*710*	*158*

Source: 'Work Report on the Principles of Interdisciplinary Law', Board of National Law Development, Jakarta, 1980, p. 21.

In this paper, we are only considering how close the laws enacted by the legislative body are to the basic human rights of the poor. We will not analyse here the Government Regulations, Presidential Decrees, or Presidential Instructions, since any such analysis would consume much time and many pages. For the present, we shall just focus on Acts of Parliament.

Of the 16 Acts which were passed in 1969, we see only four directly related to the protection of the BHR of the poor. These are the Act concerning the Formation of the High Courts in Bandung and Jakarta, the Act concerning Acceptance of Convention No. 20 of the International Labour Organization, the Act concerning Public Servant Pensions and Widow/Widower Pensions, and the Act concerning Labour Power. Further, of the 14 Acts enacted in 1970, we find only two closely concerned with upholding BHR, namely, the Act on Work Safety and the Act repealing Presidential Decree No. 2/1959 (which prohibited membership of political parties by public servants who are citizens of the Republic of Indonesia).[18] In 1971, we find only one Act, that on Combating Acts of Corruption;[19] then in 1972 we also find only one, namely, the Act on Basic Principles of Transmigration. In 1973, no Acts related to BHR were enacted, while in 1974 we find the Acts on Marriage, on the Basic Principles of Social Welfare, and on the Basic Principles of the Public Service. In 1975, 1976 and 1977, there were none that we could take note of, whereas in 1978 we see two Acts concerning the Formation of the High Courts in Pontianak, Denpasar and Kupang. Finally, in 1979 we find an Act on Child Welfare.

Other Acts passed during the first two Five-Year Plans were more often concerned with matters such as the national budget (*Anggaran Pendapatan dan Belanja Negara*);[20] extradition agreements with friendly nations; reports on several international conventions; Acts on state enterprises, foreign capital investment, meritorious conduct medals, and so forth. It is unfair to say that all these other Acts are totally unrelated to BHR in general; but our concern here is: how far is all this enacted legislation particularly concerned with the BHR of the poor? Why doesn't our government endeavour to pass Acts concerning legal aid, land reform, compulsory education, and such issues which, *nota bene*, are more relevant to the BHR of the poor? Is the upholding of BHR the last concern of government, something which may only come after economic development is completed?[21]

A point to be noted here is the fact that the number of Acts alone does not constitute a guarantee of the upholding of BHR. It very much depends on the type of legislation enacted. The test is, are those Acts tentatively identified by subject matter definitely weighted in favour of the poorer strata of our society? In addition to that relevant criterion, much also depends on the operation of those laws. The question of whether an Act is effective or not in achieving its stated purpose is vital, since it is often the case that existing Acts of Indonesia are ineffective due to the lack or the malfunctioning of mechanisms to carry them out.

Many Acts need an 'Implementation Regulation' to make them effective. The reality is that a number of Acts have never been followed up by an Implementation Regulation – so they cannot operate in practice. An example is legal aid which, according to Act No. 14/1970, forms one of the basic rights of the accused. However, this fundamental 'right' cannot be exercised simply because there is not the requisite Implementation

Regulation. And Public Prosecutors and the police always rely on this fact to deny a request for legal assistance: 'if it is to be exercised, there must be an Implementation Regulation.'[22]

So we are trapped in a vicious circle. The Indonesian government often uses such two-faced strategies in its politics of law making. With one hand, the government incorporates basic human rights in the body of the Act but, with the other hand, cancels them by indefinitely postponing the necessary Implementation Regulation. The impression we get is that the government merely wants to give verbal recognition to BHR and not to grant them. Such a symbolic style of government is not new in the developing countries. If we went to Latin America and Africa, we would see styles, like Indonesia's, which are often called the 'policy of non-enforcement'.[23]

BHR and Five-Year Plans I and II

Before speaking about BHR during the first two Five-Year Plans, we need to consider the goals and aims envisaged by those Plans. After that, we will move on to questions directly concerned with how far the goals achieved by those two Plans have approached or upheld BHR, especially those of the poor.

Indonesian debates during the past ten years about strategies of development, which most critics consider to have placed too much emphasis on increasing the Gross Domestic Product (GDP), physical construction and concrete capital, are actually very important. The planners and executors of Indonesian development believe too strongly that what is crucial is that we must first 'develop', and then the benefits will trickle down.[24] Our development planners believe this to be the best, most direct path out of the environment of poverty afflicting this nation.

Economic development can only be achieved, however, if supported by non-economic development.[25] A concept of development which places economic, legal, political and cultural problems all together is, unfortunately, not likely to find a place in the development planners' dictionary.[26] It is as if our development planners and executors are racing ahead with the desire to repeat the 'success stories' of development *à la* South Korea, Brazil and Taiwan. It is a shame that they close their eyes to what has been happening in Pakistan and Iran.[27]

What has happened in Indonesia in its Five-Year Plans I and II? Economic development has shot far ahead, while non-economic development has been left almost at the original starting-point.[28] GDP has increased, to be sure, but 'equalization of income' has stagnated. Many of our people remain poor, and many are made poor by development.[29] Illiteracy remains high, as do unemployment and the number of people without adequate nourishment or homes.[30] These are all touchstones of the basic human rights of the poor.

The imbalance in Indonesia is so great that social unrest has emerged in various places. The mothers of Siria-ria are angry, so are the agricultural workers at Jenggawah.[31] Social protest has erupted in Ujung Pandang and Medan.[32] All this unrest has occurred because our strategies of economic development have disregarded BHR and have disregarded the principle of 'social justice' which is supposed to be the spirit of that development.

The government, of course, is not unaware of the possible costs of social disturbances, and has consequently formulated what we Indonesians know as the 'Eightfold Path of Distribution'. This consists of establishing equality in the fulfilment of the basic needs of the masses, particularly food, clothing and shelter; equal access to education and health services; equality in the distribution of income; equality in employment opportunities; equality in business opportunities; equality of opportunity to participate in development, especially for women and the young; equality in the distribution of development throughout the entire territory of the nation; and equal opportunity to obtain justice.[33]

How far this 'Eightfold Path of Distribution' can be carried out in everyday life, we still have to witness in coming years. We really hope that the government executes this policy consistently, so that we are not caught in another frustrating trap, like the 'policy of non-enforcement'.

The Right to Obtain a Reasonable Wage

The level of wages in Indonesia is still quite low, both for public servants and private employees. And if we look further down the hierarchy at the wage level of our labourers, it is especially low. It is almost inconceivable, but today there are still labourers who receive a wage of 300 rupiahs a day (i.e. less than US $0.50).[34]

Without having to calculate specifics, we can easily see that for a small family with two children, Rp. 300 does not mean very much. Even an income of Rp. 1,000 per day for a small family still does not suffice, if the cost of rent and transport, and other payments are to be deducted.[35]

If there were scientific evidence that Indonesian children are less intelligent than those of other countries, we would conclude that we faced an insoluble problem; but how can malnourished children possibly be intelligent?

The available data indicate that the income of Indonesian labourers is between Rp. 300 and 1,000 per day, varying from region to region and sector to sector, as shown in Table 7.2, following.

Of course, the wage-rates shown in the table had changed by 1981, although no dramatic improvements occurred. The government-decreed minimums – which for the vast majority of workers tend also to be the maximums – had increased, but in the vast majority of categories they still had not passed Rp. 1,000 per day. And in the meantime, the price of basic goods had risen rapidly, particularly as a result of *Kenop 15* ('The 15th November Policy' of 1979) by which the government decreased subsidies and so increased prices for staple foodstuffs and transportation and also as a result of the rise in the price of oil fuel (for cooking) following the second world-wide 'oil shock'. Meanwhile, in this same three-year period (1978–81), we note that the rupiah lost somewhat more than half its value relative to the dollar. Therefore, basic human rights are not being observed in regard to the level of wages. In short, Article 27 of the 1945 Constitution of the Republic of Indonesia, which reads, 'Every citizen has the right to employment and a livelihood fitting for humanity', is still far from reality.

Table 7.2
Indonesian Labourers' Minimum Daily Wages

Province	Sector	Rate (in Rp.)	Date in force
Aceh	Industry	500	3/1/78
North Sumatra	Building	525	2/1/78
West Sumatra	Hotels	500	8/1/78
Riau	Building	600	7/1/78
Jambi	Lumbering	650	7/1/78
South Sumatra	Textiles	400	6/1/75
Lampung	Plantations	300	5/1/78
Special Capital Territory	Industry	600	6/1/78
West Java	Textiles	385	—
Central Java	Beverages	300	—
Yogyakarta	Building	250	—
East Java	Kretek Cigarettes	250	8/1/77
Bali	Building	350	4/1/77
North Sulawesi	Plantations	500	5/1/77
South Sulawesi	Beverages	225	8/1/78
Central Sulawesi	Building	500	7/1/78
West Kalimantan	Lumbering	700	1/1/77
South Kalimantan	Lumbering	750	2/1/78
The Moluccas	Lumbering	1,250	10/1/77

Source: *Monitor*, Vol. II, No. 1 (May 1979).

Land Reform

The data concerning the ownership of land in Indonesia are very incomplete. The existing data are only for several regencies and villages, and are not for the most recent year(s). Meanwhile, we have perceived changes in the pattern of land ownership. It is common knowledge that more and more villagers have been selling their land to city dwellers. Ownership of land *in absentia* is becoming an increasingly common phenomenon, not only in Java – the largest and most densely populated island of the archipelago – but outside Java as well. The trend in Java is towards a large number of landless villagers; and this has led to processes of political polarization in those villages where the proportion of landless is high.[36]

The equalization of land-ownership opportunities for the public has clearly stopped, and the land reform programme which was launched at the beginning of the 1960s is no longer heard of in practice. On the contrary, the trend in our land ownership is now reversed, from 'going public' to 'going private'.[37] Speculation and rumours that official X and business person Y have land holdings in K, L, M and N circulate more and more frequently; and the probability that official corruption is involved seems high. Accompanying these, there is a number of cases where control of people's land has been taken over by foreign corporations, particularly for plantations and lumbering.[38]

As a consequence, many cases of conflict arising from forcible dis-possession have occurred. We could mention, among these, the cases of Pajang Cenkareng (August 1978), Cikopomayak Bogor (January 1979), Lubuk Pakam Deli Serdang (February 1979), Lubuk Dendan South Sumatra (March 1979), Sesajpanjang Bogor (April 1979), Angsana Banten (April 1979), Indragira Hilir (May 1979), Mentul Cepu (May 1979), Siria-ria (July 1979), Jenggawah (July 1979), and Barang Siang (1980).[39]

The above incidents took place because of changes in the pattern of land ownership, as a consequence of which many former owners were forced to relinquish their land and many workers on the land were forced to leave. An agricultural census of 1973 – the most recent – stated that 83% of the peasants on Java possess on average less than ½ hectare of farmland per head, and that more than half possess less than ⅓ hectare per head.[40] But is the figure *still* anywhere close to 83%?

It is currently not possible to provide a quantitative answer, because the land problem is very hard to evaluate. Not only are the figures very incomplete and out of date, but those figures which do exist are some-times confusing. We only know that our land is 'going private' and that land reform has become an empty slogan of past history. In fact, Act No. 7/1970 has already abolished the Court of Land Reform that had been previously established to deal with the problem.[41] Clearly, the people's right to land still has to be continually fought for.

Equality in Education

The 'path of distribution' in education really means the realization of social justice in the field of education. This noble idea is also consistent

with our ideal of upholding basic human rights, because through education we can make people aware of their rights and obligations. The world
of education will open people's eyes to the environment around them,
and if that environment is unjust they will react. The swiftness of
someone's reaction is largely determined by the level of their ability to
read and write.[42]

At the beginning of Five-Year Plan I (in 1969)[43] approximately 28% of
all elementary school-age children could not be accommodated by the
existing school system. In addition, 32% of elementary school graduates
could not be placed in junior high schools; 23% of junior high school
graduates could not be placed in high schools; and 85% of high school
graduates could not be accommodated at the college and university level
of education.

Since that time, according to government statistics, between the end
of Five-Year Plan I (1974) and the end of Five-Year Plan II (1979),[44] the
numbers of school-age pupils and students actually in schools rose from
15,487,459 to 23,362,819 and the government claimed it had finally
achieved its target of attaining an enrolment figure of 85% of school-age
children. Most of this increase in enrolment – some 76% – was at the
primary level through a massive construction programme of elementary
school and *Inpres* elementary school (i.e. established by Presidential
Instruction) buildings in the villages. Yet it is an illusion to hope that
equality in education will be achieved through the construction of
elementary schools and *Inpres* elementary schools alone because, like
most economic development projects, the programme favours the most
urban and richest areas of the country. Additionally, we do not only need
school buildings and benches, but more particularly we need teachers
(and wages to permit them a decent living), books and other facilities. In
short, equality of access to education remains very uneven and some 30
million adult illiterates[45] are simply ignored by the Five Year Planners.
The government should have furnished much more time, energy and
funds for upholding basic human rights in the field of education.

Equality in Health

The Basic Health Act (Act No. 9/1960) incorporates an understanding of
'health' as not merely freedom from disease, deformity and other infir-
mities but as physical, mental and social health as well. This concept is
very broad, with both individual and social dimensions, and represents
the stated objective of Act No. 9/1960: a society which is both physically
and spiritually healthy. From the point of view of basic human rights, the
aim of that Act could be described as ideal; but the question here is, how
far is that aim realized in the community?

As indicated in Table 7.3, by the end of Five-Year Plan II, the
Indonesian government had constructed a large number of new physical

facilities for public health and had also increased the numbers of trained personnel. But other data for this same period suggest that apparently these increases in facilities and personnel are not enough to serve a swelling population now totalling 147 million. For example, the number of sick hovers around 50 people for every 1,000 inhabitants; yet only 50% of those who are ill have access to medical treatment of any kind. Moreover, a mere 20% of the sick can be accommodated by the existing Public Health Centres.[46] This shows us how limited are the resources provided for the people's health care.

Table 7.3
Total Numbers of Medical Facilities and Personnel

	1973–74	1978–79
Public Health Centres	2,343	4,353
Medical Clinics	7,424	4,180*
Maternity & Child Welfare Centres	6,801	2,412
Doctors	6,221	10,456
Nurses	7,736	31,061
Midwives	8,323	—
Medical supervisors	24,248	35,577

*The reduction in these figures is the result of these smaller facilities having been incorporated in the Public Health Centres.

Source: 'State Address of President Suharto of the Republic of Indonesia, at the session of Parliament on August 16, 1979', Jakarta, Department of Information, pp. 917–33.

Moreover, data obtained from the National Symposium on Food show that 9 million children below the age of five, a half-million pregnant women, and 200,000 breast-feeding mothers suffer from protein-calorie deficiency; 100,000 children each year suffer from vitamin A deficiency (which can cause blindness); 12 million inhabitants suffer from endemic goitre, due to iodine deficiency; and 12.5 million pre-school children, 9 million school-age children, 14 million women, and 5.5 million male labourers suffer from iron deficiency (which can lead to anaemia).[47] These data show us how limited the health services for our society are.

Despite a population of 147 million, the national health budget available for the year 1978–79 was Rp. 17,688,500,000, an estimate which included expenditure on increasing medical services, expenditures on supporting programmes, and routine expenditure.[48] This in fact constituted less than 0.5% of the total national budget for that year. Basically, we must face up to the fact that BHR in the field of health are still far below our expectations.

The Rights of Assembly and Participation

Article 28 of the 1945 Constitution guarantees the right of assembly and both verbal and written freedom of speech. This article forms one of the principal foundations of the life of a dynamic nation in which the people are free to establish associations and free to express opinions. Ever since this republic was formed, that article has given rise to much political discussion and to the emergence of many non-governmental organizations. It seemed that independence had brought us a climate of liberty. And, at least until 1959, we had achieved freedom of assembly.[49] But after the Decree of 5 July 1959, that freedom began to be threatened by all sorts of interference from the government. Even the judicial system, which should be independent, became a prime target for executive interference.[50] Thus, in Indonesia now, people are no longer free to express their thoughts in speech and writing. Everything must pass through censorship and control from the authorities. To be sure, opinions may still exist, but they must be on the same lines as government thinking.

More recently, at the beginning of the 'New Order' of the present government of Indonesia, we saw a regrowth of the climate of freedom of assembly and speech. The government began to act as if it thought that legitimization and therefore participation were necessary. There seemed to be a close relationship between the government and the people. But, unfortunately, that closeness proved to be merely a short honeymoon. For after a brief period of relaxation, the government began to insist upon 'Development first and Equality second, through the Five-Year Plan', and the honeymoon drew to a close. Freedom of assembly began to be curtailed, not only for government employees but, especially, for villagers. In addition to that, there has been a 'simplification' (*sic*, meaning forced reduction) of the political parties into only three, namely, the Indonesian Democratic Party, the Development Unity Party, and the so-called Functional Group.[51] Furthermore, professional associations and occupational organizations have experienced new governmental restrictions: for any one occupation or profession there can be only one legitimate organization. Thus, in labour, we find the All-Indonesian Labour Federation; amongst peasants, we find the Indonesian National Peasant Farmers' Association; and for the young, there is only the Indonesian National Youth Association. The central theme of our government's policy is 'simplification' of the realm of assembly and association, because a small number of organizations is easily monitored.

We also meet restrictions on the expression of opinions. The policy is that we are to use the institutional channels provided by the government to express our opinions; and if one persists in using non-institutional means, these opinions must be 'moderate' – meaning not measurably different from the government's. We are implored to tolerantly allow 'Development to go first' and, if we are patient, at some future time we may discuss such matters as equality and basic human rights. The government really takes this policy seriously; this is proved by the harsh actions it has taken against those elements of the press who dared to hold opinions different from its own.[52] Community leaders who have spoken on these matters of equality and BHR have often experienced interrogation by government agents and even detention.[53]

Apparently, we have not yet reached the right time for participation by the Indonesian people. They will have to wait until economic development is pronounced a success. Only then will socio-political participation find a proper place. And only then will we be able to discuss basic human rights in the socio-political field.

A Road without End?

From all that has been described above, we may conclude that the situation of BHR in Indonesia is in fact alarming. There is much we still have to do in many areas: the law, the economy, education, health and politics. An excessive emphasis on one area would result in imbalance. It is important to realize that as well as needing nourishment for the body we also need legal certainty, health services, reading materials, and freedom to assemble and hold an opinion. All this means that we should change our development policy. We should not believe that Five-Year Plans are going to solve the problem of our basic human rights, particularly when those Plans continue to put the economy as the highest priority – which determines the development of all other sectors of society. It seems that the road confronting us is still rather long.

Notes

1. T. Mulya Lubis, 'Pembangunan & Hak-hak Asasi Minusia' ('Development and Basic Human Rights'), in *Prisma*, No. 12 (December 1979), pp. 11–20.
2. To understand how wide is the scope of basic human rights, see the International Covenants on Civil and Political Rights and on Economic, Social and Cultural Rights.
3. Lubis, op. cit.
4. We are referring here to the renowned legal principle, 'equality before the law', which is contained in Article 27 of the 1945 Constitution of the Republic of Indonesia.
5. C. J. M. Schuyt, 'Keadilan & Efektifitas dalam Pembangunan Kesempatan Hidup' ('Justice and Effectiveness in the Development of Life's Opportunities'), an address translated into Indonesian by Paul Mudigdo.
6. Sajogyo, 'Masalah Golongan & Pembangunan' ('The Problem of the Poor and Development'), a working paper delivered at a seminar held at the Institute of Legal Aid, Jakarta, in 1979.
7. Schuyt, op. cit.

8. This group of colonial laws is still in force, based on the authority of Article II of the Transitional Provisions of the 1945 Constitution, which reads, 'All existing Government Bodies and Regulations are to remain in force provided that no new ones are created in accordance with this Constitution.'

9. The Indonesian government has long planned to replace the Commercial Code which was drawn up in 1883 by the Netherlands. A committee for reformulating a new Commercial Code has been formed and has met repeatedly, but to this day it has consistently failed to come up with one concrete result.

10. A rather comprehensive report on this proposed Act on Criminal Law Procedure can be found in H. Imron Rosjadi and H. Zain Badjeber, *RUU Hukum Acara Pidana* (*Proposed Act on Criminal Law Procedure*) (Jakarta: PT Bumi Restu, 1979).

11. Among the regulations contained in the Commercial Code, for example, there are many which are biased in favour of the owners of large capital.

12. In this context, it is interesting to examine our legal history and note that colonial law (what is known as Article 163 I.S., for example) essentially provided three categories of law for three basic groups: the Europeans enjoyed many advantages over the Orientals, while the latter had advantages over the native-born. In short, the principle of 'equality before the law' has never been an integral part of our legal history, either before or after the arrival of the colonialists.

13. See Act No. 1/1967.

14. See Act No. 3/1975.

15. Rosjadi and Badjeber, op. cit., particularly the opinions expressed there by the Indonesian Bar Association and the Institute of Legal Aid.

16. Lubis, op. cit.

17. There have been complaints publicized from a number of capital investors who have said that more regulations are to be found in Indonesia than in any other country. This abundance of regulations is not of great social utility but rather is bewildering, especially because of inconsistencies in many regulations.

18. This repealer Act, however, is basically meaningless because of the principle of monoloyalty whereby the government compels all its employees to become members of the Indonesian Public Service Association (KORPRI) which, *nota bene*, has been made legally a part of the 'Functional Group' (*Golongan Karya*).

19. The reason for considering this Act as one that is close to upholding BHR is the fact that corruption violates those principles of equality which are fundamental to any consideration of basic human rights.

20. Actually, fiscal policy – decisions on taxing and spending which go to make up a national budget – is connected to our concept of BHR to the extent that it defines and provides for the fulfilment of the basic human needs of the population.

21. In economic terminology, we can ask: is the distribution of income a final target which can only be reached through 'trickle-down' effects once 'development' has already been successful?

22. See Articles 35, 36 and 37 of Act No. 14/1970. A discussion of this problem may be found in T. Mulya Lubis, 'Gerakan Bantuan Hukum di Indonesia' ('The Legal Aid Movement in Indonesia'), a working paper delivered at the Faculty of Law of the Islamic University of Indonesia, Yogyakarta, 11 March 1980.

23. An interesting discussion of these points may be found in Robert C. Pozen,

Legal Choices for State Enterprises in the Third World (New York: New York University Press, 1976), pp. 143–51.

24. Lubis, op. cit. See also Adi Sasono, 'Pelita III: Tiga Isyu Pembangunan Nasional' ('Five-Year Plan III: Three Issues of National Development'), in *Profil Indonesia 1979* (*Indonesian Profile 1979*) (Jakarta: Institute of Development Studies, 1979), pp. 19–27.

25. See *Tap No. IV/MPR/1978* (Decree No. IV of the People's Consultative Assembly, or *Majelis Permusyawaratan Rakyat*, 1978), concerning the 'Broad Outlines of State Policy', especially Chapter III on 'General Patterns of Development in the Long Term'.

26. Lubis, op. cit.

27. For the case of Pakistan, see Mahbub ul Haq, *The Poverty Curtain* (New York: Columbia University Press, 1976), pp. 12–26.

28. Lubis, op. cit.

29. Ibid.

30. Ibid.

31. A portrait of social unrest is to be found in the report, *Dari Jenggawah ke Siria-ria*, by the Joint Defence Body of Indonesian University Students, Jakarta, 1980.

32. See *Tempo*, 26 April 1980.

33. See the 'State Address of President Suharto of the Republic of Indonesia, before the Parliament, 16 August 1979' (Indonesian Department of Information).

34. See *Prisma*, No. 12 (December 1979), pp. 38–48.

35. A pedi-cab driver, to whom this writer spoke, stated that, from an average daily income of Rp. 1,000, he can save only around Rp. 600 – all of which has to be sent to provide for the needs of his family in their village.

36. See William L. Collier, Soentoro, and Irna Soetomo Basuki, 'Pengamatan Tentang Pemilikan Tanah serta Landreform di Jawa', ('A Survey of Land Ownership and Land Reform in Java'), in *Prisma*, No. 9 (September 1979), pp. 17–31.

37. T. Mulya Lubis, 'Pembelaan Tanah di Kota: Sebuah Telaah Mengenai Kasus Simprug' ('The Expropriation of Land in the Cities: An Analysis of the Simprug Case'), a working paper delivered at the Conference on Land Laws held at Cibubur, 10–28 March 1980, by the National Peasant Farmers' Association and the Village Progress Association.

38. A number of these cases were handled by the Institute of Legal Aid.

39. See *Monitor*, Vol. II, No. 5 (September 1979).

40. Ibid.

41. See *Government Gazette 1970*, No. 41.

42. See Paulo Freire, *Education for Critical Consciousness* (New York: Seabury Press, 1973), pp. 1–58.

43. See *Monitor*, Vol. I, No. 3 (July 1978).

44. See 'State Address of President Suharto, 16 August 1979', op. cit. p. 866.

45. See *Monitor*, Vol. I. No. 3 (July 1978).

46. See *Monitor*, Vol. I, No. 10 (February 1979).

47. Ibid.

48. Ibid.

49. T. Mulya Lubis and Fauzi Abdullah, *Annual Report on Fundamental Human Rights, 1979* (Jakarta: Institute of Legal Aid, 1979), pp. 1–13.

50. Ibid.
51. See Act No. 3/1975.
52. The cancellations of the Publishing Permits of several of our newspapers in 1974 and also 1978 are examples of the unhealthy conditions under which the Indonesian press seeks to survive.
53. Lubis and Abdullah, op. cit.

8. Access to Justice

H. J. C. Princen

If in this meeting, or workshop as it is called in the invitation sent to us, we are to talk about the promotion of procedures for the implementation of internationally recognized human rights, the Indonesian delegation will be in full support of that idea.

We give that support because: 'Everyone is entitled to all the rights and freedoms set forth in this Declaration, without distinction of any kind, such as race, colour, sex, language, religion, political or other opinion, national or social origin, property, birth or other status' (according to Article 2 of the Universal Declaration of Human Rights); and because in all our countries we face much the same difficulties.

The similarity of those difficulties need not amaze us, because of our common dependence on a global economic system which favours the strong and therefore is apt to oppress the weak.

It is good for us to realize that, as long as that dependence lasts or even increases, and as long as we do not take steps to end that dependence, we will not be free agents. And in that case it is quite senseless to talk about the struggle to defend human rights.

It is therefore necessary to take a look at the real situation in South East Asia in general, and in Indonesia in particular, to be able to define just how far this dependence extends and threatens the interests of the common people.

One of the consequences of the policy of the Indonesian government, for instance, is the renewed subjugation of the country to the economic interests of the Western world, of the United States and Japan in particular.

The export of Indonesia's raw materials and the systematic destruction of its forests have become a fundamental element of neo-colonial relations. In exchange for foreign assistance, we were forced to agree to the import of consumer goods and could do practically nothing to stop the export of most of our natural wealth, which was sold at sometimes laughably low prices.

The exploitation of Indonesia's raw materials by Western and Japanese capital takes place on a larger and more drastic scale than in the former, colonial times because the technical means of exploitation have been greatly improved, on the one hand, and because the Indonesian governing élite shows practically no responsibility at all, on the other.

Foreign investment was mostly directed at the ever-increasing acquisition of raw materials, the vast forestry resources, and fish. But now most of the attention of foreign capital is directed towards Indonesia's oil riches, which form about 70% of Indonesia's exports.

Not very much of this foreign investment income has flowed back to the people via our national budget or has been used for projects which, not only in the short run but also in the future, will be profitable to the Indonesian people.

With this short introduction and statement on the present state of regional affairs in mind, we wish to state that we indeed feel very much attracted by the title chosen for this workshop. Because this title proposes that we accentuate *activities*: *promotion*, which is an activity, of *procedures*, which implies agreement on ways to act, for the *implementation*, which is the result of thse activities.

The workshop conveners have stressed the active role that we strive to play in the campaign for the recognition of human rights. This leads us to the immediate conclusion that an analysis of the actual situation is of prime importance; so also is an analysis of what can be done to end this situation if, indeed, the actually existing situation has such influence on the access to justice of all people.

If we agree that we are living in a neo-colonial society, which consolidates the capitalist economic system, that oppresses the middle-size and small entrepreneurs, who in turn oppress the majority of the people (as A. B. Nasution has put it), then it follows that we cannot sit with our arms crossed and wait for something to happen which will change that condition.

Thus it is clear that things should develop, because we want them to develop in a certain direction that we must determine ourselves. Yet we all know that discussion about infringements or transgressions of human rights and, especially, specific accusations against the people who commit these violations have become very difficult in our countries.

It was therefore an excellent initiative for the workshop conveners to invite us all here to Manila, to talk about the necessity of the kind of activities which could lead to a change in the situation in our countries and about what means of persuasion would be best suited to convince the ruling groups in those countries that the present situation is not a healthy one and easily could lead to civil war or revolution.

There is clearly a difficulty here: ruling groups are practically never persuaded peacefully, neither do they often voluntarily surrender the privileges which go with their positions of power. It is very easy for them to keep us out of the representative bodies of our countries or to win overwhelming majorities in elections which are entirely organized and therefore manipulated by them.

It is also easy for them to silence voices of dissent and protest and to keep those voices out of the newspapers. It speaks for itself that criticism is called 'subversion' or 'incitement to rebel' and may even result in arrest or long jail terms, or sometimes in 'civil death' (as in Indonesia) which means that people are not allowed to work or to take part in any national eonomic activities.

I would like to invite you to think about 'human rights' organizations as organizations which really involve themselves in this fight to uphold or restore human dignity, and to work out a common strategy for this region which could be used by all of us as a means to liberate not only our countries but also the hundreds of millions living there.

In these liberation efforts, we should carefully guard against becoming a tool of foreign influence and instead try to find our own way towards that liberation.

If the Universal Declaration of Human Rights is considered to be a set of values which could be used to bring about a number of important changes in the social and economic structures and in the institutions of our countries, we have a choice of two strategies.

One strategy would have us make known all our goals immediately and to press for as many of them as we could, in the hope of obtaining as much as possible. The alternative strategy is a 'foot-in-the-door' approach of concealing our aims, separating the reforms we ask for from each other, and pushing for only one change at a time. The former is a comprehensive, 'root', or *blitzkrieg* approach; the latter is an incremental, 'branch', or Fabian approach.

At various times in history, people pressing for change or reform have tried both methods. The results of their efforts suggest that, for most countries subjected to the strains and dissensions involved in modernization, the most effective method is the combination of Fabian strategy with *blitzkrieg* tactics.

To achieve our goals, then, we should separate and isolate one issue from another, but having done this we should, when the time is ripe, dispose of each issue as rapidly as possible, removing it from the political agenda before our opponents are able to organize their forces. The ability to achieve this proper mix of Fabianism and *blitzkrieg* should be a good test of our organizational efforts and our political skills.

In terms of overall reform programmes, one can, however, make a logical case for a *blitzkrieg* strategy alone. Why should we not make clear our whole set of demands immediately, arouse and mobilize the groups which favour change, and through a process of political conflict and political bargaining settle for as much as the balance of forces between change and conservatism permits? (This is my free translation from Samuel Huntington's book, *Political Order in Changing Societies*, which tries to give us an answer as to which methods are preferable for achieving the general objectives of human rights groups in our countries.)

Anticipating your answer that this *blitzkrieg* approach might well be applicable in societies where there is still some kind of social and democratic order and where institutions are still able to function more or less normally, but that none of this is true of our own societies, I will point out to you that the Universal Declaration of Human Rights, whilst warning against injustices committed by government which might easily lead to rebellion and revolt, also contains warnings against the individual use of violence and clearly prefers a juridical process to other methods.

Is this ambiguous? I don't think so. Not even contradictory, if you think in terms of self-defence – which is also a juridical principle, one which allows us to defend ourselves if our survival is attacked or threatened.

This principle of self-defence against the many injustices committed by our governments makes it necessary that we fall back on the principles of the Universal Declaration which have already been accepted by most of the member-states of the United Nations.

We must, therefore, point out to our governments that they have a duty to fulfil, namely to provide genuine access to justice for all of their people. Also that, for the government, this is a never-ending duty and that the safeguarding of these rights should be incorporated within the bodies of our constitutions or at least should be added to them in the form of Bills of Rights. Because, if that is the case, the Universal Declaration could indeed become a set of values that should be held up to our governments and to our peoples, and could become an ever-lasting inspiration for the necessary reforms in our countries. Further, local and regional organizations would then have a permanent basis for action (or reaction, if necessary). And these local and regional organizations also could decide on which strategies and tactics are most useful at a given time, in a given area.

We, from the Indonesian Institute for the Defence of Human Rights, also want this occasion to be used for the exchange of reports on the situations in our countries, because the possibility to do so in Indonesia is very limited.

It seems to us that, first of all, we have not done enough to improve the situation or help others to uphold their prestige and dignity as human beings. As in years past we must draw the conclusion, as we look about us, that the human rights situation is not getting better. It is getting worse.

Let us not be betrayed by appearances. Our judiciary is only in name independent from the executive or state power. There are practically no judges to be found in Indonesia who have the integrity and therefore the courage to make decisions which are not favourable to the government. The influence of high-ranking officials can clearly be felt by anyone who has a case against them or against the government. In Indonesia, people do not trust the courts any longer. Courts are only seen as a hindrance to obtaining justice. Justice is also very expensive, if not in money then in time, and even then it is not always sure that you get a just verdict.

Our Parliament's acceptance of our new law on criminal procedure, which indeed provides protection of very fundamental and basic human rights, is a proof that there are many members of the existing political parties in Indonesia who believe that the common people should be protected against harsh and inhuman treatment by police or military authorities. This is certainly something which must give hope for the future.

This fight for human rights includes practically all fields of human activities and all segments of our society.

The intensification and extensification programmes in the agricultural sector of the Indonesian economy, for instance, give more benefits to rich peasants or landowners, and are strengthening village élites. This in turn means more oppression of people without land or other property. Modernization also deprives a large portion of the population of employment: the rice-hulling machine has taken over the work of women rice-hullers. Profits resulting from the use of these machines go to the capital owners. The harvest-contract system adds further to the benefits enjoyed by the landowners and village aristocracy, but causes unemployment, especially among female agricultural workers.

Who is going to end this kind of oppression? Who is going to show the people that there is no access to justice unless they learn how to organize themselves, that they have the right to do so, and that there is no salvation from this situation except by and through themselves?

In the fishing sector, we can see that, due to modernization, fish catches have increased tremendously but this has meant disaster for Indonesian fishermen. A year ago, 80% of fish and prawn production was in the hands of the modern sector, signifying the end of the role of the local labour force in an industry which traditionally provided a living for millions of small fishermen and their families. The government is now trying to forbid trawler fishing; this also hurts workers employed in the modern sector of this industry.

Ordinary people also suffer from other injustices. Modernization – the building of factories, general infrastructure works like dams, roads and markets – drives them away from strategically located areas but gives them no restitution or only a little, hardly in proportion to the real value of the place which they are forced to leave.

Industrial workers do not have a protected minimum wage and even the All-Indonesian Labour Federation is not too willingly accepted by existing companies and firms. The general wage situation in Indonesia is still very far below standard. Some 37% of the workers have reached a minimum daily wage of 600 rupiahs, which is about US $1, but 63% still receive less.

By making comparisons of the price indexes received and paid by the peasants, we can conclude that the terms of trade have hitherto been detrimental to the peasants. The price index paid by the peasants is far higher than that they receive. This, therefore, indicates the decline of the living standard of the village community compared with that of the urban community. It is certainly contrary to the purpose of agricultural development – a rise in the living standards of the village communities.

We can draw the conclusion that the rights of Indonesians, especially the poorer groups, to obtain a proper living in accordance with humanitarian standards have been seriously infringed by: loss of jobs in the villages; forcible transfer of land; transfer of working capital from the weak to the strong groups; closure of small industrial businesses; the selling of cheap labour power because of the sparsity of job opportunities; and the decline of living standards because of sectoral shifts.

Our 'New Order' government, which started to reign in 1966–67 under the banner of 'human rights', giving broad and repeated promises that the rule of law would be restored and that the government wanted everybody to keep to the rules of the game, does not seem too willing to let the population participate in the government of the country. Instead, it makes the simple excuse that too much meddling by too many groups might prove harmful to the implementation of the development plans set forth by the 'New Order'.

This is a situation with many implications in all fields of life and in all parts of our society. It is clear that this endangers the position of human rights in our society and that we should fight with all our strength against this ongoing injustice.

9. Law and the Decline of Freedom in Malaysia[1]

Azmi Khalid

> *Whereas* the peoples of the United Nations have in the Charter reaffirmed their faith in fundamental human rights, in the dignity and worth of the human person and in the equal rights of men and women and have determined to promote social progress and better standards of life in larger freedom . . .
>
> Now, therefore, THE GENERAL ASSEMBLY proclaims THIS UNIVERSAL DECLARATION OF HUMAN RIGHTS as a common standard of achievement for all peoples and all nations, to the end that every individual and every organ of society . . . shall strive . . . to promote respect for these rights and freedoms and . . . to secure their universal and effective recognition and observance . . .[2]

The question of freedom and human rights in society is an important issue throughout the world. It is no less important in Malaysian society than it is in other developing – or indeed more advanced – countries.

Under international law, as well as under municipal law, freedom often becomes a very heated and controversial issue because of diverse approaches and meanings given to the principle of the rule of law. This principle is regarded by lawyers as of primary significance for the preservation of the values of freedom; yet it has, unfortunately, often been given wholly unsatisfactory meanings such that the deterioration of human rights – their suspension or elimination in fact – has been authoritatively justified on the sole basis of enacted legislation – without any consideration for justice, equality or fairness, or for universal standards which ought to be observed for all peoples in all nations.

This paper seeks to present the current situation of freedom under the law, to analyse the progressive decline of freedom as viewed from universal perspectives, and to consider the future of the freedom of the people under the law in Malaysia. Following analysis in terms of these legal perspectives, there can then be further discussion of socio-political issues, such as whether the current Malaysian government position and the Malaysian people's attitudes towards an observable decline of freedom endanger that nation's future, or whether these can be justified by the constantly evoked imperatives of security, development and communalism.

Constitutional 'Guarantees'

Malaysia's supreme law is no different from most other constitutions, especially those of the newly independent nation states, in that it explicitly includes a 'Bill of Rights' which guarantees virtually all of the human rights and fundamental freedoms enumerated in the 1948 Universal Declaration of Human Rights. But that guarantee is only a superficial formality: the actual legal position of these expansively declared individual rights is very different when practical political reality is taken into account. For example, a lengthy enumeration of traditional liberal-democratic rights may be found in Articles 5 to 13 of the 1957 Constitution, but this same Part II of the Constitution, on 'Fundamental Liberties', immediately adds that such rights may be restricted by ordinary legislation enacted by the Parliament when deemed by it 'necessary orexpedient' with regard to one or more of a variety of stated interests. Thus, while 'every person has the right to freedom of speech and expression' according to Article 10(1)(a), the second section of the same article immediately provides for restrictions

> in the interest of the security of the Federation or any part thereof, friendly relations with other countries, public order or morality and restrictions designed to protect the privileges of Parliament or of any Legislative Assembly or to provide against contempt of court, defamation, or incitement to any offence . . .

Clearly, this kind of constitutional logic, which in the process of formulating a right simultaneously negates that right, leaves little of substance to 'free speech/expression' beyond what the Parliament permits at its discretion. Under normal constitutional procedures, there would, however, remain an implicit legal presumption that the Parliament act in 'good faith' in exercising its discretionary powers. Such a presumption provides one of the principal means by which an active judiciary can justify its independent review of governmental action (whether legislation or executive action). Nevertheless, even this implied requirement that the Parliament act in good faith is apparently rejected in an earlier section of the Constitution. That is, Article 4(2)(b) – on 'Supreme Law of Federation' – states that 'the validity of any law shall not be questioned on the ground that . . . (b) it imposes such restrictions as are mentioned in Article 10(2) but those restrictions were not deemed necessary or expedient by Parliament for the purposes mentioned in that Article.'

To the extent that human rights include a private sphere in which the human personality is protected against invasion by governmental action, it is necessarily an independent judiciary – institutionally separated from the political branches of the government and supported and assisted by an autonomous, organized legal profession – that must render the protection. Article 4 has made it enormously difficult for the Malaysian courts to assume this necessary and proper role. For the point of Article 4 seems to be precisely to disallow any attempt by the Federal Court of Malaysia (or any lower court) to decide whether or not an Act of Parliament bearing upon the civil rights of Article 10(1) is constitutionally 'necessary or expedient' in accordance with Article 10(2). Earlier post-independence struggles (in some of which courts were successful) over this central issue of democratic government have now been ended; and they have been resolved in favour of a powerful executive which in practice defines the political party system, controls the ruling coalition party, and thereby controls the legislative branch. For recently there has appeared a new trend in restrictive parliamentary enactments, for example in the Industrial Relations Act (Amendments of 1980) and the Societies Act (Amendments of 1981), which reveals an intent to reduce judicial review even further. In both of these statutes, it is flatly declared that the discretionary powers of the designated minister are absolute, his executive actions are 'final and not subject to question in any proceeding in any court of law'. Therefore, while Section 1 of Article 10 purports to guarantee freedom of speech and expression, of peaceable assembly, and of forming and joining associations of one's choice, in fact there is no constitutional mechanism or process provided by which the Malaysian citizen could attempt to seek redress for the denial of one or more of these crucial civil and political rights through a parliamentary enactment.

Powers of Constitutional Amendment
Apart from the enactment of ordinary legislation of a restrictive nature, the executive power can also rely on the function of constitutional amendment which is allocated to the Parliament. To date, there has been on average at least one major Amendment Act passed every year since independence in 1957. This reflects the fact that in every general election the ruling coalition party (formerly the Alliance Party, now renamed the *Barisan Nasional* or 'National Front') has won control of well over the two-thirds majority necessary for amending the Constitution. (In 1978, the most recent general election, candidates of the National Front won 55.3% of the total votes cast and gained 85% of the seats in the lower house and all of the seats in the upper chamber of the legislative body.) Most recently, for example, in April 1981 the Parliament enacted two major constitutional amendments which received little debate and no public notice. It amended Article 150 of the Constitution to make it even easier to invoke a 'state of exception' such as emergency or martial law. Simultaneously, it amended Article 149 to permit the government to confiscate without compensation any and all private property used for 'subversive activities'. Indeed, in the latter instance the Parliament acted, against the attempted protests of constitutional lawyers and practising attorneys alike, in diametric contradiction to the pre-existing Article 13 of the Constitution which states flatly that 'no law shall

provide for the compulsory acquisition or use of property without adequate compensation'!

Emergency Powers

Part XI of the Constitution provides for 'Special Powers Against Subversion and for Emergency Powers'. The two major articles of this Part, Articles 149 and 150, provide for the suspension of constitutional guarantees of individual rights (as well as of the Parliament, the Legislative Assemblies and elections) under certain contingencies. The first section of Article 149, for example, reads as follows:

> If an Act of Parliament recites that action has been taken or threatened by any substantial body of persons, whether inside or outside the Federation –
> (a) to cause, or to cause a substantial number of citizens to fear, organized violence against persons or property; or
> (b) to incite disaffection against the Yang di-Pertuan Agong (the King, a constitutional monarch, whose position as Head of State is largely symbolic, elected by a council of the hereditary rulers of the 13 states every five years) or any Government in the Federation; or
> (c) to promote feelings of ill-will and hostility between different races or other classes of the population likely to cause violence; or
> (d) to procure the alteration, otherwise than by lawful means, of anything by law established; or
> (e) which is prejudicial to the security of the Federation or any part thereof, any provision of that law designed to stop or prevent that action is valid notwithstanding that it is inconsistent with any of the provisions of Article 5 (providing for liberty of the person), 9 (prohibiting the penalty of banishment and providing for freedom of movement) or 10, or would apart from this Article be outside the legislative power of Parliament . . .

It will be seen that the very loose wording employed in the Article (e.g. 'recites', 'taken or threatened', 'substantial body', 'fear', etc.) leaves the widest imaginable latitude for interpretation – interpretation made by the Parliament at the behest of the executive power (i.e. Prime Minister and Cabinet) and constitutionally immune from judicial scrutiny. Indeed, Article 149 provides such a relaxed operational definition of 'subversion' (for which the penalty can be execution by hanging) that it is extremely difficult to differentiate it from the practically identical definition of various 'speech crimes' inherited from the British in the form of the 1948 Sedition Act. To be sure, the Federation and its Constitution were born in turmoil, towards the end of a 12-year period of internal guerrilla warfare waged by the Communists (mainly ethnic Chinese). None the less, the anti-guerrilla campaign was successfully concluded, and the pre-independence 'Emergency' finally declared ended, in 1960. Since that year, despite evidence of the increasing stability of the country, the government has exhibited by its actions an increasing counter-tendency to make it progressively easier to declare emergencies – and so to rule by repressive legislation or mere executive decree.

Article 150 (as amended in 1981) provides for the declaration of a state of exception: an Emergency can be proclaimed if 'the Yang di-Pertuan Agong is satisfied' – meaning, so advised by Prime Minister and Cabinet – that there exists a threat to 'the security or economic life or public order of the Federation or any part thereof . . .' Since 1960, four Emergencies have been declared, the first and third of which extended over the entire country:

> 1) in 1964, during the Confrontation (with Indonesia, in the 1963–66 period, concerning the latter's claim to sovereignty over Sarawak, the twelfth state of the Federation, in the northern portion of the island of Borneo; and, to a lesser extent with the Philippines' claim to Sabah, the thirteenth state, also in the northern portion of Borneo);
> 2) to overcome a federal-state political conflict in Sarawak in 1966;
> 3) in 1969, as a result of the 13 May incidents (communal rioting, partially in response to the 1968 elections);
> 4) and in Kelantan (a dissident state on the northern peninsular boundary with Thailand) in 1977.

These Emergency situations continue in legal existence to this day because none of these proclamations has ever been terminated. As a consequence, it is not inaccurate to note that Malaysian society has been under Emergency rule now for 21 of its first 25 years of independence. Malaysian experience also appears to be unique ('appears' because the comparative research to prove the point is lacking) in that ordinary laws still continue to be enforced, subject to being suspended and replaced temporarily with Emergency laws regarded as more suitable. A major example is to be found in criminal procedure laws for security cases which are now regulated by the emergency-based Essential (Security Cases) Regulations of 1975.

Originally, Emergency powers could be implemented only in a limited manner, subject to specified constitutional conditions; however, such limiting conditions have now been eliminated – repealed by successive constitutional amendments. For instance, prior to 1960 a Proclamation of Emergency remained in force for only two months unless specifically renewed by the Parliament after its determination that such extension was necessary. But in 1960 this condition was repealed so that now a Proclamation remains in force so long as Parliament does not specifically terminate it. A further condition of limitation on the definition of emergency (i.e. as 'a condition caused by war or external threats or internal disturbances') has now also been eliminated by means of constitutional amendments in 1963 and 1981. The definition of 'emergency' today is therefore extremely wide-ranging: a Proclamation can be made even before the occurrence of events causing the threat; separate

Proclamations can coexist in concurrent or overlapping fashion; and the Yang di-Pertuan Agong's satisfaction in proclaiming Emergencies is final and not questionable in any court of law.

Wide powers have thus been 'granted' to the executive without effective institutional safeguards. The potential for abuse of such enhanced powers can only be limited by reliance primarily on the intelligence, integrity and goodwill of the executive power. Protection of the people's freedoms from abuses of power equally depends upon such a dubious basis.

The Internal Security Act of 1960

This particular law is well-known in Malaysia because it has vested the executive power with broad powers of preventive detention and also because it defines the offence of unlawful possession of a firearm which carries with it a mandatory death sentence. Such legislation is permitted by Article 149 of the Constitution with its stated aims of 'preventing subversive activities, and acts prejudicial to the public order within, or security of, the Federation or any part thereof'. Yet such legislation is clearly contrary to the individual's freedom of physical movement, speech and expression, peaceful assembly and association. None the less, this obvious inconsistency is sanctioned by the Constitution itself as an exception to enjoyment of those individual freedoms because of the importance of security and public order for society. Exceptions are therefore regarded as sacrifices to be made by the individual.

Though such sacrifices are permitted, and indeed anticipated, an attempt at the general protection of the individual has been provided by Article 151 of the Constitution so as not to infringe his or her rights to 'natural justice'. It is within this context, for example, that one finds provision within the 1960 Internal Security Act for an Advisory Board to the Minister of Home Affairs (i.e. to the executive officer empowered to order preventive detention). This Advisory Board is an independent body to which the detainee or his representative may plead his case. And the Advisory Board has several times exhibited its independence, advising the Home Affairs Minister to release all long-term detainees. However, the Home Affairs Minister is under no obligation to act on the recommendations of this Advisory Board and, in fact, in no major case has he done so. This illustrates quite specifically the general point stated above, that the only protection for the rights of individuals rests upon the unfettered discretion of executive officials. Thus far the Malaysian governmental élite has been unwilling to provide institutional mechanisms and procedures which might invest the constitutional declaration of rights with substantive meaning.

Legislative Restrictions

The actual scope of fundamental rights that remain to be enjoyed can best be understood by an awareness of how each is restricted. Much of the restrictive legislation has existed since British colonial rule; some has even been increased. Suffice at this juncture to list the primary legislation so that a clear picture emerges (see Table 9.1).

Table 9.1
Legislative Restrictions on Human Rights

Article	Right or Freedom	Legislative Restriction
5	Liberty of the person	Internal Security Act, 1960; Restricted Residence Enactment (CAP. 39); Sec. 117, Criminal Procedure Code (CAP. 6)
6	Protection against slavery and forced labour	Essential (Self-Reliance) Regulations, 1975; National Service Ordinance, 1952
9	Protection against banishment; freedom of movement	Internal Security Act, 1960; Banishment Act, 1948; Immigration Acts, 1959 and 1963
10(1)(a)	Freedom of speech and expression	Sedition Act, 1948; Printing Presses Act, 1948; Control of Imported Publications Act, 1959
0(1)(b)	Freedom of peaceful assembly	Public Order (Preservation) Ordinance, 1958; Police Act, 1967; Preservation of Public Security Ordinance, 1968; Emergency (Preservation of Public Order) Ordinance, 1969
10(1)(c)	Freedom of association	Trade Unions Act, 1959 (and 1980 Amendments); Societies Act, 1966 (and 1981 Amendments)
12	Right to education	Universities and University Colleges Act, 1971 (and 1975 Amendments); Discipline of Students Rules; Discipline of Staff Rules
13	Right to property	Land Acquisition Act, 1969

Though some of the above laws might be regarded as necessary to preserve 'law and order', it cannot be denied that, since independence, the increase of legislative restrictions has significantly reduced the scope of individual liberties. At the very least, the outlook of the executive regarding rights and freedoms must be considered quite negative, owing to the existence of so many restrictions imposed by law. Perhaps most important is the fact that the citizen is denied access to the Malaysian courts to challenge any of these legislative or executive restrictions. There is a supreme court of the land, established by the Constitution of Malaysia, yet almost every statute affecting the individual's civil rights also denies the courts the jurisdiction even to interpret the laws, much less to strike them down as unconstitutional.

Analysis and Conclusions

The Rule of Law
The true meaning of the rule of law is rule which emphasizes individual rights and freedoms; it is the function of judges and lawyers to keep this meaning constantly predominant, for the rule of law is trivialized when made subservient to the transient needs of government and the administration of the day. If it is still necessary to limit specific rights with the aim of overcoming grave threats during exceptional circumstances, then measures of protection ought to be observed so that a reasonable balance may be achieved between individual freedoms and genuine 'national interests'. In this way, the rule of law in Malaysia could then be said to be in accord with the precepts of justice according to law.

General Attitudes and Outlook
It is believed that the populace has generally become disillusioned when faced with legal restrictions upon its rights and freedoms. A negative outlook, accompanied by ignorance, sometimes becomes the basis for voicing partial and hesitant criticism (i.e. without at the same time trying to assert remaining rights). These negative attitudes and criticisms, in turn, have been regarded by Malaysian governments as indicating a lack of public desire to prevent individual rights from being further eroded. If a more positive attitude were displayed and more often acted upon, either through the judicial process or other democratic channels, this would definitely enhance public awareness, dispelling ignorance about individual rights and freedoms; at the same time it would provide explicit feedback to the Malaysian government on the degree of significance attached by the public to its rights in society.

Opposition to Laws
Laws that are believed to be unjust and in violation of individual rights should be challenged. The 'tradition' of according respect to, and abiding

by the actions of, the government would not be compromised if the people expressed their views on the laws passed by their representatives. The Constitution and the legal system allow for questioning of laws; courts appear to have the authoritative power to invalidate any laws inconsistent with the Constitution and should act so as to establish this as fact; meanwhile, Parliament itself can amend or repeal any law opposed by the people. The role and responsibility of informing the executive of this desire lie mainly with those groups which have already achieved awareness of the importance of freedom to society and the nation. It is thus critically important that the rights of such tutelary groups be preserved and promoted however much this may inconvenience or anger members of the government of the day.

The Spirit of Constitutionalism
The nation and society of Malaysia have sworn to uphold belief in the supremacy of the Constitution as well as the rule of law as both are enshrined in the Principles of the Nation. If we desire that the principles of nationhood be realized, then the legal system must emphasize not just the letter of the Malaysian Constitution but also a spirit of constitutionalism showing love of freedom, justice, and truth.

Notes

1. This is the translation into English of a working paper previously presented by the author at the National Symposium on 'Freedom and Society in Malaysia' organized by the Co-ordinating Committee of Societies Opposing the Societies Act Amendments of 1981, held at Kuala Lumpur, 29–31 August 1981. The Societies Act Amendments are discussed in more detail in Dr Chandra Muzaffar's paper in this volume. The Co-ordinating Committee, an umbrella organization of some 115 registered societies (i.e. private associations), spans the major ethnic and religious groupings in Malaysia. In particular, it includes registered organizations ranging over the full spectrum of functional specialization: professional societies, law, medicine and engineering in particular; trade unionists; merchants' guilds and trade associations; organizations to assist the physically handicapped; environmentalists, consumers' organizations, and co-operatives; university professors and students; religious and youth groups.
2. Universal Declaration of Human Rights, 1948.

10. Notes on the Domestic Legal Remedies Available in Malaysia to Protect Human Rights

Any realistic consideration of the legal remedies available in Malaysia to an aggrieved individual must begin by taking into account the severe limitations imposed upon the scope of such remedies by two overriding factors: 1) the very limited protection offered by the Malaysian Constitution to the fundamental liberties of citizens; and 2) the attitude of the Malaysian courts towards the exercise by the executive of its powers of preventive detention.

First, while the Malaysian Constitution, in common with other modern written constitutions, proclaims the fundamental rights and liberties of the citizen, it does not, in many cases, afford any significant protection against their violation. In fact, in many cases, the very clauses which spell out the nature of these fundamental rights invariably contain some stipulation (termed 'clawback' clauses by a number of scholars of international public law) which recognizes the right of some body, usually Parliament, to take away that very right. Thus, Article 5(1) of the Constitution provides that 'No person shall be deprived of his life or personal liberty *save in accordance with law*.' What this simply means is that the government of the day can freely violate the personal liberties of an individual provided it can enact a law to sanction such breaches. So long as such an enactment exists, the individual is helpless against violations of his personal liberties and, generally, legal remedies will not avail him.

The position is the same with regard to many other liberties. Thus by Articles 9(a) and 19(2), freedom of movement, and freedom of speech, association and assembly are all made subject to the complete discretion of Parliament (meaning, for all practical purposes, the incumbent administration) to restrict them. And in each of these cases, a government which seeks to enact legislation to restrict such rights has the benefit of an additional provision – Article 4(2)(a) and (b) – which 'relieves Parliament of the necessity of care in drafting and protects Parliament from any impugning of its motives.'[1]

Second, in cases of detention without trial under laws which sanction detention by order of the executive, the Malaysian courts have consistently held that there can be no judicial review of whether there was reasonable cause for such detention. Thus, for example, if a person is held under the Internal Security Act of 1960 (which empowers the Minister of Home Affairs to detain a person if he is 'satisfied' that his detention is necessary to prevent him from carrying out activities that are prejudicial to Malaysia's security, or the maintenance of essential services, or to the economic life of the country), he cannot challenge the order of detention by adducing evidence that there is indeed no basis for the Minister's alleged belief that he is a threat to the security of the country or to its economic well-being. Nor is it open to the detainee to challenge the detention order on the grounds that the allegations of fact set out in the order of detention are vague or untrue, or do not establish any such threat. In all such cases, the Malaysian courts have studiously refused to intervene by adopting the view that the detaining authorities 'in making their decision . . . have *complete discretion* and it is not for a court of law to question the sufficiency or relevance of these allegations.'

While some very minor qualifications have to be made to the above general proposition (in view of the fact that courts in Malaysia still claim the right to review a detention order on the grounds that the alleged reason for detention is not within the scope of the enabling legislation), the present state of the law can be summed up by saying that if the Home Affairs Minister states that he is 'satisfied' that a person is a threat to the security of the country (and hence has to be detained), the courts, too, will also be 'satisfied' that he is indeed such a threat.

However, and subject to the above limitations, there are in the Malaysian system four major remedies open to an aggrieved person, remedies which derive from the earlier English colonial period.

1) There is firstly the well-known remedy of the writ of *habeas corpus*. A person who is detained *unlawfully* can always apply to a court for this remedy and if his detention is indeed not sanctioned by law, he will be ordered to be released. However, given the fact that the government of Malaysia has at its disposal early exercisable, sweeping powers of preventive detention (which are perfectly legal and the exercise of which, as we have seen, is unfettered either by the Constitution or by the intervention of the courts), it has no need to resort to illegal means to detain people. Since the police, too, are vested with extensive powers of detention for the purpose of criminal investigations, the occasions for the successful use of the above remedy are strictly limited. It is a useful remedy where there has been an abuse of power at the local level, e.g. some police officer has unlawfully locked up a local 'bad hat' even though there is no evidence against him of any wrongdoing.

2) Secondly, an aggrieved individual can always seek a *judicial declaration* from the courts when his rights have been infringed. However, the fact that the Constitution does not really offer protection against the violation of personal liberties – as we have noted above, it recognized the right of some body, usually the Parliament, to restrict such liberties – has reduced the scope of this remedy. For example, a person detained under

the 1960 Internal Security Act (ISA) cannot successfully obtain a declaration that his constitutional right to the liberty of person has been infringed (per Article 5 of the Constitution) or that the ISA is inconsistent with such a right, since the Malaysian Constitution recognizes the right of the government to enact laws violating such a right.

3) Thirdly, there is the equally well-known remedy of a writ of *certiorari* (i.e. an order of the High Court removing a decision or judgement of an inferior court or other body or person exercising judicial or quasi-judicial function, in order for the High Court to review and possibly quash those proceedings). The order will only be made if there is a defect on the record of the lower court or tribunal. However, the scope of this remedy has been severely restricted by the ubiquitous tendency to include an ouster clause – a clause specifically ousting the right of the regular courts to judicially review the proceedings and decisions of the inferior tribunal – in all legislation governing the powers and proceedings of the 'inferior' tribunal or body. Although the High Court of Malaysia can, in such cases, still consider the question of jurisdiction (i.e. whether the inferior body or tribunal has the jurisdiction to deal with the matter), the inclusion of the ever-present ouster clause certainly limits the scope of the remedy. There is also a time-limit on the use of this remedy: application for leave to institute this remedy must be made within six weeks of the decision of the inferior tribunal – although the time-limit can be extended by an application to the court, if sufficient reason can be given.

4) Finally, a fourth remedy available to an aggrieved individual is a writ of *mandamus*, that is, an order of the High Court to compel an official to carry out an official act (on pain of contempt proceedings if he does not). While formerly courts would entertain such an application without leave, it is now settled practice in Malaysia that leave is first required before an application for a writ of mandamus itself may be made.

Apart from these major remedies, there are a host of 'common law' remedies for specific torts or wrongs committed to an individual. For example, an individual whose liberty has been unlawfully curbed may beable to bring an action for false imprisonment or, in appropriate circumstances, an action for damages for malicious prosecution.

When all is said and done, however, there are precious few means afforded by the Malaysian legal system for effective protection of the great rights enshrined in the 1948 Universal Declaration of Human Rights and subsequent International Covenants, conventions and treaties. Especially is this so where the government of the day views an individual and/or his actions as so politicized as to threaten vaguely-defined national interests.

Note

1. Harry E. Groves, 'Fundamental Liberties in the Constitution', in Tan Mohd. Suffian, H. P. Lee and Trindade (eds), *The Constitution of Malaysia* (Oxford: Oxford University Press 1961), p. 29.

11. Recognition of Human Rights under Thai Laws

Viboon Engkagul

Thailand has always formally subscribed to the principle of civil rights. And to some extent the human rights of the Thai people have always been officially recognized by every Thai government. In the United Nations Thailand voted for the adoption of the Universal Declaration of Human Rights in 1948. And Thailand has a Westernized form of government modelled on that of a democratic country; it also has a written Constitution as the basic law of the land, a Constitution which recognizes certain fundamental rights and liberties of Thai citizens.

The Universal Declaration of Human Rights

Thailand, like almost all other member-states of the United Nations, voted for the General Assembly resolution adopting the Universal Declaration of Human Rights in 1948. In fact, the motive behind this decision was a political one, rather than a true commitment to the principles of the Declaration. At that time, the Japanese military occupation of World War II having ended and Thailand having been admitted to the United Nations one year after its founding in 1945, the Thai government was desperately anxious to be considered a full-fledged member-state of the UN so as to ensure its survival as an independent nation. To achieve this goal, the Thai government conformed; its support for the Universal Declaration was therefore inevitable.

In fact, Thai governments since then have never been active in any way to implement the Declaration; they have consistently shown their passiveness towards programmes on human rights organized by the UN and its specialized agencies. Thus, there are very few international conventions relating to human rights to which Thailand is currently a contracting party.

In addition, the fact that so many prominent Thai legal scholars have shown little faith in the purposes of the Declaration has rendered the promotion of international human rights in Thailand much more difficult than would have been expected. Most Thai lawyers pay very little attention to the field of international human rights. Even worse, some of them do not regard these as the lawyer's proper concern at all.

The Thai Constitution and Bill of Rights

The current Constitution of Thailand was promulgated on 22 December 1976 (following a bloody military take-over). It is the country's tenth Constitution since its political revolution in 1932, a bloodless revolution which limited the powers of the traditional monarchy. Theoretically, the Thai Constitution is the highest law of the land. It provides for a modified parliamentary system and specifies the other institutions of government. It also guarantees certain individual rights and freedoms which are in accordance with the ideas of a democratic society. Essentially, the Constitution is the source from which all laws, regulations and executive orders can derive their legitimacy.

Chapter 3 of the current Constitution may properly be regarded as the Thai Bill of Rights, since a number of basic rights and liberties are officially recognized there. It is only fair to say that most of the rights in the Universal Declaration are acknowledged in Chapter 3 and some of them are implemented in full.

The basic rights and liberties set forth in the Thai Bill of Rights can be listed as follows:

1) the right of all citizens to equal protection by the law and to enjoy political rights (Sections 23 and 24);

2) the rights to freedom of religion, of religious sects, and to worship as one believes (Section 25);

3) the right to be secure from unlawful arrest or detention (Section 28);

4) the right to be secure in one's dwelling against unlawful search and seizure (Section 32);

5) the right of the alleged offender to be presumed innocent until proven guilty by final judgement (Section 27), including prohibition against *ex post facto* laws (Section 26); the right to obtain legal assistance (Section 29); and the right to compensation upon false conviction (Section 30);

6) the right to freedom of speech, writing, printing, and publication (Section 34);

7) the right to own property (Section 33);

8) the right to be free from forced labour (Section 31);

9) the right to peaceful assembly and association (Section 37);

10) the right to form a political party (Section 38);

11) the right to education (Section 35);

12) the right to freedom of communication by post (Section 39);

13) the right to freedom of movement, for travel and settlement (Section 40);

14) the right to found a family (Section 41); and

15) the rights to file a petition of grievance (Section 42) and to sue a government agency or official (Section 43).

Restrictions on the Thai Bill of Rights

The specific rights listed above are subject to a number of restrictions.

Apart from any specific restriction on a designated right, there exists a general principle of restriction on the Thai people's enjoyment of their rights. Thus Section 45 of the Constitution states that: 'No person shall exercise the right and liberty under the Constitution against the Nation, religions, the King and the Constitution.'

It is understood that the basic rights of the Thai people under Chapter 3 are subject to other overriding considerations, namely, national security, religion and the monarchy. Yet, as a matter of fact, Section 45 is quite vague and can be interpreted broadly. Practically all actions can be interpreted as endangering national security, religion, or the monarch. It is doubtful, therefore, whether the recognition of the rights of the Thai people will be of any value in practice.

May I turn then to a separate issue: that of specific restrictions on the exercise of one's rights and liberties?

With regard to the political rights of Section 24, for example, no specific definition is provided of 'political rights'. Furthermore, Section 24 provides that political rights must be exercised in accordance with 'the provisions of the law'. To grant a right yet immediately qualify that its exercise must be *in accordance with the provisions of the law* is to create ambiguity, leaving that 'right' subject to the interpretations of transient governmental majorities.

It must be noted, further, that the other main sections of Chapter 3 have been subjected to similar restriction. The constitutional phraseology may vary: 'conditions and means required by laws', 'must be in compliance with' the laws', 'by virtue of the law provisions', 'to preserve the national security or the protection of other persons' rights, liberties, and reputation', and 'in the maintenance of public order or good morals' are only some of the exceptional formulae employed throughout the Thai Bill of Rights. But in each case, the result is the same.

There is a further constitutional problem. Contemporary Thai jurisprudence has now recognized the legitimacy of the military mechanisms which have toppled previous lawful governments. According to the precedent established by the present Supreme Court of Thailand, the (military) leader of any *coup d'état* who successfully takes over power from the lawful government is deemed the supreme ruler of the government. Therefore, any decrees or commands issued by him during his rule are now regarded as of equal status to the lawful actions of the Parliament. In the past 50 years in Thailand there have been numerous successful coups and revolutions, yet all legislation enacted by means of revolutionary decrees are considered valid laws. There is no doubt that almost all of these decrees, etc. were enacted in contradiction to the ideology of human rights; none the less, in the context of the current Thai Constitution, all are regarded as valid, as integral parts of 'the provisions of the laws'.

Enforcement of Human Rights

In many parts of the world today, it can be easily seen that the human rights of the people cannot be enforced. In some countries, it is impossible to think that the condition of the people can be improved: their situation is hopeless. However, one can be optimistic about Thailand and say that the trend is now towards the enforcement of human rights.

Furthermore, it seems to be a universal problem that people lack suitable means to enforce their rights. Therefore, people around the world should exchange their experiences of means of attempting to enforce their rights. The means which I would like to discuss here are: 1) judicial review; and 2) the Constitutional Tribunal of Thailand.

Judicial Review: The present Thai judicial system was patterned on that of Western countries. At the time of its establishment during the reign of King Rama V (i.e. only 50 years ago), the country was under an absolute monarchy. Given Thailand's long history as an independent kingdom, even today most Thai judges naturally hold passive views on human rights issues. In consequence of these attitudes and of present political conditions, access to judicial remedies against any violations of human rights in Thailand seems quite difficult.

Constitutional Tribunal: Under the current Constitution, the Constitutional Tribunal of Thailand is comprised of seven members, i.e. the Speaker of the Parliament, the President of the Supreme Court, the Director-General of the Public Prosecution Department, and four other highly qualified persons selected by the parliamentary body. The Speaker of the Parliament acts as Chairman of the Tribunal.

The main duty of the Tribunal is to determine whether any of the legislation of the Parliament is in contradiction with any constitutional provisions. It therefore has no duty to grant any remedy for any violation of the rights of the Thai people.

Conclusion

From what has been discussed above, we may come to the conclusion that the legal protection of human rights in Thailand is still quite inadequate. The main reason for this inadequacy is the lack of effective remedies and procedures to protect against any breaches of rights.

In any event, the state of human rights in any society will depend on the political development of that society. And, at present, Thailand has not yet achieved political maturity according to a Western-style yardstick.

12. The Present State of Human Rights in the Philippines

J. B. L. Reyes

The United Nations members have entered into two covenants that are fundamental to the question of respect for human rights. First is the International Covenant on Economic, Social and Cultural Rights, opened for signature on 1 December 1966. It was ratified by the Philippines and it entered into force for this Republic on 3 January 1976.

Second, but not in order of importance, is the International Covenant on Civil and Political Rights, and its Optional Protocol. The Philippines signed it on 19 December 1966 but has not ratified it.

The reasons for the failure to ratify this basic document are given in a Letter Opinion (No. 44) of the Honourable Ricardo C. Puno, Minister of Justice, dated 20 March 1980, addressed to the then Acting Minister of Foreign Affairs. Because of its authoritative character, permit me to quote extensively from it:

> It is stated that the International Covenant on Civil and Political Rights was signed by the Philippines on December 19, 1966. The Covenant enumerates certain civil and political rights of peoples in general, and individuals in particular, and imposes upon signatory-states the obligation of observing and/or protecting such rights. It also provides for the creation of a Human Rights Committee and the appointment of *ad-hoc* conciliation commissions to consider communications from member states regarding non-compliance therewith. The Covenant allows a member-state to take measures derogating from their obligations in time of public emergency which threatens the life of the nation, although derogation from certain articles is not allowed. The agreement in question has an accompanying Protocol which confers upon the nationals of member-states the right to seek the intervention of the aforesaid administrative bodies in connection with violations by their respective countries of their obligations under the Covenant. Adherence to the Protocol is optional.
>
> We do not find any legal objection to the enumeration of rights under the Covenant. Nearly all the individual rights and civil liberties mentioned therein are fundamental rights already recognized by our constitution and statutory law and/or well-recognized in Philippine jurisprudence. Compliance with the provisions of the Covenant therefore would not pose a serious conflict with our municipal law.

However, the following provisions require further consideration in view of the financial implications:

(1) Article 9(5):

'Anyone who has been the victim of unlawful arrest or detention shall have an enforceable right to compensation.'

(2) Article 14(6):

'When a person has by a final decision been convicted of a criminal offence and when subsequently his conviction has been reversed or he has been pardoned on the ground that a new or newly discovered fact shows conclusively that there has been a miscarriage of justice, the person who has suffered punishment as a result of such conviction shall be compensated according to law, unless it is proved that the non-disclosure of the unknown fact in time is wholly or partly attributable to him.'

It is also noted that full compliance with obligations under the Covenant in time of public emergency is not always required, as it allows member-states to take measures derogating from their obligations thereunder to the extent strictly required by the exigencies of the situation, provided that such measures are not inconsistent with their other obligations under international law, and do not involve discrimination solely on the ground of race, colour, sex, language, religion or social origin. (Art. 4) While no derogation is allowed from certain articles, the rights included in these articles, namely: the right to life (Art. 6), the prohibition against torture, cruel or inhuman punishment (Art. 7), slavery and servitude (Art. 8), imprisonment for inability to fulfil a contractual obligation (Art. 11), *ex post facto* laws (Art. 15), the right to recognition as a person before the law (Art. 16) and to freedom of thought or conscience and of religion (Art. 18) have not been affected by the existence of emergency conditions during martial law.

In fact, the President has disclaimed in a public statement ('The Challenge of Liberty', delivered by Pres. Ferdinand E. Marcos, at the 8th World Law Conference, Manila, 21 August 1977) that the failure of the Philippines to ratify the Covenant in question, as well as the Optional Protocol, is due to the fact that the country is under martial law, as the Philippine position, taken as early as the deliberations on the draft Convention in 1966, was that the authority given to other states by the Covenant to petition where the petitioning state considers another state as not complying with the provisions of the Covenant, may constitute a derogation of national sovereignty, and may result in the interference of the super-powers in the affairs of less-developed countries, without advancing the cause of human rights. The President also stated in the same speech that this position is shared by the other developing countries, and that the Philippines expressed its preference for 'a regional approach to the problem of ensuring human rights protection'.

In view of these reservations expressed by the President, the bases of which remain valid to date, it is believed that the advisability of ratifying the Covenant at the present time should take into account not only legal considerations but political realities.

But while the Constitutions of 1935 and 1973 enshrined in their Bills of Rights most of the human rights expressed in the International Covenant, these rights became unavailable on the proclamation of martial law on 21 September 1972. Arbitrary action then became the rule. Individuals by the thousand became subject to arrest upon suspicion, and were detained and held for indefinite periods, sometimes for years, without charges, until ordered to be released by the Commander in Chief or his representative. The right to petition for the redress of grievances became useless, since group actions were forbidden. So were strikes. Press and other mass media were subjected to censorship and short-term licensing. Martial law brought with it the suspension of the writ of *habeas corpus*, and except for members of the Supreme Court, judges lost independence and security of tenure. They were required to submit letters of resignation and were then dismissed. Torture to extort confessions was practised, as has been declared by international bodies like Amnesty International and the International Commission of Jurists. Investments from abroad, conditioned upon a cheap labour market, were encouraged, external debt attained unprecedented heights, and poverty and crime increased. This lasted for nine years.

What was the outcome of the lifting of martial law?

On 17 January 1981, by Proclamation No. 2045, President Marcos declared the termination of the state of martial law throughout the Philippines. This declaration, joyfully received, was, however, subject to important restrictions expressed in the same proclamation:

1) That the call to the armed forces of the Philippines to prevent or suppress lawless violence, insurrection, rebellion and subversion should continue to be in full force and effect;

2) That in the two autonomous regions of Mindanao, upon the request of the residents therein, the suspension of the privilege of the writ of *habeas corpus* should continue;

3) In all other places, the suspension of the privilege of the writ should also continue with respect to persons at present detained as well as others who might thereafter be similarly detained for the crimes of insurrection or rebellion, subversion, conspiracy or proposal to commit such crimes, and for all other crimes and offences committed by them in furtherance or on the occasion thereof, or incident thereto or in connection therewith;

4) Military tribunals created under martial law were to be dissolved upon final determination of pending cases that might not be transferred to the civil courts without irreparable prejudice to the state in view of the rules of double jeopardy, or other circumstances which might render further prosecution of the cases difficult, if not impossible;

5) Last, and most important

pursuant to Article XVII, Sec. 3, para. 2, of the [1973] Constitution, all proclamations, orders, decrees, instructions and acts promulgated, issued or done by the incumbent President constitute part of the law of the land

103

and shall remain valid, legal, binding and effective even after the lifting of martial law, unless modified, revoked or superseded by the President or unless expressly and explicitly modified by the regular National Assembly.

Thus, all restrictions and limitations on human and civil rights of the people under martial law still subsist; and most important among the repressive legislations is the Public Order Act, Presidential Decree No. 1737, dated 12 September 1980, that expressly provides:

SEC. 2. Whenever in the judgment of the President/Prime Minister there exists a grave emergency or a threat of imminence thereof, he may issue such orders as he may deem necessary to meet the emergency including but not limited to preventive detention, prohibiting the wearing of certain uniforms and emblems, restraining or restricting the movement and other activities of persons or entities with a view to preventing them from acting in a manner prejudicial to the national security or the maintenance of public order, directing the closure of subversive publications or other media of mass communications, banning or regulating the holding of entertainment or exhibitions detrimental to the national interest, controlling admission to educational institutions whose operations are found prejudicial to the national security, or authorizing the taking of measures to prevent any damage to the viability of the economic system. The violation of orders, issued by the President/Prime Minister pursuant to this decree, unless the acts are punishable with higher penalties under the Anti-Subversion Act, the Revised Penal Code or other existing laws, shall be punishable by imprisonment for not less than thirty (30) days but not exceeding one (1) year.

The President/Prime Minister may authorize the Minister of National Defence to issue, in accordance with such regulations as he may prescribe, search warrants for the seizure of any document or property subject of the offence or used or intended to be used as the means of committing the offence pursuant to this section.

SEC. 3. The incumbent President/Prime Minister, any Cabinet member or any other public officer shall not be held responsible or liable in any civil, criminal or other proceeding for any act or order issued or performed while in office pursuant to the provisions of this Act.

Note that the Presidential discretion in Section 2 above is untrammelled by any restriction; while Section 3 is confirmed and amplified by Section 15, Article VII of the Constitution as amended in 1981, and reading as follows: 'The President shall be immune from suit during his tenure. *Thereafter, no suit whatsoever* shall be made for official acts done by him *or by others* pursuant to his specific orders during his tenure' (Emphasis supplied).

Of similar importance is Presidential Decree No. 1498, dated 11 June 1978, but not published until 1980, entitled National Security Code, compiling and reiterating, *inter alia*, previous regulations for the Control of Mass Media (Sections 24–31); Control of the Mail, including censorship (Section 32); control of foreign travel (Section 37); restriction on rallies, demonstrations, strikes, picketing and group action (Section 46); penalizing malicious dissemination of false information (Ch. IV, Section 3); establishment of checkpoints (Ch. IV, Sections 8 and 9); etc.

The people's rights appear now still subject to the same restrictions as existed under martial law. Whatever liberties they are allowed to enjoy appear more as a matter of grace than of right. And in fact conditions are essentially unchanged. The country's economy is still stagnant and controlled by its creditors and by powerful foreign interests, especially multi-nationals. Persons arrested for offences against state security remain without recourse to the privilege of the writ of *habeas corpus* and often disappear without trace: for the first six months of 1981, after the lifting of martial law, the Task Force Detainees of the Philippines has documented 161 cases of prisoners 'salvaged' (executed without trial) and 12 cases of involuntary disappearance. About 80% of pre-school children suffer from malnutrition; and even by government statistics, nearly one-quarter of our workers are not gainfully employed. Wages are the lowest in Asia. The Philippines stands foremost among countries receiving subsidy payments from the IMF on account of balance of payment deficits.

Worst of all, peasant and farmer demonstrators are fired upon, wounded and killed for failure to disperse on command: thus in Guinayangan, Quezon, on 1 February 1981; Bassud, Camarines Sur, on 14 June 1981; and also in Culasi, Antique, on 19 December 1981. In Davao people are being concentrated into population centres, away from their farms and sources of livelihood, and kept for indefinite periods in sites without sanitation facilities or medical services or adequate food, by local military commanders, on the pretext of military operations against rebels, and apparently without the knowledge of superior officers in Manila, and without any prospect of relief, since military chiefs could not or would not even conjecture when such operations would be finished or concluded. In San Vicente (previously called Laac), Davao, the Integrated Bar of the Philippines' Commission on Due Process and Human Rights found thousands of persons thus indefinitely concentrated since October 1981, under inhuman conditions, without any soldier having been killed or injured during the interval. [See next chapter for more details.]

13. Strategic Hamletting in Laac: An Overview, January 1982

The area known as Laac in the rugged, rolling hills of the northernmost section of Davao Province on the island of Mindanao has become the testing ground of a new military strategy of 'total pacification' being used by the Armed Forces of the Philippines (AFP) against the rebel forces of the New Peoples Army (NPA). [The New Peoples Army is the military wing of the Communist-led National Democratic Front (NDF); a second insurgency exists in the Philippines in the form of the Moro National Liberation Front (MNLF), a Muslim secessionist movement.] The name that the AFP has given this strategy is 'grouping', but in reality it is the very same 'strategic hamlet' strategy which was developed and utilized by the armies of the United States and South Vietnam against the people of that country during the recent Indochina War.

In Laac and the surrounding towns of Davao and Agusan Provinces, settler families have been ordered by the military to dismantle and abandon their farmhouses in the countryside, and to move into the *barrio* (geographical sub-division, not necessarily administrative sub-unit) and town centres which are in some cases as far as 10 kilometres from their farms. This hamletting has transformed this entire area into something akin to a refugee camp, with hunger and disease and fear causing suffering and even death to the residents.

Although the expressed purpose of this hamletting is to isolate and destroy the rebel NPA forces, it is the people of Laac and the surrounding towns that have become the victims. Even more ominous than the hunger and disease that daily threaten their lives, however, the residents now fear that the real purpose of the hamletting strategy is to gain control of the land in the area for agri-business and agro-forestry projects, and to coerce the people into either participating in these projects or evacuating the area. Already several thousand people have been evacuated, considerably reducing the population from its 1980 level of 37,000.

It was only in 1979 that the Laac area was separated from the neighbouring municipality of Asuncion, and was declared a municipality with the name San Vicente. The vast majority of Laac's residents are settler-farmers who came to the area over the past ten years to establish farms in the terrain cleared by logging operations. Most of the land is still classified as 'forestal', even though logging has long since stopped. The area has been known as a base area for NPA forces who have been conducting propaganda and organization campaigns among the residents. There were sporadic encounters and ambushes between rebel and military forces, which led to a steadily increasing military presence in the area. Until July 1981, it was the Philippine Constabulary (PC) of the Davao Provincial Command, and 'striking force' battalions from the Region XI Command such as the 54th, 56th and 61st PC Battalions that were stationed in Laac.

Increasing Militarization

A dramatic and steady build-up of military forces began in July, with the eventual stationing of three battalions in the area, made up of composite forces of the Philippine Army, Marines, Airborne and Scout Rangers. By September there were some 2,500 soldiers stationed in the area. They began a campaign of forced recruitment of local men into the Integrated Civilian Home Defence Force (ICHDF), requiring each barrio to contribute at least 15 men. Those barrios which failed to fulfil this quota were to be considered sympathetic to, and supporters of, the NPA rebels, and would be raided by the military.

The (Roman Catholic) Diocese of Tagum has compiled a lengthy documentation of arrests and tortures and even killings of Laac residents during the period from February 1981 to December 1981, as the military forces hunted for NPA rebels and their supporters. Despite these cases of military abuses, Laac residents still considered the army soldiers much more disciplined and respectful of civilians than had been the PC soldiers that formerly patrolled the area. In some cases, abusive Army soldiers were publicly punished by their superiors.

On 4 September a peace conference was called by the military in *sitio* (town or rural township) Linumbaan of barrio Langtud, because the people of that barrio had not yet provided their quota of men to be trained as ICHDF members. Eight Airborne soldiers and four ICHDF members attended the conference. After the meeting, as the soldiers and ICHDF were leaving the sitio aboard a commandeered Ford Fiera, they were ambushed. Five Airborne soldiers, including Lt Pajel, were killed, along with the ICHDFs.

The next day all the residents of Langtud were summoned to the *poblacion* (administrative centre) of San Vicente for another peace conference which was attended by Gen. Alfredo Olano, Region XI Commander, and by Col Teofilo Bulosan of the Davao Provincial Command. The men were ordered to report to San Vicente to the military authorities on Monday and Wednesday of each week, even though this would severely affect their ability to maintain their work on their farms. It was soon after this that many families began leaving

Langtud and other barrios of Laac, as military operations increased and intensified.

Beginning of Hamletting

In October, the military ordered that all families would have to move into the centres of their sitios and construct houses there. A curfew was established from 5 p.m. (sunset) to 5 a.m. (sunrise), when all people would have to be within the sitio centres, or 'hamlets'. This, in effect, created a 'no man's land' in the countryside, with anyone caught in the area automatically considered an NPA rebel to be shot on sight.

Army commanders explained that this hamletting was necessary because 'Laac is like a beautiful lake, in which there are some bad fish. Thus it is necessary to drain all the water from the lake in order to catch these bad fish!' The life and work of the farmers were disrupted by this move into the sitios, since they did not have enough time to construct new houses in the sitio hamlets and also keep up their work on their farms. In most cases, however, the sitio hamlets were located within 3 kilometres of their farms, so that it was still possible, although difficult, to continue farming.

In November, however, a new order came from the military authorities. All the families would have to move again, this time into the barrio centres. The military ordered that all houses at farmsites in the countryside and in the sitio centres would have to be at least partially dismantled, by removal of the flooring and at least one wall, and that each family would have to construct a new house in the barrio centres. There are 29 barrio centres in the town of Laac, and so began a tremendous influx of families into these few hamlets. It was also in November that this hamletting strategy was expanded by the military into some barrios of the neighbouring Davao towns of Asuncion, Kapalong, Montevista and Monkayo, as well as to some barrios in the towns of Agusan Province to the north.

Effects on the People
This expansion and widening of the hamletting policy has made it almost impossible for the majority of the farmers of Laac and these surrounding towns to continue to farm their fields. Since November they have been occupied almost full time in dismantling their old houses, moving them to the barrios, collecting wood and other building materials with which to construct new shanties in the barrio hamlets, apart from, at the same time, trying to take care of their farms. In some cases these barrio hamlets are located as far as 10 kilometres from their farms, and so the farmers must start walking at 5 a.m., reaching their farms at the hottest time of the day, and then walk back in time to be inside the hamlet by sunset at 5 p.m.

Further aggravating the difficult situation of the people, the military has been requiring them to attend meetings and rallies in the hamlet centres, and also in some cases to render service by providing wood for, and constructing, the soldiers' barracks. In some barrios, each family is required to provide 50 pieces of roofing shingles for the construction of the military barracks and housing; while in other barrios there are reports that each family is required to give between 2 and 5 pesos per month towards the support of the military forces. The farmers are suffering financially, since many of them have had to spend what little cash savings they had to purchase building materials for their houses, and to buy food when their supplies become exhausted. To obtain cash for their house building and for these forced contributions to the military, many farmers have had to sell whatever food supplies they had, at low prices, thus further aggravating their food shortage. Since many farmers have been unable to return to their farms to plant their fields, or to harvest their crops, the spectre of famine in the near future hangs over the area.

False Surrenders

On 27 November, the people from the barrios surrounding Laac were required to go to the town centre to register themselves. Some 6,500 people were in the town that day, and they were given placards containing anti-NPA slogans, and made to swear that they would not support the NPA rebels and were loyal to the government. Helicopter gunships hovered overhead, with their machine guns pointed at the people massed below.

In the following days, the national newspapers reported that 7,000 NPA rebels had 'surrendered' to the government in Laac. Similar smaller rallies have been staged in the far-flung barrios of the area.

The People Appeal for Help

In late November, the farmers of Laac sent an open letter of appeal for assistance to concerned fellow citizens. Sections of this letter are quoted here:

> Since July 1981, PC battalions and striking forces flooded the barrios of our town. There are more than 2,500 regular troops, and hundreds of para-military personnel (ICHDF, etc.). First they assured us that their presence is to check the fast expanding NPA guerrilla units in this province, and to protect the civilians. But, as days passed, the ever expanding number of military troopers made life more difficult for us. Checkpoints mushroomed in many of our barrios, which restricted travel. Before we could go out from our places, we have to secure safe-conduct passes from the military authorities. Jeeps were not allowed to enter some areas. This made it difficult for us to buy our necessities and to market our products. Military operations

became frequent. Anybody under suspicion was brought to the barracks for tactical interrogation. Some were physically and psychologically tortured. A number have been SALVAGED [the Filipino euphemism for having been killed at the hands of the internal security forces].

As a result of their intensified military rule, several families of farmers have fled to unknown places to save their families. Those of us who remained are opting to face the consequences of extreme poverty, epidemics (malaria and diphtheria), hunger and even death. Sometimes during peace talks fear reigns among us, because a few who were trained for two days as ICHDFs became spies, driven by their hunger of power – and for survival.

We live a life of uncertainty, fear and utter poverty. Even if we tried to tend our farms during the day, most of our time is spent in hiking. By the time we start working on our farms it is almost noontime, and the sun would be too hot for work. We are hungry, sick and miserable now. What will tomorrow bring for us?

They described the hardships of the successive hamletting orders from the military, first to the sitio centres and then to the barrio hamlets. They spoke of the deadlines imposed by the military, who threatened to burn and strafe any houses that were not dismantled and moved in time. One family which remained in their house one evening was strafed to death. The military cut down their permanent banana and coffee plants, and uprooted their root crops, under the pretext that these might be used by the rebels. The public appeal of the farmers of Laac concluded with these words:

We realize now that it is not the NPAs they are getting rid of. It is us innocent civilians! The military has spent more effort in destroying our own organizations, which have spearheaded our co-operative efforts to maintain peace and order, and to improve literacy and health. They are hounding farmers who have begun to assert their rights. Now we are deprived of our right to a decent livelihood and shelter. With our abandoned farms, we are facing hunger. Many of us entertain the idea that it is not only the NPA they are interested in, but the land we have occupied and tilled. We are aware that big foreign corporations practically surround us. Is it remote that they want our farms for expansion for more falcatta, banana, and palm oil plantations?

On 14 December, the people of Laac sent a letter to President Ferdinand Marcos, in which they appealed that the hamletting be ended, and that the military be withdrawn from their area. To quote from that letter:

We the people of Laac suffer from intense hardships and fear because of heavy militarization in our barrios. Many have died, many more are sick, and a big number are starving . . . The military issue a lot of orders; but the heaviest order was the order to move from the sitios to the barrios . . . We were given a deadline for moving. Precisely because of our extreme poverty, the deadline came and went, and many of us had not yet built shelters for our families. Thus the common sight of people living with unfinished roofs and no walls. Many more still lived in chapels, or crowded into shelters with other families.

We are also concentrated in a place where there is no clear source of clean water, and where the surroundings are dirty. The children are the worst hit by disease and epidemics. We have no money for medicines. Thus, all we can do is watch as our loved ones slowly die.

President Marcos, we humbly ask you to allow us to return to our farms and our traditional way of life. We also ask you to order the immediate withdrawal of the Army from our barrios.

Suspicion of Land Take-Overs

What has led the farmers of Laac to suspect that the real reason for the intensification of militarization through hamletting is the take-over of their lands for plantations? In the third week of December, Col Alejandro Cruz of the 37th IB Airborne Forces, the overall commander of the Laac operation, met with the farmers of barrio San Antonio (one of the remote barrios of Laac which is located near the border with the neighbouring town of Monkayo to the east). Col Cruz informed the farmers that a 900-hectare portion of their barrio would be cleared and then planted with rubber and ipil-ipil trees. Cruz further explained that he personally would manage this plantation for the barrio, with the barrio captain serving as foreman.

All men of the barrio would have to contribute one full day's work in the plantation each week, for the clearing of the land and the planting of the trees. He said that the work was to begin on 2 January 1982; and that the clearing was to be finished within one month. Those farmers who would be displaced by this plantation would, he said, be given land to farm somewhere in the barrio. The workers would not be paid wages, but would be given food on the days that they worked, and would receive a share of the profits once the trees were harvested – some five years from now. Anyone who refused to participate in the project would be considered a supporter of the rebels.

The men would also be required to construct barracks for the soldiers, and to cut timber for this purpose. The women would provide food for the workers. Finance for the project, as well as for other poultry- and hog-raising projects of the barrio people, would come from the government's KKK livelihood programme (the *Kilusang Kabuhayan at Kaunlaran*, or 'Movement for Progress in Livelihood', a programme widely publicized by the Marcos regime as the solution to the development needs of the people). The farmers would be able to continue farming small plots of land in the barrio to meet their food needs. Cruz indicated that once this 900-hectare plantation was planted, it might be expanded to include other lands as well.

There are some 600 families living in barrio San Antonio. It is one of the barrios most severely affected by the hamletting, since some of the people's farms are as far as 15 kilometres from the barrio hamlet. Some of the residents are Tribal Filipinos of the Dibabawon tribe. It was reported that in San Antonio alone, where 120 families live, eight children had died of sickness associated with the hamletting. In barrio Inacayan, closer to the town of Laac, farmers have also been told that they would have to plant ipil-ipil and rubber trees on their land.

It might be that the military plans to designate these tree-growing projects as 'communal tree plantations' under the government's revised Forestry Code. But the manner of implementation amounts to forced participation by people in these tree plantation development schemes. It further increases the suspicion that these plantation development schemes may be the true reason for the hamletting strategy being imposed by the military – rather than counter-insurgency operations against the NPA.

Industrial Tree Plantations
There are other indications that this hamletting strategy may be part of a wider government scheme to develop these remote rural areas into agri-business plantations and tree-growing ventures. The government has announced that it plans to develop 2 million hectares of Industrial Tree Plantations (ITPs) in the Philippines over the next ten years: an average of 200,000 hectares per year. Included under this programme are ipil-ipil, falcatta, rubber and other types of trees. The primary vehicle for the execution of this programme will be the granting of ITP leases for forest lands to companies or individuals who are willing and able to implement this scheme.

Another vehicle for implementation is the granting of Communal Tree Farm (CTF) leases to barrio communities which undertake to develop tree farms as income-generating projects. Since, however, almost all cleared forest lands in the country are already occupied by settler-farmers, the government may be searching for a means to either eject these settlers from the land, or force them into participating in tree-planting programmes.

In 1980, the government announced the granting of a 27,000-hectare ITP lease to the ADECOR corporation (Aguinaldo Development Corporation), somewhere in Davao Province. Parts of the ADECOR timber concession are located in the towns of Laac, Asuncion and Kapalong – the very centre of the current hamletting strategy of the military! At least two other corporations are already engaged in ITP projects in Mindanao. The PICOP corporation (Paper Industries

Corporation of the Philippines) has ITPs in the provinces of Surigao, Agusan and Davao to supply raw materials for its expanding paper plant in Bislig, Surigao del Sur. The newly established Manila Paper Mills, Inc. (MPMI) has been granted ITP leases for some 45,000 hectares, to supply raw materials for its planned pulp and paper plant to be located in Butuan City. MPMI has entered into subcontracts with several logging concessionaires in the Agusan provinces (north of Davao) to set up ITPs within their cleared timber concession areas.

Another Davao-leased timber concessionaire, DATICOR (Davao Timber Corporation), has established a new fibreboard plant in the town of Mati, Davao Oriental, and will also need a steady source of wood as raw material for this plant. Antonio Floirendo, businessman and head of the KBL (*Kilusang Bagong Lipunan*, or New Society Movement, the personalistic political party – and official state ideology – which Ferdinand Marcos has created) in Mindanao, is building a cardboard carton factory within his TADECO (Tagum Development Corporation) banana plantation in Panabo, Davao del Norte, and will need a steady supply of raw materials for that plant. It is quite possible that agro-forestry projects planned for the Davao-Agusan areas are intended to supply these expanding wood-based industries.

Palm-Oil Plantations

Another agri-business venture which may lie at the roots of this hamletting strategy is the establishment of palm-oil plantations in the Agusan provinces. The government, through its National Development Corporation (NDC), has entered into agreements with five multinational corporations to set up a total of 30,000 hectares of palm-oil plantations. NDC will lease the land to these corporations.

As of now, only one of the five companies, Guthrie, Inc., has begun operations in Agusan. Settler-farmers in the area have been resisting the take-over of their lands for Guthrie's plantation. Another one of the five, Sime-Darby, has already pulled out of its palm-oil venture, possibly because of the burgeoning resistance of the settler-farmers in its leasehold area. This, too, may be leading the government and the military to search for ways to minimize farmer resistance, and/or to force their participation in such projects. There are reports that part of the area designated by NDC for palm-oil development lies within Davao Province.

Vulnerability of Settlers

Settler-farmers on forestal lands are particularly vulnerable to such land-grabbing schemes. Although many of them apply to the Bureau of Forestry (BFD) for release of their occupied lands for titling, this release and titling process is painfully slow and requires many 'red-tape' bureaucratic procedures that obstruct the successful processing of their applications. Alternatively, settlers who can demonstrate that they have occupied their forest lots since before 1975 can apply for 'forest occupant

113

permits' which establish their right to remain on their land under certain conditions laid down by the BFD. This, too, is a lengthy, bureaucratic process, and must be repeated annually, thus discouraging many settlers from following it through. It sometimes happens also that the BFD grants leases to corporations for agro-forestry projects, even though the land has already been petitioned for release by the occupant settlers.

Expansion of Hamletting

High-ranking military officials such as the Region XI PC Commander, Gen. Alfredo Olano, have stated that the Laac area is a testing ground for the hamletting strategy. According to him, if this strategy proves successful it will be implemented in other areas of Mindanao, especially in the more remote rural areas near the boundaries between provinces, where the rebel NPA forces often operate. Although hamlets are being created in other towns of North Davao, and in some towns of Agusan del Sur and Davao del Sur, Laac is the only place so far where the strategy is being implemented throughout an entire municipality. (Now, however, hamletting has been ordered in the whole of Asuncion as well.)

By December 1981, there were 35 hamlet centres in the 29 barrios of Laac. In other Davao towns, Asuncion had 15 hamlet centres; Kapalong had five; Montevista had 12; New Corella had three; and in Monkayo the number rapidly expanded from three to ten within the month of December alone. There were 80 hamlet centres in all in Davao del Norte Province, with indicators pointing to an ever increasing number being created in Agusan del Sur and in Davao del Sur.

Relief Efforts

Despite the tremendous suffering inflicted on the people by the hamletting strategy, neither the military nor the various government agencies have taken steps to provide the needed medical services and relief supplies to the people. The burden has fallen on concerned citizens of the private sector, including the Churches, who have begun sending relief goods, medicines and medical teams to the area.

Bishop Pedro Dean of the Diocese of Tagum visited the area on 22–23 December and immediately afterwards mobilized a more intensive relief effort by the Diocese. On 4 January, Bishop Dean appealed by letter to the National Secretariat of Social Action (NASSA) for assistance in responding to the plight of the people of Laac:

> In the past few months the military operations in San Vicente (Laac) and neighbouring places have caused terrible suffering to our people. Families were displaced, diseases were widespread, and in many instances death has taken its toll. The farmers, gathered in hamlet centres, are not allowed to go back permanently to their farms. When they go to their farms, they have to

be back to the centres before evening, even when their farms are 7 to 10 kilometres away. Shelters in the hamlet centres are small – shanties which are congested, very hot during the day and very cold at night. Water is scarce, and consequently sanitation is bad.

Dialogue

During the first week of January, Bishop Dean went to Manila and spoke personally to the Chief of the Philippine Constabulary, Gen. Fidel Ramos, about the plight of the people of Laac. Gen. Ramos advised that the Bishop consult with the government and military authorities in Davao about this. On 11 January, a dialogue was held at the TADECO residence of Antonio Floirendo, with representatives of the Church, the military, and the civil government. Present at this dialogue were: Gen. Alfredo Olano, Region XI PC Commander; Col Milton Tiburcio, PC Provincial Commander, Davao del Norte; Col Wilfredo Cruz, PC Commander, Davao City; Col Alejandro Cruz, Commander 37th Airborne IB (Laac); Gov. Gregorio Dujali, Governor of Davao del Norte; Assemblyman Rudolfo del Rosario, Davao del Norte; Mr Antonio Floirendo; Bishop Pedro Dean, Diocese of Tagum; several priests and nuns; the municipal mayors of the six Davao del Norte towns of Laac, Asuncion, Kapalong, New Corella, Monkayo and Montevista; Judge Consolacion, Davao City Court of First Instance.

The purpose of the dialogue was to hear the complaints of the Church representatives, and to explain the rationale of the hamletting strategy. The military representatives insisted that the idea of hamletting came not from them, but from the civil government. They claimed that the *Sanggunian Bayan* of Laac had passed a resolution calling for hamletting, in order to protect the civilian population from the NPA rebels. (The *Sanggunian Bayan* is an allegedly traditional Filipino, participatory municipal assembly reinvented as part of Marcos's New Society Movement.) The municipal mayors backed up this statement by the military, claiming that they had first consulted with their *barangay* captains and *purok* leaders ('traditional' local, small-area officials), and that all of these had been unanimous in requesting hamletting. The military officials claimed, therefore, that they were only implementing the expressed desires of the civil government, but that they were prepared to remain in the area for up to five years if necessary, in order to protect the people from the rebel forces. As proof of the need for hamletting, the military pointed to the 'mass surrender' of more than 7,000 NPA supporters in Laac on 27 November!

The Church representatives challenged this assertion by the military, pointing out that the people said they were forced to move to the hamlets, under threat of burning and strafing of their houses. But the military denied that force was used, or that any deadlines for the dismantling of houses had been set by them. They admitted that the people were ordered to remove the flooring and part of the walls of their houses, but they denied that any farmers had been prohibited from returning to their fields.

Rationale of Hamletting Strategy

Then the military explained what they referred to as the 'rationale' for the hamletting strategy. It has four aspects: 1) 'Mutuality in Security', meaning that in the hamlets the people can both protect themselves and also work together in the *bayanihan* (mutual help) spirit; 2) it is easier for the military to protect the people in these hamlets; 3) it is easier to get the people to protect themselves; 4) government services can more easily be made available to the people when they are grouped together in hamlets.

The military further explained that the 'criteria' which they use in selecting the areas for hamletting are: 1) 'critical areas', and 2) 'the economic situation of the people'. They admitted that certain things were 'overlooked' in the implementation of the hamlets, such as the provision of adequate food and shelter, but said that these were the responsibility of the local civil government.

In response to the Church representatives' description of the plight of the people within the hamlets, the military said that perhaps the situation would only be temporary. They explained that the hamlet strategy was a 'model', or a 'prototype of counter-insurgency warfare', and that it might have to be modified later. The Church representatives objected to this concept, asking what right the military had to 'experiment' with the lives of the people in this way. Gen. Olano in turn objected to the use of the word 'experiment'.

He said the military would 'reassess' the hamletting strategy as they went along, and that perhaps the strategy could be modified later. He mentioned the possibility that perhaps it would only be necessary to hamlet the people in the sitio centres, rather than in the barrio centres as they were doing now. Gen. Olano assured the Church representatives that they would be consulted in the course of the reassessment. When asked by the Church representatives whether the people, too, would be consulted in the process of reassessing the hamletting policy, Gen. Olano did not give any definite answer!

Denials

Col Alejandro Cruz was asked by the Church representatives to explain about the 900-hectare rubber and ipil-ipil plantation which is to be set up in barrio San Antonio. Cruz denied that he had announced to the people of San Antonio that they would be required to participate in any such project. He even went so far as to deny that he was in San Antonio at the time that he was alleged to have made the announcement – despite the fact that two residents of San Antonio have sworn affidavits that he was there and did make the announcement.

Gen. Olano insisted that such a story is merely NPA propaganda against the military. With regard to Col Cruz's alleged announcement that KKK funds would be utilized to finance the tree-growing project in San Antonio, Gen. Olano suggested that this was probably only a misunderstanding by the people. He explained that the military had been requested by the President only to 'disseminate' information about the KKK programme.

Mr Floirendo took the occasion of the dialogue to deny allegations that he may personally have a role in the Laac militarization scheme, in order to advance some of his business interests in that area. He also denied that he has been guilty of any wrongdoing in the Paquibato area of Davao, where Tribal Filipinos and Visayan settlers have expressed apprehension that agri-business interests are responsible for the continued violence in that area in order to gain control of the land.

Likewise, Mr Floirendo denied any wrongdoing in the case of the farmers who have been ejected from the Minda Farms area of Panabo, Davao del Norte – an area recently purchased by him. To illustrate his sincerity and concern for the small farmers, Mr Floirendo announced that he personally had persuaded President Marcos to release 2,500 hectares for the Girl Scouts-Boy Scouts Land Grant in the Laac-Asuncion area.

Assessment

The situation of the people hamletted in Laac and the surrounding towns of Davao and Agusan has deteriorated during the first two weeks of January 1982. Food supplies are dwindling, diseases have reached epidemic proportions, especially among small children, and the cool, rainy weather has brought further suffering to the inadequately sheltered families. Fear and uncertainty grip the people, and families continue to evacuate the area, many of them with no set destination. Government relief and medical assistance remain at a minimal level, placing a great burden on the Churches and private sector which try to assist the people there. It is as if a great punishment had been inflicted on the people.

In the face of this, high-ranking military officials of the region continue to deny that they are employing force against the people. They claim that they are merely responding to the plea of the civil government to 'protect' the people from the rebel forces. Despite clear indications of agri-business and agro-forestry projects being planned for the area, government and military officials continue to remain silent about the extent of these projects, the identity of their prime movers, and even their specific location. Municipal mayors of these towns, whether out of fear and helplessness or out of complicity in these schemes, continue to collaborate with the military and to declare that all this is being done in the interests of the small farmers.

The happenings in Laac provide further evidence of a situation in the Philippines where a government is at war against its own people. Until recently, it was a war characterized mainly by intimidation, manipulation and deception practised against the people. But the reports filtering in from all over the country of increased militarization reveal that the war against the people has escalated to a new level.

From Samar come reports of massacres perpetrated against entire barrios. From Agusan come reports of shadowy military groups of the 'Lost Command' liquidating people at will and guarding the business interests of transnational corporations which are seizing control of the land. And now, in places like Laac and other remote areas of Davao and Agusan, the military are readily admitting they are testing a 'prototype strategy' of strategic hamletting of entire municipalities, which will be implemented in more and more areas of Mindanao. Despite the shallow denials being given by the military, the message is painfully clear – force to keep the semblance of peace.

Part III:
Particular Rights,
Special Problems

14. Particular Rights, Special Problems

This section presents a group of papers, again seven in number, which more directly focus on particular human rights and/or special problems of relevance to Third World nations.

The first paper deals with freedom of association. In our view, this right – along with the rights to opinion, to expression, and to assembly – is one of a core bundle of fundamental rights of individuals in society. Without this core bundle, it is extremely difficult to see how government, even at its best, can be anything more than a benevolent despotism – where life as a 'well-fed' and 'happy' slave is contingent on the daily whims and caprice of the ruler. Without these rights, governmental institutions and processes never develop beyond a self-aggrandizing executive power; paternalism and a claimed sense of *noblesse oblige* degenerate into full-blown élitism, isolated and insulated from the mass citizenry, increasingly fearful and distrustful of it; political history becomes the dreary chronicle of coups and counter-coups at the top, and the bloody record of attempted rebellion and secession, or full-scale revolution and civil war, at the bottom.

If the long-term world-wide struggle for human rights is to have success, freedom of association is an essential pre-condition. 'Modernization', by which more is meant than sheer economic growth, both causes and requires social differentiation. If under these emerging conditions ordinary citizens cannot lawfully associate together, they will be less able to discover, articulate and seek peaceful means to defend their perceived collective interests; but they will in time come to appreciate their common experience of oppression, driving them towards a mutinous, subterranean politics of violence. If lawyers cannot freely associate on the basis of their professional expertise, norms and interests, it is highly improbable that an independent judiciary and the rule of law can be either established or maintained. Moreover, the right to freedom of association is perhaps *the* right which most clearly marks the indivisibility of, and the artificiality of, attempts to catalogue separately 'civil and political rights, on the one hand, and economic, social and cultural rights, on the other'. For the process of human association is simultaneously both political and economic in its implications; and the skills, talents and techniques that individuals develop through acting in organized human endeavours are of equal and direct utility in both the economic and the political realms – which 'worlds' themselves are separable only at the level of academic conceptualization. The continuing struggle over Solidarity in Poland is the most recent, well-documented evidence of the multi-functional nature of an apparently unitary right. However, the right to freedom of association also constitutes something more than a fusion of first- and second-generation human rights; it marks more than a blending of liberal democratic, and Marxian Socialist, political philosophies. This is so because freedom of association also crucially relates to concepts of third-generation rights. That is, for example, if there is a right to development or to any other such 'human and people's' right (in the language preferred by the black African nations), such a collective right will prove meaningless in the absence of the individual's right to freedom of association. Otherwise, the alleged collective right will remain a global abstraction, possibly of use as a word-weapon in inter-state politics but in reality nothing more than one further version of a 'national interest' to be defined by the political élite(s) of one or a group of nation states and asserted against the élite(s) of one or another category of such entities. But a claimed state's right is most frequently something different from, and less than, often contrary to, a human's right. In short, without freedom of association, 'development' cannot rise above serving as a euphemism for central economic planning, and sometimes annual growth in the Gross Domestic Product, commanded from above.

If freedom of association is such a crucial human right, then the paper by Chandra Muzaffar makes a valuable contribution to our further understanding of this complex concept with his documented insistence that the analyst must be concerned with both the right to form associations and the further freedom of associations to function effectively. To hedge private voluntary associations about with so many legal restrictions as to render them functionless, or functional only symbolically and that in terms of the interests of the political élite, which is the same result, is as grave a violation of human rights as the flat, outright banning of them all. In drawing attention to this equation, Chandra underlines the point, that in both politics and law it is more important to *see* what the élite is in fact doing than merely to *hear* what that élite says it is doing. 'We permit all sorts of citizens' associations to exist in our country' can be a very deceptive claim. Increasingly in the Third World, therefore, the goal of promoting and protecting international human rights hinges on the outcome of the struggles involved in this second meaning of freedom of association.

Freedom of the press, as indicated above, is equal in importance to freedom of association in the continual effort to expand and ensure human rights. Without the concept and practice of a legitimate political opposition, so that dissent and public criticism are *not* automatically equated with treason and sanctioned accordingly, governments tend naturally to indulge in wide-ranging and high levels of official corruption and to foster mismanagement, inefficiency and waste in their operations. In Third World nations, like the five of the ASEAN region, where governments pursue a policy of state capitalism, seeking to control and guide the domestic investment function, these tendencies become magnified; and, in the absence of opposition, continued incumbency in governmental office becomes the sole assured route to both income and wealth in the individual's occupational career.[1] Therefore, it is precisely at this juncture that the motivation to repress physically incipient opposition becomes intensified and joined to the institutional means for engaging in political repression (i.e. executive control over the police, military and courts). On the other hand, the probability of such wide-scale violations of human rights is significantly reduced where institutions and processes exist to render governmental leaders broadly representative of, responsive to, and held accountable by, the non-leaders in the system. These, of course, are the instrumental goals of democratic governance. These goals are furthered when there exist institutionalized bases for the public criticism of government, its policies and personnel. Such bases can be genuine opposition parties, that is, those with a plausible – not merely 'theoretical' and mathematically possible – opportunity of becoming the majority party in the foreseeable future; private voluntary associations which can exert 'pressure' for or against governmental policies; and/or independently owned and managed media of communication, particularly newspapers.[2] Ideally, the concept of a 'loyal opposition' embraces all three of these elements – the moderation of élite behaviour in response to actual or feared public criticism is maximized where all three bases coexist – because they are mutually interactive, with each functioning over time as both effect and cause of the other two. Finally, however, when one (or more) of these bases does exist and is functioning and the government then embarks on a course of massive violation of freedom of the press, it does more than destroy or damage a single political right. That is, governmental censorship is a pre-condition to the effectiveness of its official propaganda; and the two processes together, both censorship and propaganda, permit the repressive government to conceal or obscure the fact that it is engaged in concurrent violations of economic, social and cultural rights as well. This is the lesson of the paper prepared by Abraham F. Sarmiento. While his case study is of the impact of martial law upon the press of the Philippines, the human rights problem posed is universal.

Women comprise approximately half of the world's population – and do considerably more than half of the world's work. Women in the Third World are engaged in the struggle to overcome the multiple burdens of endemic poverty, yet they suffer a double disability in having simultaneously to break the shackles of sex-role stereotyping inherent in traditional societies. It is appropriate, therefore, that the next two papers in this section focus on the problems of women in the Third World. The first of these, by Amarjit Kaur, presents a detailed analysis of the status of women in the legal systems and in education and employment in all five ASEAN countries. In all those areas where reliable statistics exist, actual practices are demonstrated to fall far short of the formal dedication to the legal principle of equality claimed by the governments of these societies. Kaur's comparative analysis is followed, and confirmed, by that of Sister Soledad's case studies on multinational corporations and women in the Philippines. These case studies focus on electronics (TMX Corporation), the garment industry (Triumph Corporation), women in agriculture (Castle and Cooke), and sex-orientated tourism (the World Safari Club). Both papers indicate that the development strategies currently pursued in all ASEAN nations, worked out in concert by governmental technocrats, World Bank-IMF planners, and the multinational corporations and large Western banks, have perpetuated – and in many instances magnified – the inequality of the sexes in this region of the world.

The final three papers with which this section concludes are of a somewhat different nature from those above. We view these three as initiating, yet hardly resolving, a necessary debate concerning what domestic and international strategies to adopt in opposition to rights-violating Third World regimes.

In almost all instances where authoritarian governments have come into existence in the Third World, they have sought to preserve a façade of democracy, usually retaining an atrophied and manipulated electoral process to present the appearance of a legitimate grounding on the consent of the governed. In some real but unquantifiable degree, this unhappy result has been caused by policies of the United States government which, as in Central and South America, have been satisfied by a minimal formalistic threshold, as a consequence of which *de jure* recognition and more material benefits have been readily granted to otherwise illegitimate regimes. This fact poses a problem and, simultaneously, identifies a potential target, for North Americans concerned with human rights. But what course of action should non-American human rights advocates take domestically, when they must live and function within an authoritarian system operating with pseudo-elections? Should the non-violent opposition lend itself to these fake demonstrations of public participation and popular will? These, broadly, are the questions posed in a second contribution by Sarmiento in which, quoting extensively from the political philosophies of Thoreau, Tolstoy and Gandhi on civil disobedience, the author argues that electoral boycotts constitute a legitimate and effective mode of opposition to illegitimate governors. Indeed, Sarmiento writes specifically in justification of the electoral boycott led by the United Democratic Opposition (UNIDO), of which he was a founder, against the controlled re-election of President Marcos on 16 January 1981. Yet since such a boycott technique seems a rather limited 'weapon' of the oppressed, we leave open the question of whether additional, and more effective, forms of 'non-cooperation' may not yet be invented by a new generation of Gandhis, Paulo Freires, and other strategic thinkers for the powerless.

The following paper, by Randolph S. David on 'developing the power of communities to defend themselves', suggests two additional oppositionist techniques with which human rights activists have recently experimented. The first of these is that of the community self-survey which combines research and documentation of community-identified problems undertaken as a means to consciousness-raising, community self-defence organizing, and simultaneous expansion of the public that is attentive to 'local' human rights violations. (We note that, although this approach is often proposed by individual members of academic institutions, the approach itself is predicated upon an implicit distrust of academic social scientists. That is, their stripped-down techniques and basic methods of research are useful, and the underlying epistemology of the social sciences is fundamentally sound, yet, by and large, academic social scientists have not employed their talents and techniques for advancing human rights. This is as true in the United States and the Soviet Union as it is in Thailand and Indonesia. It is true because higher education has increasingly become an instrument of state policy the world over. Academic social scientists thus function to serve the interests of the powerful, whereas to focus on human rights violations would be to identify the manifold consequences of vast power differentials within one's society and to cast one's lot with the powerless.) And the second technique, which complements the first, is the use of the 'peoples' tribunal' device, initially popularized by the Bertrand Russell and Lelio Basso Foundations in response to the Vietnam War. The device entails the effort to form and shape an effective 'world public opinion' to which law – and the behaviour of governors – must ultimately conform. Underlying the use of this technique is the premise that the nation state is the prime perpetrator, and certainly the proximate cause, of massive human rights violations. Consequently, to appeal (for an end to violations) to intergovernmental forums *alone*, in which the self-same sovereign state is the unit of representation and of voting power, is to invite defeat.

The paper by David, in dealing with the Chico Dams hydroelectric project and the Kalinga Tribals, also raises a specific problem to which human rights advocates have become increasingly sensitized in the past decade. Almost every nation today, and certainly the more populous and extensive ones, contains within its territory one or more 'Little Societies' formed largely on the basis of ethnic, religious and linguistic differentiation. However, development, in almost all forms currently practised in the Third World, threatens to destroy such cultural islands without at the same time aiding their members to be assimilated into the larger society into which they are involuntarily pushed. The task for human rights advocates therefore is a most difficult one: to demand, and help devise, development policies which preserve the cultural integrity of such indigenous groups (and to do so without inventing a new type of zoo!), but which at the same time positively prepare those former members who

consciously and voluntarily opt for assimilation into the larger, modern-
izing, society.

Finally in this section, the strategy of self-reliance that remains
somewhat sketchy in the last paper (or in the earlier contribution by
Princen) is fleshed out in Wanee Bangprapha's treatment of the Co-
ordinating Group for Religion and Society (CGRS) in Thailand. The
history of this particular non-governmental organization (NGO) indicates one type of development of human rights activism, and a pattern
which could be readily duplicated in many of the less developed nations.
First, within the context of Thai history, culture and politics, the CGRS –
which is a broad, religiously-based ecumenical group – was formed in
reaction to the harsh repression resulting from the bloody military coup
of 6 October 1976. For the first three years of its existence, the group
provided legal and humanitarian assistance to the many thousands of
victims and their families. After almost three years of such emergency
human rights work, when most of its aims had been achieved (i.e.
prisoners released, harshest decrees rescinded), the CGRS then paused,
reflected and took a longer-term view of the problems Thai society faced.
As a result of this analysis, the group redefined its functions to include
both rural and urban development in order 'to fight against the root
causes of human rights violations and oppression'. With these broadened
goals, the Co-ordinating Group for Religion and Society now operates as
a catalytic agent, stimulating a children's nutrition programme, the
formation of rice co-operatives, slum self-organization, research on the
laws and practices concerning the problem of child labour. It conducts
these projects in such a manner as to foster self-reliance among bene-
ficiaries and participants, permitting the CGRS itself to withdraw and
assume new tasks. It is this self-development, as both process and goal,
which provides the substance to the author's insistence that 'we do not
believe that development is produced with money.'

Notes

1. This is *not* to say that there are no pathological tendencies, which produce
   serious violations of international human rights, that occur in those Third
   World nations where the political élite professes to be guided by the scientific
   principles of Marx, and especially of Lenin and Stalin, and where the political
   economy takes the form of state Socialism. However, the pattern of human
   rights violations is different in these countries, from what occurs in the five
   ASEAN nations, and requires separate treatment which cannot be undertaken
   here.
2. Governments everywhere, in the Second and First Worlds as in the Third, have
   expressed concern for – through their varying controls over – the electronic
   media. Therefore, our concern here is with freedom of the printed media,
   particularly of daily newspapers and public-affairs magazines and journals.

15. Freedom of Association: The Malaysian Situation

Chandra Muzaffar

Any discussion of freedom of association should be concerned not only with the right to form associations but also with the freedom of associations to function effectively. The latter is in a sense more important than the former. This chapter will be concerned with both aspects of the freedom of association.

After analysing the extent to which 'the freedom to form' associations and their 'freedom to function effectively' are respected, I shall examine the various forces that have shaped the nature and character of the freedom of association in Malaysia. This aspect cannot be studied in detail since such a discourse will take us beyond the limits of this chapter. Then, in conclusion, I shall provide some reflections on likely future trends that may influence this fundamental liberty.

In order to understand the freedom to form associations and their freedom to function effectively, we have to divide the post-independence period in Malaysia into two phases.

Legislation and Reality: 1957–69

In the 1957–69 phase, it was the constitutional stipulation on freedom of association and the Societies Act (1966) which determined the legal parameters for the exercise of that freedom. Article 10 of the Constitution recognizes the right of all citizens to form associations. This right, however, is qualified. It can be restricted by law if Parliament deems it necessary or expedient, in the interest of the security of the nation, public order or morality. Parliament can then even pass laws which are contrary to Article 10 and other articles on fundamental liberties. Equally important, the King can proclaim an emergency and then enact laws inconsistent with fundamental liberties.

The Societies Act of 1966 regulated the right to form associations even further. Under the Act, the Registrar of Societies, a mere bureaucrat, was given wide powers to approve, refuse and cancel the registration of societies. He could also order a registered society to include certain provisions in its constitution or rules and could prohibit affiliation or connection with any society established outside the Federation.

However, laws alone do not provide a complete picture of how the state regarded the formation of societies. One has to look at the actual situation as well. Apart from the Malayan Communist Party (MCP) which remained banned from colonial times, certain extreme religious and cultural groups were denied registration in the pre-1969 phase. Most other organizations, including opposition political parties, obtained registration – though in some instances after an unjustifiably long delay. The Democratic Action Party (DAP) was one such example.

Worker groups seeking to form trade unions, too, had to wait a long while for their registration. Here again, the power to register was vested with a government servant, the Registrar of Trade Unions. There was no mechanism by which citizens could compel the Registrar of Societies or of Trade Unions to expedite registration.

Though there were these difficulties, it is true that on balance the right to form associations was honoured most of the time. If the government sought to control societies and trade unions, it was not through this right but rather through the freedom to function effectively. It is perhaps cleverer to allow associations to exist and yet ensure that they do not succeed.

Opposition political parties, for instance, seldom found it easy to publish journals or organize public rallies – since both require permission from the authorities. There were frequent cases of active party members or able trade unionists being transferred to some other state or city. There were also other forms of harassment and victimization. Most of all, opposition politicians were detained under the Internal Security Act (ISA) which allows a person to be held indefinitely without being charged or tried.

It is this approach rather than direct curbs upon societies which adversely affects the freedom of association. Nowhere is this indirect approach more clearly illustrated than in the question of access to the media. Although in the pre-1969 phase groups critical of the state were given some coverage in the national newspapers, the overwhelming dominance of the government and organizations favourable to it was most apparent. The law that requires newspapers and other periodicals to renew their licences every year deterred most of them from attempting to adopt a more balanced approach. There was even less access for groups outside the Establishment to radio and television, which are both state-owned. When associations have so little opportunity to communicate with the public, they cannot hope to be effective.

Insurmountable as these obstacles were, one must recognize never-theless – especially after the experiences of the last decade – that the pre-1969 phase did provide some openings for associations to function. For even if permits for public rallies were delayed, opposition rallies could take place. In spite of everything, opposition party journals and trade union periodicals made their appearance. Political parties could organize and trade unions could expand. In fact, a major public-sector union, the Railwaymen's Union of Malaya (RUM), launched a nation-wide strike for weeks, yet the government did not retaliate with the harsh, punitive measures common elsewhere. Neither did the harassment and detention of politicians become so serious or severe as to prevent the opposition from mounting an effective challenge in the 1969 elections. Indeed, even university students were allowed to participate in elections. They had their own political clubs on campus and issued statements and demonstrated on a whole variety of national and international controversies.

Legislation and Reality: The Post-1969 Phase

The situation began to change after 1969. To start with, laws affecting the freedom of association were tightened. Various pieces of labour legislation from 1969 to 1980 have had the effect of making it more difficult to form unions in certain industries. The right of unions to associate with one another, to form confederations within the trade union movement or to affiliate with other private associations, either inside or outside the country, has also been subjected to severe curbs. The right of trade unionists to be active in politics is controlled through laws which prohibit them from holding office in political parties.

The freedom of association of students has not been spared either. Through the University and University Colleges Act (UUCA) of 1971 and subsequent amendments in 1975, students are not only prohibited from any form of involvement in politics but are also barred from membership in civic associations unless permission has been given by the university authorities. Even within the campus, the establishment of any student organization must be sanctioned by those authorities.

Like students, university academics are also restricted in their involvement in politics. Though they can be ordinary members of political parties, they cannot hold office or stand for election or engage in campaigning. This is a classic example of allowing an individual to associate but making sure that the act of association will remain ineffectual.

The prohibition pertaining to lawyers belongs to this same broad category. Lawyers who are members of any of the legislatures or office holders in political parties cannot sit on the Bar Council or the state-level Bar Committees. Other rules pertaining to the quorum for meetings and the like impede attorneys as a community from spearheading the struggle for social justice.

More than all these rules, however, it is the 1981 Amendments to the Societies Act whch have had the greatest impact upon the right to freedom of association. It is not the formation of societies that is affected but the capacity of societies to function effectively. Under these Amendments, societies that comment on or seek to influence public policy are classified as 'political societies'. In this manner, criticism of the government and challenges to authority can be controlled since very few civic organizations would want to be known as 'political societies'. This is partly because politics connotes the quest for power which is prohibited to government servants, teachers, academics and other similar groups which at present play prominent roles in civic associations. Furthermore, it is not inconceivable that, once the amended Act is fully implemented, the various categories just mentioned will actually be prohibited from holding office in such political societies.

Even as it is, other aspects of the Amendments constitute serious encroachments upon the freedom of associations. The already vast powers of the Registrar of Societies contained in the 1966 legislation have been further enhanced. He has now been given the authority to approve every foreign affiliation or connection, to determine foreign funding for societies, to remove office holders from non-political societies and to decide whether a society has violated certain entrenched clauses of the national constitution. His right to interpret the constitution in particular amounts to a usurpation of the function of the courts.

These enhanced powers of the Registrar assume grim significance when it is recalled that under the Amendments societies have been denied access to the courts. In the past, a society that was dissatisfied with a decision of the Registrar or the Minister concerned could seek redress from the courts. This right has been expressly repudiated in the 1981 Amendments. Now the Minister is the final arbiter. This must surely place all societies, whether political or not, in serious jeopardy.

So far we have examined the legal situation pertaining to freedom of association after 1969. Once again, we must analyse actual practices in connection with the right to form associations and the right of associations to function effectively in order to discover whether realities are as restrictive as the laws that exist today.

Since 1969, there have been at least three occasions when societies with aims that had nothing to do with Communism, led by individuals who were in no way linked to subversive activities, failed to obtain registration certificates. The first was an unsuccessful attempt in 1974 by five academic staff associations from the five national universities to establish a confederation to be called *Tenaga Akademik*; its purpose was to protect the rights of academics and to enable them to play a more effective role in nation building. The second was an attempt by a handful of academics and other professionals to establish a society committed to the advancement of knowledge of human rights and social justice based upon a rational, scientific study of the social sciences and humanities. This was in 1975. The society was to be called *Liga Reformasi* but the application for registration was turned down without reason. A third endeavour, also in 1975, was the establishment of the Malaysian Human Rights Organization (MHRO). This was initiated by a group of writers, academics and relatives of political detainees. Again, no reason was given for the rejection.

These three examples suggest that human rights have become suspect. Yet it is ironic that the right to freedom of association does not extend to those who wish to protect human rights.

When we analyse the actual functioning of societies, it is evident that those organizations concerned with human rights as part of a larger quest for social justice have been placed under severe stress and strain. It is often impossible to organize public forums or seminars on major social issues. Most civic associations are now compelled to hold private seminars on an invitation basis even if they are dealing with consumer or environmental problems. Organizations which are more directly involved in social reform or 'conscientization' find it difficult to obtain permits to publish periodicals. ALIRAN (*Aliran Kesedaran Negara* [Society for National Consciousness, or National Consciousness Movement] of which this author is President) is a non-electoral society with a small membership devoted mainly to raising public consciousness. ALIRAN has not only been denied a permit to publish its own journal, but since October 1980 has also been threatened with deregistration by the Registrar of Societies. Apparently, the government was provoked to act when ALIRAN's studied criticisms of various aspects of national life were favourably received by the public. Though the organization continues to exist, surveillance of it has not abated. Like leaders and members in some other non-electoral associations – notably the Muslim Youth Movement (ABIM) – ALIRAN personnel are also sometimes subjected to undue harassment.

However, active trade unionists have been victims of harassment on a much more serious scale, and so have opposition politicians. It has been suggested that the principal leaders in the major opposition parties are closely watched by the government's Special Branch.

In fact, opposition parties are confronted with many obstacles. Since 1978, for example, public rallies have not been allowed even during election campaigns. Indeed, even small discussion sessions, *Ceramah*, confined to a few hundred people, require police permits. A number of stringent conditions on the type of issues that can be discussed, the identity of the speakers, the length of time of the meeting, and so on, are often imposed quite arbitrarily.

As in the pre-1969 phase, these direct controls upon societies are perhaps less significant than the indirect curbs upon public expression. The media remain controlled, though some newspaper editors, on their own initiative, have tried to exercise a certain degree of independence.

The reasons for this attempt at independence (which will be examined below) also explain in part the government's own slight change in attitude. Recently, a number of political detainees were released unconditionally – although the ISA continues to be used. Newspapers are now allowed and even encouraged to publish the administrative shortcomings of governmental departments and agencies. In fact, even before this new attitude appeared, it is irrefutably true that certain freedoms continued to be enjoyed. Trade unions have not ceased to recruit members, organize training courses and, most of all, demand better wages and working conditions. Everything considered, political parties continue to seek new recruits, open up branches, and issue statements on political matters. Even students – the UUCA notwithstanding – are actively involved in organizing political forums on their campuses.

All this indicates that freedom of association and action still exists. At the same time, it is a fact that societies and trade unions outside the Establishment are far less effective today than they were in the pre-1969 phase, though even then they were not completely free to be truly effective.

We should now try to explore the underlying reasons for the situation surrounding freedom of association in Malaysia. What are the causes of the decline of this fundamental liberty over the years?

Explanation of the Decline of Freedom in Malaysia
It is possible to argue that the nature and character of freedom of association, and indeed of most fundamental liberties, are conditioned by four main factors: the beliefs, values and attitudes of the ruling class; the interests of the ruling class; changes in economic and social structures; and the political culture of the society in question. Further, these four factors are not only interrelated but together constitute a united whole.
The Beliefs, Values and Attitudes of the Ruling Class: There are four distinct elements in the psychological make-up, or belief-system, of the ruling class which have influenced the character of freedom of association in Malaysia.

First, the ruling class at the time of independence in 1957 believed that the nation should practise parliamentary democracy. If they had felt otherwise, there might not have been any right to freedom of association. The decision to adopt parliamentary democracy as the system of government was, however, not the product of a conscious, deliberate reflection on political values and ideals. It was preferred simply because the leaders of the Alliance, the coalition that inherited independence, were familiar with it, given their educational background. Since parliamentary democracy was a British institution and since they admired the British, it was worthy of emulation. (There were, of course, other reasons too, to be discussed later.)

For the post-1969 leaders, especially the present group, the British origin of parliamentary democracy holds no such attraction. In so far as this origin had played some role in the attitude of the first generation of leaders, its rejection today may help to account for the greater readiness of the present élites to restrict fundamental liberties.

This difference in attitude between first- and later-generation leaders is also found in many other post-colonial societies. One must hasten to add, however, that admiration for an institution associated with the colonial overlord has never been a sufficiently strong basis for continued loyalty to it – as is proved by many Third World élites. It is only when adherence to parliamentary democracy emerges from intellectual and spiritual sources that it can withstand the tribulations of political upheaval.

Another belief of the ruling class in 1957 which contributed towards freedom of association was related to the economic system. By perpetuating a capitalist economy which by its very nature endows the owners of capital with freedom of association, the new state had to recognize that particular freedom as a value in itself. This is not unlike the economic history of Europe where the struggle of the bourgeoisie for their economic rights got equated willy-nilly at a certain point with the general quest for human rights. Even in the Third World, it is not a coincidence that some of the states that have managed to sustain certain fundamental liberties for a period were invariably those which bestowed freedom upon the market.

In Malaysia, as in those other states, freedom of association with a market connection predictably favoured the economic élites while tolerating other groups which happened to be around. It explains to some extent why from 1957 onwards trade unions have been subjected to various curbs and controls. Indeed, it is this economic orientation of the ruling class which is partly responsible for the character of freedom of association in the country: a fundamental liberty that does not provide much liberty to the fundamental groups in the society.

While it is true that the overall thrust of the economy and what it implies for trade unions and the like has not changed, it is evident that there have been discernible shifts within the economic stratum. These shifts have produced more freedom for some groups as against others. This, in turn, has resulted in restrictions and regulations which have affected freedom of association and other fundamental liberties in the post-1969 phase. However, this process is more appropriately analysed under 'changes in economic and social structures', our third factor.

Thus we shall turn to the third element in the values and beliefs of the ruling class. This is its commitment to the ethnic characterization of society. From 1957 on, the élites, presiding over a multi-ethnic society *par excellence*, approached all major issues in politics, economics and culture from ethnic perspectives. Whatever the justification for this, it created a situation whereby ethnic associations discovered that they had legitimate roles to perform. They operated with the sort of freedom which progressive political groups based on non-ethnic ideologies could not hope for.

Of course, ethnic organizations associated with the state had greater room for manoeuvre. Among these, Malay societies were freer if only because the dominant party in the Alliance was the United Malays National Organization (UMNO) whose goal was the advancement of Malay ethnic interests. UMNO's dominance, in turn, was due largely to the fact that the majority of electoral constituencies were rural and

Malay. For mobilization of votes in such areas, societies like the Malay teachers associations – which campaigned during the 1960s for wider use of Malay as the official and national language – were crucial.

Non-Malay societies close to the non-Malay parties within the Alliance – the Malaysian Chinese Association (MCA) and the Malaysian Indian Congress (MIC) respectively – could also express themselves freely as long as they did not question some of the constitutional and political principles which guided inter-ethnic ties forged by the government. To a lesser extent, Malay and non-Malay societies outside the Establishment could function too, provided they did not become effective to the point of threatening the Alliance's conception of ethnicity.

Since the now expanded yet still ethnic coalition (termed the *Barisan Nasional*) continues to maintain ethnic dichotomies in public policies, the significant role of ethnic associations has not diminished in any way. The difference is that ethnic groupings with an Islamic slant have become more prominent recently, in line with rising Islamic consciousness elsewhere. However, since a number of these are not really with the government (which they see as un-Islamic) and some are very critical of it, the government has tried to curb their activities. Consequently, there is less freedom for Islamic societies as a whole.

Similarly, non-Malay groups in the post-1969 phase are confronted with more serious obstacles than in the past. Apart from constitutional impediments to raising certain issues which they perceive as important, these groups are finding it difficult to articulate publicly their anxieties about their future in the country. This is largely because their sentiments and demands are diametrically opposed to those of emerging Malay middle-class groups advocating Malay ethnicity. These Malay groups enjoy a symbiotic relationship with the UMNO-led government. Hence, they – more than anyone else – have the widest scope for their activities.

Our analysis of the influence of ethnicity upon freedom of association has shown that this aspect of the ruling class's belief-system gave rise to the participation of ethnic associations on a large scale in the pre-1969 phase. Since then, however, various changes involving Islamic consciousness and non-Malay interests have brought about a situation in which Malay ethnic groups espousing the *Rukunegara*, or official state ideology, appear to have greatest latitude. This demonstrates that the dynamic of ethnic politics is capable of restricting freedom of association.

Finally, a fourth element, one with a cultural dimension: the 1957 élites manifested a sense of restraint in their attitude towards political power which meant that they did not seek to control or dominate the entire system. Consequently, other groups were able to enjoy some degree of freedom.

This sense of restraint was due largely to the élites' traditional background. Malaysia is one of those rare cases in the Third World where the group that inherited power was linked to the traditional administrative-aristocratic leadership of Malay society. As an élite group it had known power in pre-colonial society and even during the colonial period it had some semblance of authority through its collaboration with the British. Whatever the many disadvantages of such a background, it at least helped cultivate a restrained attitude to power since the exercise of authority was not something new to these élites.

Tradition was responsible in yet another way for restraint. Being leaders whose positions in society were guaranteed by their administrative roles or aristocratic lineages, they enjoyed the sort of deference that gave them a sense of confidence and security. It was certainly true of Tunku Abdul Rahman, a prince, who was the founder of the Malaysian state and the first Prime Minister. Given this confidence, there was a willingness to tolerate differences of opinion, to allow others some leeway – as long as it did not lead to a challenge to authority which the traditional, feudal psychology would interpret as an act of supreme disloyalty. (We shall return to this element as part of our study of political culture and freedom of association.)

Although the Tunku and the first-generation leaders have been replaced by others, restraint as a political characteristic has not disappeared altogether. This is partly because in an evolutionary situation, new leaders – whatever their backgrounds – eventually become socialized into the dominant ethos. They acquire the values and attitudes held by the core of the initial leadership group. However, as time passes, as political circumstances change, these founding values tend to atrophy. This may be one of the reasons why, as is increasingly alleged, there is less of a sense of restraint today.

If we reflect on these four elements that form part of the central beliefs and values of the ruling class, it is evident that all four have undergone considerable transformation over the last two decades. This explains to some extent why freedom of association is more restricted today.

The Interests of the Ruling Class: More important than beliefs and values are the interests of the ruling class. It is almost an axiom of politics that if fundamental liberties are restricted it is because the ruling class wishes to perpetuate itself.

Indeed, it might be argued – other reasons notwithstanding – that the 1957 élites adopted parliamentary democracy precisely because the system appeared to confirm their power. The series of elections held before independence resulted in huge victories for the members of the Alliance. Even after independence, every election from 1959 to 1969 gave the Alliance comfortable two-thirds majorities in the Parliament. It was only in the 1969 general election that the coalition suffered some setbacks. The suspension of democratic rule and the declaration of an emergency following a riot that took place in the wake of the election were events that were not unrelated to the results of the election.

The ruling class's reaction to the 1969 election showed that it regarded parliamentary democracy as a system that should legitimize its rule. This attitude has remained. The 1974 and 1978 general elections which were resounding successes for the *Barisan Nasional* restored the confidence of the new élites in the efficacy of parliamentary democracy. Indeed, it is partly because the democratic system seems to serve the interests of the ruling class that it has been allowed to continue to exist.

Since the system is expected to help keep the élites in power, it follows that critics and opponents should not be allowed to use the system to mobilize support or mount an effective challenge against them. Even in the pre-1969 phase, this attitude was apparent. If there was greater tolerance of diverse opinions it was not only because of the values and beliefs of the élites which we have examined. Perhaps it was due even more to the control that they exercised over the Alliance and the political environment as a whole. In other words, the élites knew that they could afford to provide some latitude since it would not affect their interests, which, as usual, were paramount.

The Alliance leadership had an effective grip over the coalition and national politics for a variety of reasons. As the party that had won independence, the Alliance commanded immense respect which helped it to dominate the situation. Through the independence movement, the coalition had also forged inter-ethnic links which were strong and stable. Except for a brief crisis in 1959, relations among the coalition partners were excellent to a point where the Alliance itself had a distinct identity of its own. Within UMNO there were hardly any cliques or factions. The Tunku himself commanded total loyalty.

Apart from all this, a fairly efficient administrative machinery and a prosperous economy also made it easier for the leadership to control the political environment. The political culture, which we shall examine shortly, with its emphasis on obedience, security and mobility further enabled the ruling class to dominate. It gave them the confidence to relax a little, since their position was unassailable.

It is partly because the situation within the *Barisan Nasional* and in the political environment is less stable that the post-1969 leadership has become less tolerant of challenges. Though there have been impressive electoral victories, there are today more problems among the *Barisan* partners, just as there are easily identifiable cliques within UMNO. These signs of internal instability have been accompanied by changes in the larger environment. The non-Malay middle class has expanded, a Malay middle class has come into being, the economy is not doing as well as it formerly did, the administrative structure reveals weaknesses, and ethnic and political perceptions are beginning to change. The upshot of all this is that the ruling class is finding it more difficult to dominate and control the total situation. Consequently, it has become more and more hostile to criticism. Thus in the post-1969 phase the ruling élites have become extremely wary of associations which are potentially effective in spite of an ever shrinking arena for expression and action.

For in the ultimate analysis it is the interests of the ruling class that matter.

Changes in Economic and Social Structures: It is perhaps altogether appropriate that our discussion on structures follows our reflections on the values and beliefs of the ruling class and its interest in self-preservation. For there are many unexplained changes related to the emergence of new groups and new demands which will now be made clearer.

To begin with, in contrast to many other newly independent states, Malaysia's social structure in 1957 was fairly straightforward, apart from its ethnic dimension. Within the Malay community there was an upper class of aristocrats and administrators (called 'administocrats' in my other publications) and the Malay masses, largely rural and poor. There were intermediary groups of teachers, lower-level government employees and the like, who did not, however, constitute a class as such. Among the non-Malays, in contrast, there was a middle class distinguishable by income and life style, in addition to a wealthy and influential upper class and a lower class of urban and rural workers.

As in other countries, educational and economic growth, which has been phenomenal, has altered this structure. Today there is a Malay middle class comprising bureaucrats, professionals and executives. Similarly, the Malay upper class has also changed its character through the infusion of new elements originally from the lower strata of society. Among the non-Malays too, the middle class has grown tremendously, while the upper class has witnessed a decline in the traditional coteries of wealth and their replacement by new economic élites. Within both communities, however, the majority of the people remain poor and powerless.

These changes within the middle and upper classes are extremely relevant, not just to freedom of association but to freedom as a whole. We shall look at their economic and then at their political consequences.

While changes within the non-Malay social structure are part of an ongoing process, the emergence of the Malay middle class is a different proposition. It is its misfortune that this class has arrived at a time when there is already an established non-Malay middle class initiated through the colonial educational and economic system. Its late arrival has, in a sense, forced it to depend much more upon the state to consolidate its economic position in particular. Since the state is in any case committed to the creation of a Malay commercial and industrial élite as outlined in its New Economic Policy (NEP), its ideological goals are in complete harmony with those of the new Malay middle class. Consequently, state political and bureaucratic power has been used to carve an economic niche for this new class. This has meant creating new rules on private enterprise, new regulations on private capital, and new institutions to assist the advance of Malay entrepreneurship. The total impact of all this has been the bureaucratization of private enterprise or, to put it differently, the growth of state capitalism in the post-1969 phase.

State capitalism is by its very nature restrictive. Whatever may be the merits of controlling the sort of private enterprise that exists in countries like Malaysia, the involvement of the state in the market leads inevitably to the diminution of certain economic freedoms. Traditional owners of capital, whether foreign or local, in the plantation and tin sectors for instance, lose out to state capital. Big non-Malay businesses feel confined by new rules and eventually surrender to state enterprises. Even Malay private firms, unable to match the capitalization of government agencies, close down their genuinely entrepreneurial activities.

All this has an effect upon freedom; for if autonomous economic groups, which in a capitalist society help to keep autonomous social and political activities going, come under bureaucratic control then freedom itself will be lost. There is ample evidence to support this contention. A cursory analysis of the political opposition in Malaysia and of non-electoral groups critical of the Establishment will show that many of the individuals involved are economically independent of the state. Economic autonomy then is closely linked to political freedom.

This becomes even more apparent when one considers the position of workers in state-owned companies. They are not only prohibited from active participation in opposition politics but are also punished harshly if they resort to industrial action to support their demand for better wages. This was proved in the case of the Airlines Employees Union (AEU) in February 1979. There is no doubt at all that workers in state-owned companies face more severe restrictions than their counterparts in private firms.

Thus far we have examined the consequences for freedom which result from the economics of state capitalism; but the growth of the Malay middle class is also a political phenomenon with overt political consequences. Unlike the earlier Malay upper class to whom power came naturally, the new Malay middle class has to struggle much more to establish itself, partly because it does not have the same aura and partly because it is in a more competitive environment.

The competition is in fact a consequence of the expansion of the middle class itself. As any middle class expands there is bound to be greater rivalry among its members for the limited material and intangible goals of position, power, mobility, respect, deference and honour. This had begun to happen to the non-Malay middle class in the 1960s. The birth of Islamic groups within the Malay middle class in the 1970s is to some extent a manifestation of the same phenomenon.

As these Islamic and other non-Establishment groups challenge the dominant Malay middle-class elements associated with the state and its economic ideology, the latter are bound to react with anger and hostility. For they feel that even before they have secured their positions properly, attempts are being made from inside and outside the community to dislodge them. Consequently, they decide to use the power of the state to curb and control the dissident groups. This is precisely what has been happening in the last few years. Therefore, the emergence of the Malay middle class at a certain historical juncture, and its relationship with the state in which it is coupled with the state's ideology, have led to a series of economic and political actions that have had the effect of reducing freedom of association and other fundamental liberties.

The Political Culture: While the ruling class and social structures provide the main explanations for the condition of freedom, one should also evaluate the mass-based political culture to determine whether there are certain attitudes, beliefs and values held by the people at large that have a bearing upon fundamental liberties.

It has been hinted above that, within the Malay community, there is the notion of unquestioning loyalty to the leader. A traditional feudal trait which was sustained throughout the colonial period, it has survived to this day mainly because the ruling class that inherited independence was from an administocratic background. Successive UMNO leaders have perpetuated this aspect of leader–led relationships since it serves the interest of the élites.

As an attitude of mind, unswerving loyalty affects freedom of association in a direct manner. Because of unwillingness to accept that questioning the leadership is a legitimate activity, any dissident attempt to chastise the authorities for curbing fundamental liberties does not normally receive significant support from the Malays. Indeed, in a community where such a psychology is pervasive, the idea of individual rights, of human rights for the masses, will not take root easily. For these rights must be seen in relation to institutions and individuals associated with the state. Given the attachment to authority and the aura of the state, any endeavour to enhance the power of the ordinary human being would be regarded as lese-majesty. Of course, this attitude is changing with various transformations taking place in Malay society.

Among the non-Malays, their position as second- and third-generation citizens whose active domicile began only after World War II has conditioned their attitude to freedom. While individuals and groups here and there are seriously concerned about fundamental liberties, non-Malays as a whole have very little commitment to basic rights and freedoms. The security of their positions and the mobility of their occupations are by far the dominant considerations. But here again, as the future comes to appear less secure and as they become more settled, more and more middle-class non-Malays are beginning to understand the importance of fundamental liberties. Certain newspaper attitudes in the 1970s and 1980s prove the point.

From a different perspective, Malaysia's multi-ethnic character is also an impediment. In a society where genuine ethnic dichotomies are exaggerated beyond reason, a point is soon reached when people become afraid to discuss fundamental issues for fear of hurting ethnic sensitivities. Often the issues involved have little to do with the ethnic situation. It seems to me that within our political culture there is a psychology of fear linked to the multi-ethnic character of our society. It dampens public enthusiasm for fundamental liberties. This is to be expected when the authorities keep on reminding the people, every time there is a major public controversy, of the danger of the 1969 riot repeating itself.

Finally, the long period of economic prosperity for the middle and upper classes which has lulled most of them into slumber, the constant fear of a Communist threat to national security, and the absence of an intellectual tradition of freedom have all contributed towards the perpetuation of a passive political culture. And yet, it must be repeated, elements of that culture are beginning to change.

Conclusions

It is ironic that one of the crucial factors that may stimulate the political culture to become more active in the future is further state penetration. For the Achilles heel of this penetration of the economy, which is being accompanied by more rigid control over politics, is that it is being carried out on behalf of a segment of the rising Malay middle and upper class. Whatever its short-term benefits, it will not help the Malay masses in the long run. This is because it does not envisage any holistic structural transformation aimed at creating an economically egalitarian and politically participatory society. Similarly, while the economics of state capitalism which works in tandem with sections of private capital will provide some gains to selected non-Malay groups, it will be antithetical to the interests of the majority of those communities as well.

With this scenario, Malay and non-Malay groups outside the citadel of power, however different their starting-points, may well realize as the situation develops that they should co-operate to protect their autonomy and independence. Malay elements in the middle class who adhere to a different vision of society or are being edged out will have no choice but to continue to oppose the penetration of the state. After all, they would be perceived by the forces around the state as real rivals for political power. Non-Malay elements, too, who have continually to submit to the dictates of these new forces, may come to prefer resistance to acceptance of their domination.

It is not inconceivable, then, that for the first time in our history Malay and non-Malay groups may have a sound, rational basis for forging an indestructible link: the need to protect their freedom. In the past, it was often the desire to seek power that brought them together. Now, at last, they will realize that freedom of association will achieve its ultimate purpose only when human beings associate with one another as human beings to defend that most exalted of human values – freedom.

16. Freedom of the Press in the Philippines

Abraham F. Sarmiento

Any discussion of freedom of the press invariably begins with an appeal or allusion to the fact that the fundamental charters of all democratic societies uphold and guarantee freedom of speech and expression. Indeed, the press is honoured as the *only* profession that has a constitutional mandate for its practice. This guarantee appears as the First Amendment of the Constitution of the United States. In the Philippines, the mandate is enshrined in all the charters enforced – first as Article III of the Philippine Autonomy Act, then as Article III, Section 1, Paragraph 8 of the 1935 Constitution of the Philippines, and finally as Section 9 of Article IV of the 1973 Constitution.

The governments of the world which avow adherence to the tenets of democracy recognize freedom of speech and a free press as essential and indispensable to the discovery and the dissemination of political truth. The basic assumption is that the stewards of government derive their powers and privileges from the sovereign will of the people. The aspirations, needs, opinions and criticisms of the people should, therefore, guide and govern state authority. A great anomaly emerges when this relationship is reversed: when government officials impose their own opinions and policies upon the people, without due regard for the sovereign will of the people. Even if one grants that men ascending to public office are capable and upright, they are not totally infallible. Moreover, public officials can never totally divest themselves of their personal, material, political and intellectual stakes and biases. The best defence against the triumph of the personal and subjective wishes of public officials over the public good is still a healthy and unbridled public opinion.

Free speech and a free press are, therefore, the essential cornerstones of good, efficient and honest government. Furthermore, the paramount duty of state authority is to abide by the popular will.

Propitious insights are provided by philosophers and writers. In his work *On Liberty*, the liberal democrat John Stuart Mill argues that 'all silencing of discussion is an assumption of infallibility.' Mill submits further that the contest of opinions is necessary for societies to arrive at political truths, since man is 'not sufficiently capacious and impartial' to make one specific approach to problems, the best and only correct one. According to Mill: 'Truth, in the great practical concerns of life, is so much a question of reconciling and combining of opposites . . . and it has to be made by the rough process of a struggle between combatants fighting under hostile banners.' The English writer, Junius, in the 18th century wrote – in terms that may now seem trite – that 'the liberty of the press is the palladium of all civil, political and religious freedom.'

In decisions penned by the courts of law, the unswerving commitment to press freedom from government repression is a recurring theme: 'The protection given speech and press was fashioned to assure the unfettered interchange of ideas for the bringing about of political and social changes desired by the people' (*Roth v. United States*, 354 US476, 484). Then again, in *Whitney v. California* (377): 'If there be time to expose through discussion the falsehood and fallacies, to avert the evil by processes of education, the remedy to be applied is more speech, not enforced silence.'

People have fought and died in the search for truth and for freedom of speech. At the base of discussions about the free flow of ideas among people in society is the concept of intellectual liberty. The right of individuals to freedom of expression evolves from their basic right to be free to think what they will. Struggle has always preceded state recognition of freedom of speech and of the press, despite the fact that the final end of the state should be to make people free to develop their faculties to the maximum.

No other institution in society better illustrates the tensions between the interests of government, private enterprise, and the public than the institution of the press. A quasi-public agency held accountable to the public, the press has to contend with its basic identity as a private enterprise, as well as confronting government regulation. Thus, when we talk about freedom of expression and the free flow of information in a mass society, we must also talk about access to the media. This cannot be avoided inasmuch as private business assumes control of mass media facilities. Owners of media agencies, no less than government officials, should respect the public's right to know and be informed. Yet, too often, the media become beholden to the commercial interests of the owners and ignore their responsibility for the public welfare. An even more complicated scenario emerges when private corporate interests in the press converge with government interests. In this instance, the public good often suffers.

Some examples of the divergence between the theory of freedom of the press and the Philippine reality will sharpen the above discussion.

* * * * *

In his book, *Press of the Philippines: Its History and Problems*, the American scholar, John Lent, describes the Philippine press in the following manner:

When one speaks of the Philippine press, he speaks of an institution that began in the 17th century but really did not take root until the 19th century; which overthrew the shackles of three governments but became enslaved by its own members; which won a high degree of freedom of the press but neglected to accept the responsibilities inherent in such freedom.

A Filipino historian, Renato Constantino, contributes his own insights:

> Given the realities of our time, the press in a society like ours plays a subordinate role to the institutions and levers of power that dominate society; in effect, the press is just one of the conduits of the aspirations and thought of persons who conduct that society.

Hailed as 'one of the freest' in the world before 1972, the Philippine press was forced to give up all its rights and to neglect its responsibilities towards the public, when martial law was declared in September 1972. Proclamation No. 1081 enforced one-man rule and military sovereignty over the people, avowedly 'to save the republic and reform society' (according to Mr Marcos). In truth, however, military rule was a response to increasing resistance by the Filipino people to the corrupt and dictatorial Marcos regime.

From the moment that martial law was declared the press became the most controlled of social institutions and it remains so today. In the earliest days of martial law, the first act of Mr Marcos was the closure and take-over of all newspapers, magazines, radio and television facilities by the Defence Secretary. Affected by this arbitrary and repressive measure were 404 offices, 26 major-circulation magazines, six television channels, and 312 national and provincial radio stations. Letter of Instruction No. 1 ordered the arrest of journalists and media people. 'Rumour-mongering' or the spreading of political rumour was decreed a crime by Presidential Decree No. 90, punishable by *prision correcional* (imprisonment for anything between six months and one day, and six years).

The collusion of private business and state authority in the Philippine press today is one of the greatest scandals of our time. After a period of enforced prior censorship under the Media Advisory Council, co-chaired by the Secretaries of Defence and Public Information from 1972 to 1975, the Philippine press was allowed by Mr Marcos to regulate itself. This was done, however, only after media facilities were put under the control and ownership of the friends, relatives and business associates of the Marcos couple. By such apologies as 'freedom with responsibility', journalists in the Philippines have been forced to practise 'self-censorship', even as others have expressed opposition. The Philippine authorities have maintained a policy of repression against protesting journalists.

Celebrated examples of the Marcos dictatorship's assault on press freedom include the arbitrary arrest and prolonged detention of many editors and journalists who dared write against the Marcos regime, the

Marcos family, Marcos cronies, and Marcos sycophants. One of these was Abraham F. Sarmiento, Jr, my eldest son and the editor-in-chief of *The Philippine Collegian* from 1975 to 1976. He was imprisoned for seven months and seven days, first in Fort Bonifacio and later in Camp Crame Stockade. He died shortly after his release from the Camp Crame Hospital at the age of 27 years. The 4 February 1978 issue of *Ningas-Cogan* (published in New York City) carried the following account of his editorship:

> Just before the *Collegian* was temporarily closed, its editor and staff summarily put under arrest, Ditto [Abraham P. Sarmiento, Jr] had managed to elevate the paper into the sole saving grace of the Philippine press. The *Collegian* had become the only newspaper in the country that dared to print the truth and everything else that was unpleasant to those who wielded power. So well did the *Collegian* live up to this task that Ditto and his courageous staff could not have gotten away without paying the heavy price they paid for their audacity.

Other examples of repression against defiant journalists include the expulsion of Associated Press correspondent Arnold Zeitlin, the harassment of *Far Eastern Economic Review*'s Bernard Wideman, the closure of five Church media facilities in 1976, the forced resignation of Letty Magsanoc of the *Bulletin Today*'s 'Panorama', and countless cases of articles and issues arbitrarily banned.

At present, I and several correspondents – Manuel Concordia, former Delegate, Congressman and Under Secretary of Justice, and former Congressman Rogaciano Mercado – are still under 'house arrest' for allegedly publishing (in the case of Sarmiento and Concordia) in 1979, and for translating (in the case of Mercado) from English into Tagalog, a book written by the former President of the Philippines and President of the 1971 Constitutional Convention, Diosdado P. Macapagal, entitled *Ang Demokrasya Sa Pilipinas*, very critical of the Marcos dictatorship. The English version, *Democracy in the Philippines*, was published and circulated in 1976.[1]

Faced with conditions of intense political competition between the public and a repressive government – a government in collaboration with the media owners – the committed press is bound to come down on the side of the public. The boundaries of press freedom should be circumscribed only by the laws covering libel, obscenity, *sub judice* litigation, and national security, with the latter sparingly and reasonably applied. When 'national security' becomes a catch-phrase for all criticism that the government wishes to quell, then press freedom is prostituted. The constitutional guarantee of the liberty of the press is thus violated, often because of the political whims and caprices of an abusive and corrupt government.

In a democracy, the press should enjoy freedom from prior censorship, free access to information, free and unhampered circulation, and freedom from subsequent punishment. It is no democracy when a government discourages these freedoms. Only a regime that does not enjoy the people's support penalizes critical opinions. In this light, the press should stand by its public's resistance movement and seek all paths to liberation.

When the pen has failed in all its efforts at asserting press freedom, no recourse is left for journalists except the road to active protest.

Note

1. All four (President Macapagal, and Sarmiento, Concordia and Mercado) were charged in 1979 (SPI No. 79–347) before the military for 'Inciting to Sedition' (Violation of Article 142, Revised Penal Code, as Amended by Presidential Decree 942 and Presidential Decree 970) and 'Rumour Mongering' (Violation of PD No. 90). On 12 May 1980, the Special Investigating Panel composed of the Judge Advocate General, the Deputy Judge Advocate General, and the Executive Officer of the JAGO found a *prima facie* case against the four noted above, and three others (the owner of the printing press, the manager of the printing press, and another translator). President Marcos approved the preliminary investigation of the case by the military and its trial by the Military Tribunals. In the meantime, the four respondents went to the Supreme Court and obtained a restraining order. Meanwhile, 12 libel cases were filed in the Rizal Provincial Fiscal's Office against Macapagal, Sarmiento, Concordia and Mercado by 12 military officers whose reputations were allegedly besmirched by the book. All these cases are still pending.

17. The Status of Women in ASEAN: Some Observations

Amarjit Kaur

This paper represents a modest attempt to stimulate some discussion on the status of women in the five ASEAN nations, an issue which appears to have been grossly neglected hitherto. The paper does not undertake an exhaustive review of the literature on women in ASEAN; nor does it claim to be a definitive work on the subject.

As a preliminary to the main discussion, the term 'status' requires some explanation. The usage of the term has often been contested on the grounds of imprecision. In this paper, it is used in its generally accepted meaning of 'standing', and of ascribed respect which, though essentially abstract concepts, are understood in all communities.

In 1972, the United Nations proclaimed 1975 as International Women's Year. The three themes of International Women's Year – Equality, Development and Peace – indicate that women today still suffer discrimination, and for the most part neither participate fully nor share equally in the benefits of economic and social progress and development.

While women in the ASEAN region share many, if not all, of the problems of women in the more developed countries, they have additional problems of their own, problems which have arisen from their participation in the global economy. It is ironical that, in recognizing that it is particularly wasteful and shortsighted to make only marginal use of the energy and talent of over half the population in these areas, Western development schemes have served only to accentuate discrimination against women.

The aim of this paper, therefore, is to discuss some recent trends in the situation and status of women in the legal, social and economic spheres in the ASEAN region.

Legal Status

There is, of course, no one system of law prevailing in Indonesia, Malaysia, the Philippines, Singapore and Thailand. The systems of law followed in each of these countries are related to its cultural-religious background. In none of these countries is there any uniform national law which applies to all citizens, irrespective of their religion, in the personal sphere affecting property, inheritance and marriage. At the same time, it appears that the system of law governing a religious group in one country is not necessarily the same as that governing a group professing the same religion in another country.

Political/Civil Rights

Suffrage: Except for Thailand, the other four ASEAN nations were until recently under some form or other of colonial rule. Generally speaking, their independence has been followed by new written constitutions, guaranteeing equality of political rights with adult franchise to all citizens.

Political rights include the right to vote and hold public office and the right to exercise public functions on equal terms without any discrimination.[1] These rights were laid down in the new constitutions of the newly independent countries but their full implementation is held back by factors including lack of education and economic freedom. Although adult franchise was introduced without literacy tests, the electoral participation of women – though encouraging – cannot be taken as an indication of their political awareness. Modern methods of mass education and mass communication, as well as traditional loyalties, have minimized the importance of formal education. Additionally, party organization and party systems have reduced to an absolute minimum the freedom of individual choice in elections. None the less, it is recognized that a minimum standard of education, including the ability to read, is essential for the development of political interest and awareness among women voters.

Women participate in all stages of elections, both as party members and as members of non-party organizations interested in the political education of women. However, women (and men) often vote in accordance with decisions reached by the leaders of villages. It is often recorded in rural areas that the party which secures the support of the leaders of the village will be likely to win the votes of the overwhelming majority of the people. This tendency is particularly evident in Malaysia, the Philippines and Thailand.

Leadership of women still comes primarily from the leisured and educated class. Owing to economic factors and the heavy responsibilities of the family, many women are prevented from taking much interest in electoral events.

In all these countries, women's organizations are engaged in the political and social education of women. In Indonesia, there are political parties for women only, which are meant to prepare them for participation and leadership in the political life of the nation. However, these are only in the experimental stage, and are intended to search out the best way for women to participate in Indonesian political life.[2] In Malaysia, women's sections are organized by the political parties, and progress in political education among women bears witness to the effectiveness of their activities.[3] Nevertheless, the number of female candidates offering themselves for election bears no relation whatsoever to the proportion of women voters. Some of the reasons for the reluctance of women to enter the legislature include lack of political ambition, lack of economic freedom, fear of the disruption of family life consequent on absence from home, lack of adjustment to the techniques of party politics and lack of experience.

In no ASEAN country is there constitutional or statutory reservation of legislative seats for women. In Thailand, which is a constitutional monarchy, the problem is slightly different. There have been no opposition parties and the Thai legislature is only partly elective. Women have, however, found a place in that legislature as elected members on the basis of merit. Meanwhile, the electoral law requires an educational qualification for candidates to the legislature in Thailand.

To summarize, the principle of equal political rights of men and women has been recognized and written into the basic laws of these five countries.

Citizenship: On the issue of citizenship in these countries, women generally enjoy fewer privileges than men. A woman married to a male citizen can become a citizen but no corresponding privilege is extended to a man married to a female citizen. In addition, citizenship is not generally transmitted by a woman to her children. Only recently in Malaysia, Singapore and the Philippines was provision made for a woman to transmit her citizenship to her children. In Thailand and Indonesia, a woman still cannot transmit her citizenship to her children under normal circumstances.

Personal Law

In the field of family law, the principle of equality has not yet won universal acceptance in ASEAN.

The patriarchal family structure and society prevail generally in the ASEAN countries with only few exceptions, which are confined to small areas in some of the countries; in others there are no exceptions to the rule of patriarchy. The personal laws affecting women in regard to residence after marriage and property rights are, therefore, generally permeated by the norms of a patriarchal system.

Marriage: In the Philippines, Singapore and Thailand, marriages are primarily monogamous.[4] In Indonesia and Malaysia, however, Muslims are allowed to have more than one wife. Polygamous marriages among non-Muslims in Malaysia have become a thing of the past with the enforcement, from 1 March 1982, of the Law Reform (Marriage and Divorce) Act, 1975.[5] In Indonesia, one reason for the practice of plural marriages is that Indonesian society accords a higher status to a married woman than to a single woman. In actual practice, however, economic factors and public opinion in both Indonesia and Malaysia act as restraints on polygamy. Furthermore, provisions have been introduced in

Indonesia and in some of the Malaysian states which stipulate the necessity of the consent of the first wife before a man legally contracts a second marriage.

Age of Marriage: Generally, parental consent is required for the marriage of a person who has not attained the age of consent. In all five countries, the minimum age for marriage is higher for males than it is for females.

In the Philippines, the age of consent is 14 years for females and 16 for males, but the law requires the consent of the parents if the bride is under 18 and/or the bridegroom under 20. In Thailand, the legal age is 20 years without the consent of the parents but 17 years for a boy and 15 for a girl with parental consent.

In Malaysia, for non-Muslims the age of consent is 18 for both males and females except that, for females over 16, a marriage can still be solemnized if it is authorized by a licence granted by the Chief Minister. However, for Muslims there is no minimum age for marriage. According to Muslim law, the age of consent for a woman is the age of puberty, which is deemed to take place at 15.

It is clear from the legal provisions for the minimum age of marriage in these various countries, excepting only Malaysia and then only for non-Muslims, that the law still assumes that a woman should contract marriage at an earlier age than a man, hence the two-year difference. This two-year difference is not entirely a physiological consideration. Rather it is based upon the assumption that, since a woman's role is solely that of wife and mother, she can accept the responsibility of family life at a much younger age. The man is perceived as the sole (or main) breadwinner of the family and, consequently, he has to improve his earning capacity by prolonging his education and training. Thus, the legal systems in these countries have strong implications for the status of women. They perpetuate the traditional stereotyped sex-roles and deprive women of the opportunity of pursuing higher educational goals and learning advanced skills useful for the development of a career outside the home.

There are other obstacles to career-orientated women. In the Philippines, a wife can work so long as her husband does not object to her working. In Thailand, the law stipulates that the husband's approval be obtained before the wife can establish a business or engage in a profession different from the one she was engaged in at the time of her marriage.[6] In the other countries, there are no legal provisions to prevent a woman from having a career, although informal social constraints exist. On the other hand, in Singapore, and in Malaysia to a lesser extent, economic necessity has resulted in women sharing the burden of financial support of their families.

Divorce: In the Philippines, the sole Roman Catholic nation of the region, marriage is an inviolable social institution and the law does not permit divorce. However, legal separation is permissible, mainly on evidence of guilt: although adultery by the woman is a legal cause for separation for the man, the woman can file a petition for legal separation against the husband only for concubinage.

In the other countries, marriage constitutes a civil contract and consequently divorce is permissible. For Muslims, in both Indonesia and Malaysia, divorce by the husband may take place on insubstantial grounds, yet the possibilities for women to initiate divorce are limited. In Singapore and Malaysia, for non-Muslims since the 1975 Law Reform (Marriage and Divorce) Act, a marriage can be dissolved either by mutual consent or by judicial decree.[7] In Thailand, adultery is ground for divorce for the husband, but not for the wife, unless there are other grounds as well.

In all the ASEAN countries, therefore, the law is based on a double standard which permits men much more freedom than women from marriage commitments.

Property: In all these countries, the husband generally is given the power to manage and administer the conjugal property while the management of the household is bestowed upon the wife. Ownership and complete rights of a woman in respect of her separate property appear to characterize the laws in each of the countries. Marriage thus does not diminish her right of disposal of her own property. In Thailand, however, there is an important distinction. The wife's property is automatically merged with that of her husband and becomes common property. The wife is no longer free to manage or control her own property and cannot dispose of it without the consent of her husband. The only way she can circumvent this law is by declaring the property as separate property at the time of marriage and refusing to allow it to be merged with the conjugal property.[8]

Inheritance: In Singapore and Malaysia (for non-Muslims), if a husband dies intestate, the wife is entitled to one-third of the estate if he leaves issue, and half if he leaves no issue. But if a woman dies intestate, the husband is entitled to the whole of her estate. In the Philippines, there is no inequality of treatment in inheritance based on sex. In addition, in Thailand a woman cannot enter into a legal agreement without the consent of her husband. And, in the Philippines, a woman cannot sue or be sued in her own name without her husband's involvement. Meanwhile, the inheritance law of Muslims is unreservedly partial towards males: a male is entitled to two shares for every one share bestowed on his sister. However, application of the rules of inheritance is rather flexible in both Indonesia and Malaysia and is governed by *Adat* (i.e. customary) law as well.

Guardianship: In the ASEAN countries, descent is normally traced through the male line and the law is accordingly partial to the father. The father either has first priority in claiming guardianship over children and property (as in Indonesia, Malaysia, Singapore and Thailand) or both parents jointly exercise parental authority but, in the case of disagreement, the father's decision prevails (as is the case in the Philippines).

To summarize, since the personal laws affecting women in regard to residence after marriage are permeated generally by patriarchal norms, they discriminate against women. This is essentially because these laws are based on the assumption that a woman's primary role is that of wife and mother and that the husband is head of the household. It is also assumed that women are inferior to men.[9]

Social Status

A commonly used indicator of the social status of women is their educational opportunities. In the field of formal education in the ASEAN countries, girls have traditionally lost out to their brothers. Since women are expected to be wives and mothers primarily, parents have frequently judged it not worth while to educate their daughters for a place in the professional or business worlds. Moreover, while women may on occasion be considered the social equals of men, they are not thought to be their intellectual equals.

Table 17.1 below indicates the percentage distribution of female student enrolment at the various levels of education for the period 1975–76. It is clear from the table that education at the primary level is almost equally available to females and males. With the exception of Indonesia, girls constitute almost 50% of the total primary-school enrolment in the region. The enrolment of females at the secondary-school level tends to decrease, while at the tertiary level a substantial decrease is evident. With the single exception of the Philippines, the proportion of female undergraduates for the other countries drops to between 28% for Indonesia and 44% for Thailand. (In 1980, the proportion of female students enrolled in tertiary-level education in Singapore rose to 33%.)

Table 17.1
Percentage Distribution of Female Student Enrolment at Various Levels of Education, 1975–76

Country	Primary	Secondary	Tertiary
Indonesia	45	36	28
Malaysia	48	41	31
Philippines	48	49	56
Singapore	47	52	28
Thailand	47	42	44

Sources: UNESCO Regional Office, *Progress of Education in the Asian Region, 1975*, quoted in UN, *Economic and Social Survey of Asia and the Pacific, 1976*, p. 55. Figures for Indonesia are obtained from the *UN Statistical Yearbook, 1976*, pp. 839–59 (cited in Aline K. Wong, 'The Changing Roles and Status of Women in ASEAN', *Contemporary Southeast Asia*, No. 2 (September 1979), p. 192).

Although the figures for female university enrolment may look impressive for less developed countries, data on the fields of study taken by women at the tertiary level indicate that the women tend to concentrate on the humanities, social sciences, education and the fine arts. Professional fields such as law and medicine, engineering and the agricultural sciences are still very much male-dominated.[10] This trend is consistent with the traditionally held view that the humanities, arts and social sciences, and education are 'appropriate' subjects for women, while the natural sciences and professional fields are suited to the 'realm' of men.[11] Girls also tend to be directed into academic or commercial streams while boys are guided into technical and professional training. The element of choice may be theoretically present but the trend is largely the result of socialization and Western-modelled education which inculcate sex-linked values and attitudes among the young.

This difference in the field of study leads to dissimilar opportunities in employment and occupation, resulting in the preponderance of women in the labour force in certain fields and their tiny, or complete lack of, representation in other fields (as discussed under economic status and employment opportunities, below). This further leads to differentiation in salaries, wages and occupational hierarchies based upon sex.

Economic Status

Although women's role in direct production has vastly expanded in the ASEAN countries, there has been virtually infinitesimal change in the cultural presumption that, for women, the reproductive role must take primacy over the productive role. This has repercussions for female labour-force participation, occupational choice, and lifetime career path and income.

In the period 1970–76, the percentage of women in the total economically active population of the ASEAN nations ranged from 30 to 40%. Specifically, the percentage levels of female labour-force participation were: Indonesia (1971), 33%; West (or peninsular) Malaysia (1970), 32%; the Philippines (1975), 34%; Singapore (1976), 31%; and Thailand (1976), 38%.[12] These percentages compare favourably with levels of female participation in the labour force in the more developed countries.

The employment situation of the female labour force is, of course, closely correlated with the relative importance of the agricultural and the manufacturing sectors in the economies of these countries. Table 17.2 indicates the percentage distribution of the economically active female population by occupational category in the ASEAN countries. It is clear that women predominate in agriculture, forestry, fishing and hunting (approximately 55 to 60%) in Indonesia, Malaysia and Thailand. At the other extreme lies Singapore which has become an almost entirely urbanized island-state in whose economy working women have assumed more modern roles. The data for the female labour force of the Philippines lie somewhere between these two extremes.

In four countries, as indicated in Table 17.3 following, women form a large proportion, from 40 to 50%, of the total number of workers employed in the manufacturing industries. (And in the exception – West Malaysia – the percentage of women workers in the manufacturing sector rose to approximately 41% in 1976.)

Although there is an indication, from the data of Tables 17.2 and 17.3, that women are increasingly participating in the most modern sectors of their countries' economies, such high levels of female participation actually reflect certain peculiarities of the industrial structures of the countries of the ASEAN region.

First, in these countries, most manufacturing industries are labour-intensive, export-orientated enterprises. In all five nations, women are primarily employed in textiles, garments, electronics, and food-processing industries, or in precisely those industries which require certain characteristics that are stereotypically 'feminine' and for which women may be considered particularly 'suitable' workers. This is so because women are considered patient, well-behaved and meticulous workers, good at tasks requiring careful attention to detail and tolerant of routine, repetitive and monotonous tasks which men abhor and shun.

Second, women's employment in such industries represents the exploitation of cheap labour as the women are paid near-subsistence wages only. (For instance, in the electronics industries of the Philippines, Malaysia and Thailand, in 1981 the starting daily (i.e. 8-hour) wage of women workers ranged between $2.12 and $2.35.) Industrial women work mainly as unskilled or semi-skilled operatives, positions for which only a minimum of training is required. Opportunities for promotion and up-grading are almost non-existent. Labour unions, if they exist at all and are not simply company unions, are in any event strictly controlled by their governments.

Third, most of the industrial investment in the ASEAN countries comes from foreign capital which has been attracted to the region by both the availability of a cheap labour pool and the host-government's 'incentives' and special concessions (whereby the outside investor commits itself to either no or only trivial 'sunk costs'). Since most of these foreign-owned industrial enterprises are the offshore operations of large multi-national corporations, they are indeed 'footloose' and, hence, the level of industrial employment provided by them is highly unstable. To take another example from the electronics industry, the structure of this industry 'requires' an expendable work-force because of fierce inter-corporate competition, the pace of technological change, the rapid saturation of markets for consumer electronics products, and so forth. The female employees, who constitute the majority of electronics industry workers, are consequently the most vulnerable to fluctuations in employment due to international market forces. For instance, during the

Table 17.2
Percentage Distribution of Economically Active Female Population by Occupational Groups, 1970–76

Occupational Groups	Indonesia (1971)	W. Malaysia (1970)	Philippines (1975)	Singapore (1976)	Thailand (1976)
Professional, technical, and related workers	2.1	4.9	9.2	11.5	3.0
Administrative and managerial workers	0.1	0.1	0.6	0.7	0.4
Clerical and related workers	0.9	3.7	5.5	25.5	1.6
Sales workers	13.5	4.7	17.2	11.4	15.2
Service workers	5.0	8.1	16.8	14.6	3.5
Agricultural, animal husbandry and forestry workers, fishermen and hunters	58.1	54.5	33.3	1.8	59.6
Production and related workers, transport equipment operators, and labourers	9.2	10.3	14.8	28.5	16.3
Workers not classifiable by occupation and persons seeking work	11.1	13.7	2.6	6.0	0.4
Total %	100	100	100	100	100
Total women	(13,686,119)	(912,661)	(5,168,000)	(286,433)	(5,360,540)

Source: International Labour Office, *Statistical Yearbook*, 1977.

Table 17.3
Percentage of Female Workers in Work-Forces of Selected Economic
Sectors, 1970–76

Economic Sector	Indonesia (1971)	W. Malaysia (1970)	Philippines (1975)	Singapore (1976)	Thailand (1976)
Agriculture, forestry, hunting and fishing	32.1	36.9	21.9	24.0	36.8
Manufacturing	42.6	29.0	46.9	40.4	50.2
Wholesale and retail trade, restaurants and hotels	43.6	18.1	57.6	30.3	52.0
Community, social and personal services	27.3	29.7	61.0	34.2	40.0

Source: International Labour Office, *Statistical Yearbook, 1977.*

1973–74 recession, approximately 15,000 workers – one-third of all electronics workers – lost their jobs in Singapore alone. Some factories in Penang, Malaysia, laid off thousands of workers, while others cut the working week to three days. The host-countries, therefore, have no effective controls over the durability and stability of the investments they so eagerly seek.[13]

Thus, although 'regional development' in ASEAN has meant that more employment opportunities have been created for women, these jobs offer low pay, few prospects of job mobility, and insecurity of job tenure; nor do they generate skills that are transferable and useful to women in obtaining better jobs elsewhere in the economy. The female-intensive industries are marginal to the host economy and, consequently, women are not integrated permanently into the mainstream economy. Further, and ironically, their social status is lowered because factory work has a low status in the ASEAN countries. As a result, factory women have to live with a lasting social stigma, their social status falls, and they even face overt hostility in the local communities from which they were recruited.

Female employment in trade and services – especially petty trade, hawking, and personal services – represents employment in the less organized, informal sectors of these economies. Traditionally, women in the ASEAN region have played very active roles in trade, whether in the cities or rural villages. In Thailand, for example, women own trading enterprises, either separately or in conjunction with their husbands. In Indonesia, the wholesale batik trade has long been the monopoly of upper-middle-class Javanese women. The traditional trading, as well as service, activities of women are reflected in the higher proportion of women in the category of wholesale and retail trade, restaurants and the hotel industry of Table 17.3.

Alternatively, the distribution of female employees in the various occupations (in Table 17.2 again) indicates that only a small number of women are engaged in professional, technical, administrative and managerial positions. It is assumed that women are not ambitious for advancement in their careers since paid employment is secondary to their primary reproductive role and since they benefit directly or vicariously from their husband's career advancement compared to which their own work is secondary and inferior. Women are also presumed to shy away from responsibility, to prefer a subordinate position where they take rather than give orders, to lack initiative, imagination and daring, and neither to need nor desire increased incomes and status, since they are only secondary contributors to family income, and family status derives principally from the husband's occupation and income. Thus, women in the ASEAN countries are generally employed in lower-paid occupations and are disadvantaged in employment as compared to men.

It is not surprising, therefore, that in the ASEAN countries women work longer and harder than men, even if not all their labour is rewarded by income or status returns. An oft-quoted UN estimate, that states that 'women perform more than three-quarters of all labour hours in the world but receive only one-tenth of all revenue', typifies women's position in the ASEAN nations.

Some Concluding Remarks

A number of important issues pertaining to the status of women have been dealt with in this paper. The statistical and other facts demonstrate that, despite the fact that the principle of equality between men and women is formally recognized in the five ASEAN countries, there still remains unequal treatment of women in law, education and employment. While it is acknowledged that the status of women is not solely determined by law, none the less the law can obstruct or accelerate the achievement of full equality for women.

The environment must also change if the laws are to be effective. This can be accomplished through better educational and training facilities for women, changes in attitude, and 'affirmative action' programmes undertaken by governments of the region. Small first steps have been taken but we have a long way to go.

Notes

1. In Thailand, the offices of village headman and district officer are barred to women. In August 1982, new government regulations were introduced which now permit women to become village chiefs and *tambon* chiefs (the next administrative level).
2. See UN-ESCAP, *Mechanisms for Promoting Integration of Women in Development in Indonesia* (prepared by Saparinah Sadli, University of Indonesia, Jakarta, 1979).
3. See, for example, Ramlah Adam, *UMNO: Organisasi dan Kegiatan Politik 1945–1951* (*Organizing for Political Change 1945–1951*) (Kota Bharu, 1978). See also Lenore Manderson, *Women, Politics, and Change: The Kaum Ibu UMNO, Malaysia, 1945–1972* (Kuala Lumpur: Oxford University Press, 1980).
4. In the Philippines, polygamous unions are allowed in the Muslim areas of the Southern Philippines. Although polygamy was declared illegal in 1970, the Muslim Code of February 1977 reinstated Muslim personal law where Muslim marriage and divorce customs were concerned. In Thailand, polygamous unions are allowed in the four southernmost provinces where the rules and regulations regarding marriage conform to Muslim laws.
5. Subsisting non-Muslim polygamous marriages are recognized.
6. A further impediment is that the husband has the final say as to where the couple should live or establish a domicile.

7. The waiting period for presenting a petition for divorce is two years from the date of marriage. However, before the petition can be taken to court, the petitioner has to bring the matrimonial dispute before a marriage tribunal/ conciliatory body. These bodies were set up in April 1982, and their main function is to attempt to patch up broken marriages. If, however, the members of the tribunal believe that the marriage cannot be saved, they issue a certificate to the aggrieved party who then goes to court to file a petition for divorce. As a matter of interest, ever since the conciliatory bodies were set up in the Federal Territory and the neighbouring town of Petaling Jaya, more women than men have come forward for help. *New Straits Times* (8 September 1982).

8. In Malaysia, for taxation purposes, a wife's separate property is deemed to be her spouse's; thus, for example, upon its sale, he is taxed – not her.

9. See Betty Jamie Chung and Ng Shui Meng, *The Status of Women in Law: A Comparison of Four Asian Countries* (Institute of Southeast Asian Studies, Singapore, Occasional Paper Series No. 49, October 1977).

10. The percentage levels of female student enrolment at the tertiary level in the humanities, fine arts and education were: Malaysia (1969), 69%; the Philippines (1972), 51%; and Thailand (1970), 43%. For Indonesia (1972), 51% of the female student enrolment at the University of Indonesia was in the arts and social sciences. For Singapore (1977), female enrolment at the two universities in the arts and social sciences was 32%; in science, 23%; and in commerce and business administration, another 23%. See Aline K. Wong, 'The Changing Roles and Status of Women in ASEAN', *Contemporary Southeast Asia*, Vol. 1, No. 2 (September 1979), p. 192.

11. In Thailand, women are still barred from the armed forces, the police, customs, and the public accountant's department.

12. Wong, op. cit., p. 183.

13. See Rachel Grossman, 'Women's Place in the Integrated Circuit', in *The Changing Role of S. E. Asian Women* (*Southeast Asia Chronicle* No. 66, January–February 1979)/Pacific Studies Center, Vol. 9, No. 5 (July–October 1978), p. 10. For an excellent analysis of women industrial workers in Malaysia and Singapore, see Linda Y. C. Lim, *Women Workers in Multinational Corporations: The Case of the Electronics Industry in Malaysia and Singapore*, Michigan Occasional Paper No. 9 (University of Michigan, Fall 1978). See also Jamilah Ariffin, 'Women at Work', *Third Eye* (November 1980), pp. 17–22.

18. Women and Transnational Corporations: The Philippine Experience

Sister Mary Soledad Perpiñan, RGS

A $1,000 advertisement placed by the Central Bank of the Philippines in *Time* magazine in September 1980 reads:

> Look to the fast-rising financial capital of Asia. The Philippines.
>   Consider its huge potential. Highly literate. English-speaking manpower. Cheap labor rates. Abundant managerial expertise. For expatriates, low maintenance and living costs – the lowest in the region.
>   Consider the significant tax incentives. Clear-cut ground for foreign investors. Guaranteed repatriation of profits . . . all amidst a proven and budding economic climate.
>   Bring your business over. And till some of the most fertile investment grounds this side of the globe.[1]

The door is wide open and the welcome warm for transnational corporations (TNCs) to take root in the 'fertile investment territory' of the Philippines.

If this is government policy, how has the TNC phenomenon affected Filipino women? In particular, what price do they have to pay in the TNC-dominated industrial, agricultural and service sectors? In what ways are they used for profits – and pleasure as well? Do Filipino women play the expected role, taking it for granted, or is there some awareness? Or even militant protest?

Before we tackle these questions, it is important to have an overview of transnational corporations and their impact on Philippine society. Against this background, we shall then focus on the exploitation of women industrial workers in the electronics and garment industries in a free trade zone; women agricultural workers and other rural/tribal women affected by the encroachment of agri-business or foreign-financed infrastructure projects; and women as promoters of TNC products, victimized by tourism and big business.

Incursion of TNCs

During the 1970s and especially after the declaration of martial law in 1972, transnational corporations proliferated in the Philippines. TNCs (defined as firms controlling assets in two or more countries and having annual sales of at least $1 billion) now number 297. Of these, 168 are US corporations, according to a study of the American Chamber of Commerce of the Philippines (May 1980). Transnational corporations in the Philippines overshadow domestic corporations with foreign equity, regional headquarters, offshore banks and representative offices.

According to World Bank reports, in 1980, foreign investment in the Philippines increased to more than five times the annual average for the previous decade. The investment promotion efforts of the Marcos administration have indeed attracted more investment from such companies as Ford, Shell, and American Can Company.[2] Until the 1960s, the Philippine economy had been dominated by the raw materials exporting sector. The roots of this extend back to the Spanish colonial period, the galleon trade of the 17th and 18th centuries, and the monopolies of cash crops in the 19th century. The switch to the American market occurred when the Philippines was handed over to the United States for $20 million.

From 1898 onwards, US firms have had easy access to Philippine minerals (gold and copper), food products (sugar and coconut) and other materials exploited for US consumption. Even though the Philippines was given political independence in 1946, this trade pattern was perpetuated by the Laurel-Langley agreement. This agreement was due to terminate in 1974 but was extended by the dictatorial powers of one-man rule. For a brief while, in the 1950s, an attempt was made to tighten the reins on the inflow of foreign goods and the outflow of dollar reserves through the enforcement of an import-substitution policy. This attempt ended in the 1960s when the World Bank and International Monetary Fund dictated an open door policy and when export-orientated industrialization was launched. This triggered an avalanche of foreign companies and financial institutions.

Impact on Philippine Society

Many studies substantiate the fact that foreign-owned corporations dominate RP (Republic of the Philippines) business, wield power, and reap handsome profits at the expense of the Filipino people.

Backed up by presidential decrees, treaties and executive agreements in their favour, TNCs have been having almost everything to their advantage. The government hopes to see a total of 21 Export Processing Zones (EPZs) or specialized industrial estates operating all over the country by 1985. Practically the whole Philippine territory will by then be converted into an industrial paradise for foreign investors.[3]

Recently, the World Bank and IMF designed a super scheme promulgating industrial and financial reforms. Immediately the RP government followed orders and, instead of protecting local industry, early in 1981 reduced tariffs, liberalized trade, and added still more investment incentives – to the consternation of local Filipino industrialists! And to make up for the loss of revenues occasioned by these additional privileges, the not-so-rich Filipinos have now been targeted to shoulder a tax increase of 50% over the 1980 levels.[4]

Contrary to the belief that foreign investments plough in capital, the RP Securities and Exchange Commission investigation shows that TNCs have been cornering peso loans. Subsidiaries of foreign corporations are treated as prime customers by domestic banks and investment houses and have advantageous credit standing in the Philippine money market.[5] For example, a comparison of foreign direct investments and foreign domestic borrowings from 1972 to 1974 reveals that foreign corporations brought in only US $5.50 for every $100 that they borrowed from local houses. Thus, rather than alleviating the situation, TNCs worsened the scarcity of loan capital for Philippine firms.[6] Furthermore, a recent University of the Philippines Law Centre study indicates that for every $1 invested by foreign corporations there was an earning of $3.58, of which $2 were repatriated while the remaining $1.58 represented income reinvested to repeat the cycle.[7]

After all these years of TNC-invasion, has there been any significant transfer of technology? Unfortunately, Filipinos have had minimal access to the secrets of the trade. Except for TNC subsidiaries, the general public has been kept ignorant about technological information. Moreover, imported technologies are inappropriate, being capital-intensive and heavily reliant on imported raw materials, equipment and supplies.

Has industrialization been hastened? The Philippines has not yet escaped from the rut of a backward agricultural economy. As a matter of fact, to this date it cannot even boast of a fully integrated steel industry. It suffers the fate of other Third World countries of being just a part of a so-called 'regional complementation scheme'. The TNCs and their allies, the World Bank and the IMF, would like the country to remain a mere source of cheap labour and raw materials.

Women in Industry

According to the preliminary report of the 1980 census of population, there are 47,914,017 Filipinos, of whom 24,028,523 are male (50.15%) and 23,885,494 female (49.85%). Only 1 million women belong to the industrial work-force; but before we seek to generalize about women industrial workers, let us use the case-study approach and begin with concrete situations.

Case Study 1: BEPZ Women Workers

BEPZ (Bataan Export Processing Zone) is an industrial estate designed to promote export manufacturing principally through the attraction of overseas investment. It is a physically enclosed enclave consisting of standard factory buildings erected in advance of demand and of a variety of services and facilities for the occupants.[8]

There are 58 export enterprises in BEPZ (as of January 1981) and the majority of these are units of transnational corporations. They enjoy the preferential treatment of: exemption from taxes and customs duties on exports and on imported machinery, raw materials and supplies; low rents (about P9 per square metre per month); full repatriation of foreign investment and profits at any time; and assistance from the RP zone authority in recruiting labour and keeping it docile.[9]

In 1979, there were 27,004 wage earners in BEPZ, of whom 90% were women. A total of P112 million went on salaries and wages that year, with an average annual pay per worker of P4,148 (or P17.28 daily, reckoned on a five-day working week). Included in this P112 million figure, however, are 6,827 non-factory workers including an unspecified number of administrative and technical personnel whose salaries, of course, are far above that of the common worker. The average wage of a factory worker actually ranges from P8 daily for casuals and apprentices to P13, with or without allowances.

In the same year, BEPZ factories realized a total production of US $116.8 million. This means a gross earning of US $5,789 – or P42,528 (at the official rate of US $1 to P7.3) – per employee. Even if the costs of raw materials, depreciation on machinery and equipment, rent, taxes, and the average annual salary of P4,148 are deducted from this amount, a tidy sum is still left over for BEPZ participating capitalists, local or foreign.[10]

Problem Areas

1) Wages are low – decidedly, since one of the most attractive features of BEPZ (or the Philippines, for that matter) for foreign investors is the low labour cost. As the EPZ Authority reported in 1978, one of the main reasons why Ford Philippines came to BEPZ is because of 'the Philippines' inexpensive labor which is less than $2 daily as against Norway's $8 an hour'.

2) Workers are kept docile and discouraged from unionizing.

3) Job insecurity is high. Lay-offs are frequent. Apprenticeship, which is paid less than the legal minimum wage, can extend for a year and even longer.

4) Workers' morale is very low. Workers suffer from lack of recreational and leisure-time activities, while there is an abnormally high percentage of women over men. Married female workers are discriminated against in employment, so abortions are frequent. Managers and supervisors take advantage of the very young working girls and exploit

them sexually. The choice is to give in or lose one's livelihood. In BEPZ it is a common phenomenon to find unwanted babies strangled to death or otherwise done away with.

Other Problems
A survey of BEPZ workers conducted in August 1980 revealed rampant violation of their rights, such as: forced overtime, oppressive quota systems, union busting, absence of safety measures, and violation of minimum wage laws. Among specific TNCs where women workers abound, the survey indicated these violations:

Monasteria Knitting, Inc. (German)
disciplinary action for failure to meet quota; two-day suspension for violation of forced overtime; workers not allowed to leave the factory even if they are ill; workers have no choice as to when to claim their vacation or sick-leave time.

Denzil Don Philippines (Australian)
forced overtime; threat of mass lay-offs was used by management to prevent workers from establishing a union.

Viron Garments Mfg Co., Inc. (Chinese/British/Filipino)
workers receive a mere P9.75 per day, less than the lawful minimum wage, while apprentices receive P9; and none of 300 or so employees receives a cost of living allowance; quota system; no vacation-leave benefits, even for workers beyond one year of service; harassment, suspension and dismissal to prevent workers from organizing a union.

*　　*　　*　　*　　*

Of all industries, electronics and garments have the largest proportion of women workers. It is therefore helpful to present two case studies of two relevant transnationals, TMX (electronics) and Triumph (garments), to particularize the plight and struggle of women industrial workers.

Electronics Industry
To avoid the rising wages occasioned by unionization and the growing labour shortage elsewhere in South East Asia, electronics firms have come to the Philippines. The country is the most attractive prospect in Asia because of a combination of factors: governmental incentives; a vast supply of young, relatively highly educated, cheap female labour; and a broad knowledge of English among the populace. However, only the labour-intensive and eye-straining assembly work has been relocated here. The initial and final testing stages, for example, are performed in the mother countries.[11]

A study conducted by the RP National Institute of Occupational Safety and Health reports that the third most dangerous industry, in terms of exposure to cancer-causing substances, is electronics. Throughout the production process, electronics workers in the Philippines are exposed to acids, solvents and gases which have various physically damaging effects, causing, for example, eye defects, cancer, lung disease, and liver and kidney troubles.

Meanwhile, the electronics industry remains one of the top non-traditional manufacturers of the Philippines, accounting for US $138.19 million of exports.[12] And the Philippines exports semiconductors to the United States, Japan, Western Europe, Canada, Singapore and Malaysia.[13]

Case Study II: TMX Philippines, Inc.

Address:	Aurora Boulevard, Quezon City
Activity:	Watch assembly
Status:	Commercial operations began January 1978
Ownership:	100% American, wholly-owned subsidiary of TMX Limited
Net sales:	₱70,440,000; net income – ₱3,134,000
Market:	Timex, Inc., Bermuda
Labour generation:	4,412 positions
Pay scale:	Job 1 (line operator) – ₱13.95/day; Job 2 (line operator) – ₱14.45; Job 3 (inspector) – ₱15.15; Job 4 (jobmaster, assistant supervisor) – ₱15.65; allowance – ₱12.30/day

Nana, a bespectacled 20 year old, has been working at TMX Philippines, Inc., for the past two years. Part of her earnings is sent home to her native province to augment her family's meagre income. A portion is set aside to help her continue her studies. Most of the girls at TMX are students. She says, 'It's very difficult; we get so tired!'

Soft Sell: Various incentives are given to the workers in order to increase productivity: on the annual awards night, prizes are given to the year's most outstanding operators on the basis of 100% attendance and performance. These operators usually have to maintain or even surpass their quotas in order to qualify. One award winner received a ₱100 gift certificate at Rustan's (a department store chain) and a plaque. Bonuses are also given to employees who do not avail themselves of their sick-leave and vacation privileges. As an extra incentive, raffles are held to determine the lucky employee who will be given the use of a Timex watch for nine months only. If the watch is lost, the worker is requested to pay the company its full value.

Hard Sell: The company also metes out 'remedial actions' to workers who are unable to measure up to its standards. A dismissal threat awaits those who fail to meet their quota. Preventive suspension is the lot of an employee suspected of being a source of trouble.

Anti-Union Activities: Workers have grounds for believing that the company takes measures to spy on activities leading to the establishment of a union. Phones are tapped and workers are prevented from attending meetings by the enforcement of overtime work whenever the company gets wind of any such happening.

Lay-Offs: Approximately 1,500 workers of the TMX facility in Quezon City were laid off in 1980. Some 321 were dismissed.[14] Workers have reason to attribute these measures to a move to make the Aurora Boulevard building merely a warehouse or an office and to concentrate on the newly inaugurated TMX plant in the Mactan Export Processing Zone.

Major Problems: Apart from low wages, Nana stated that the quota system is one of their major problems. 'They continually increase our quota. It has come to a point that we have to utilize our break periods for working just to meet the minimum required output. To make matters worse, if you do meet the quota, they raise it higher!'

Strike: Although such activity is banned by Presidential Decree 823, the TMX women workers went out on strike in late 1980 when management threatened them with another mass lay-off.

Filipino Garment Industry

The glowing reports about garment exports – ranked fourth in 1980 and worth US $302.29 million – do not represent the net benefits to the country from this industry. About 56% of the exports' value is actually comprised of imported raw materials and only 44% – the value added thanks to the Filipino garment workers, mostly women – originates in the Philippines. In other words, for every $1 exported, according to the reports, only 44c in fact constitutes export earnings.

Of these export earnings, about 30% are profits which may be repatriated to the headquarters company/mother country so that only 70% remains, from which wages and other local overhead expenses are paid. For every $1 of garment exports, therefore, the 'net benefit' to the country (in terms of incomes that are paid to Filipinos and that remain in the country) is only about 31c.

This 'net benefit' is wiped out entirely by the following: 1) low wages and harsh treatment of garment workers; 2) smuggling and transfer pricing through the 'consignment system'. The value of these two evils (which ultimately mean pure profit to the foreign companies) is estimated at twice the value of reported profits. And, for the 1972–78 period, this was placed at $296 million (₱2.2 billion) or an average of $42 million (₱303 million) per year. Profits are thus derived from two sources: 1) those from manufacturing, about 33%; 2) those from smuggling and intra-corporate transfer pricing, 67%. Meanwhile, the return on capital for every peso of compensation paid to garment workers in the Philippines has been increasing over the years. In 1974, it was a factor of ₱8.13. This means that a worker who received ₱8 a day in 1974 produced for the company ₱65/day in profits. For workers, it is a case of division. Each ₱8 gets subsequently divided into different items of expense (food, clothing, transport costs, etc.) among the members of the worker's family. For the company, it is a case of multiplication. Total profit is the product of P65 multiplied each day by the number of workers in the firm.[15]

Case Study III: Triumph International

Location: Food Terminal, Inc., Taguig, Metro Manila
Main office: Munich, West Germany
Branches: 48 branches around the globe
Capital: 100% German capital; in March 1975, it began with an initial capitalization of US $10 million
Products: Women's underwear, such as bras, girdles, panties, bikinis for export to Europe and Asian countries
Production: As of June 1979, a daily output of 10,500 pieces, 98% to Europe and 2% to the local market c/o Mondragon Industries
Net sales: P80,966,000 (1979); net income – P3.059 million
Work-force: 95% female; 5% male

Workers' Complaints: Very high quotas are imposed on the workers (e.g. 450 pieces daily). With minimum compensation, they work under very strict conditions.

Bambi, a Triumph worker, said: 'We are frequently watched by our supervisor. We are prevented from talking to each other and are always ordered to concentrate on our jobs. Whenever we commit mistakes in sewing, the bra is placed near our face and the supervisor sneers that it is as ugly as our face.'

Each time complaints are voiced, management threatens the workers with preventive suspension and termination.

There are no safety devices in the work-place. The working conditions are so bad that there is a high rate of tuberculosis: three out of every 100 workers get TB.

Workers' Struggle: The genuine trade union PMTI *(Pagkakaisa ng mga Manggagawa sa Triumph International)* has led in the collective bargaining of Triumph workers. From the start, it has been militant in fighting for the workers' rights as indicated by the following PMTI actions:

1) The 'Four Hour Strike' in July 1977, was to force management to comply with Presidential Decree 1123 and grant the workers a P60 increase in emergency allowance. Management conceded after negotiations, with military intervention, but retaliated by filing preventive suspensions against 56 workers and union officers.

2) The 'Boycott of Management Memo' in August 1978 protested against a new lunch-break rotation among the workers of one shift and obtained the maintenance of the old schedule.

3) The 'Boycott of Overtime' in October 1978 demanded an across-the-board increase of P1 daily, as provided by Presidential Decree 1389, and

succeeded in obtaining a P0.75 increase after two days of negotiation. However, management filed an unfair labour practices complaint against the union with the Ministry of Labour and Employment and pressured the union to accept an increase of only P0.50.

4) The 'Five Day Strike' took place during November–December 1978, in protest against the unbearable heat inside the factory and won the installation of an air-conditioning system. The brunt of management's ire fell on 71 officers and union members who were then placed under preventive suspension, which is tantamount to getting fired.

These examples of the Triumph workers' struggle prove the power of mass action as necessary to the enforcement of the law and of the Labour Code.[16]

Summing Up

Women industrial workers are a very small portion of the Filipino labour force: just 1 million, or a mere 5%, according to government statistics.

Discrimination: The fact that there are only 1 million women workers in industry shows that men are preferred to women in most cases because of the myth of the 'stronger sex' and the privileged position of the traditional breadwinner. Women naturally get edged out because theirs is considered to be a mere supplementary income.

However, TNCs capitalize on the women's virtues of patience and tolerance, endurance and perseverance in work that is complex and minute, as well as repetitive and monotonous. This is particularly true of the electronics and garments industries. Management thinks it is to its advantage to have a vast majority of women in an enclave like BEPZ. As one of them put it, 'We hire girls because they have less energy, are more disciplined, and are easier to control.'

In Philippine society, there are built-in cultural distinctions between men's work and women's work and prejudiced assumptions that men can do better than women. As a rule, women are given fewer chances to acquire new skills and to take a more responsible role in production. For this reason, women workers are generally relegated to the lowest rung in management's ladder.

Wages: In the Philippines, as in the rest of the world, the female sector helps depress wage levels. As competitors for jobs, they swell the labour force and, because there are more potential workers to choose from, TNCs can offer to pay less.

It is a fact that Filipino workers have the lowest wage rates in the whole of Asia-Pacific. The President of the Philippines is cognizant of this and, with pride, he once declared,

> Our country now has one of the lowest average wage levels in this part of the world . . . We intend to see to it that our export program is not placed in jeopardy at an early stage by a rapid rise in the general wage level . . .[17]

This promise he has kept faithfully.

Even for the same kind of work as men, women workers get lower wages: thus, for the same work for which a man receives ₱296 per week, the female worker receives only ₱160 or 54%.

Doubly Exploited: If both men and women are exploited by the capitalists (a workers' group estimated that in 1975 for every peso net output, a worker received ₱0.09 while the employer retained ₱0.91), women get doubly exploited. That same study reports that women workers not only have 7 hours and 16 minutes paid work but also face some 5 or more hours of unpaid labour at home each day of the work week!

Working Conditions: Among the complaints of women workers are the imposition of heavy workloads in terms of quotas, intolerable heat in garment factories, and extreme cold in electronics firms.

Women workers are given only 15 minutes to eat their dinner outside factory premises and are also timed whenever they have to go to the rest room. There is also the rampant practice of forced overtime.

Job Insecurity: Most female workers are hired on a temporary basis. In the BEPZ it is not unusual for workers to change jobs at least three times a year because of the short duration of work contracts. Avoidance of permanent workers is one way of avoiding payment of any fringe benefits and employer contributions – another tactic to increase profits!

Unionism: The high unemployment rate among women workers hampers to a large extent their attempts to get more benefits for themselves. Given their low level of educational attainment and the limited opportunities open to them, many production workers shy away from any real bargaining because the system works against them.

Presidential Decree 823, which bans strikes, prevents many workers from organizing for mass action. In the case of women, some still have the notion that unionism is men's prerogative.

Reduced Benefits: Under martial law, Presidential Decree 148 introduced the following revisions affecting women workers:

1) Maternity leave with pay was reduced from six weeks to two weeks before, and from eight weeks to four weeks after, delivery.

2) In cases of medically certified illness due to delivery, the leave may be extended without pay in the absence of unused vacation and/or sick-leave credits.

3) Payment of maternity leave is limited to the first four deliveries, in line with the government's family planning programme.

4) Setting up of special facilities for women, such as seats, separate lavatories and nurseries, is no longer required by law but left to the discretion of the Ministry of Labour and Employment (MOLE). Meantime, inspection teams from MOLE do not really see to it that the Labour Code's prescribed standards of working conditions are followed by management.

5) Finally, Presidential Decree 1202, dated 27 September 1977, integrated

maternity benefits into the Social Security system, in fact making it more difficult for workers to claim them.

Women in Agriculture

Since the majority of Filipinos live in the rural areas, it follows that most women are involved in agricultural work. They contribute about 21% of farm labour, or 36% of hired labour and 17% of unpaid family labour. They also devote much of their time to post-harvest activities. Hired female workers participate in almost all types of farm operations except land preparation and weeding.

Women peasants suffer mainly from the feudal exploitation of the entire peasant class. They are subjected to the exploitative landlord–tenant relationship, usury, price manipulation and obligatory menial service to the landlord: common abuses in rural Philippines.[18]

Like women industrial workers, female peasants also suffer discrimination. A comparison of wages of hired workers in rice production shows that males usually get higher pay except for harvesting and threshing (see Table 18.1).

Table 18.1
Wage Payments of Workers for Rice Production (in Pesos per Day per Person)

Activity	Male	Female
Land preparation	₱ 8.16	₱ 5.78
Transplanting and related tasks	9.43	8.72
Weeding	10.36	9.51
Other pre-harvest	—	3.28
Harvesting	12.86	14.32
Threshing	14.69	15.73
Other post-harvest	9.78	9.45

Source: Emmanuel Santiago, 'Women in Agriculture: A Social Accounting of Female Workshare'.

Although feudal oppression is more dominant and prevalent, the incursion of transnational corporations in the countryside has been very insidious. TNCs make their presence felt mainly through foreign investment in wood-based industries (logging, lumber), mining and processing plants, and agri-business (corporate farms and plantations of fruit, coconut, sugar, etc.), as well as through infrastructural projects (dams, roads, etc.) financed by foreign loans or some government aid programmes. In addition, some TNC products are practically forced into the hands of farmers, like farm inputs of fertilizers and pesticides, fungicides, etc., which are part and parcel of government credit programmes.

With reference to the focus of this paper, rural women relate to TNCs as agricultural workers in foreign-owned agri-business; as wives or family members of men engaged in wood-based, mining, and other TNC operations; or as members of communities affected by foreign-financed projects. Again we shall take case studies to put things across more concretely.

Case Study IV: Castle and Cooke in Mindanao

Castle & Cooke:[19]	43,700 employees; $36,500 sales per employee or total 1979 sales of $1.595 billion; profits of $700 per employee or total 1979 profits $30.1 million
RP operations:	100% American equity – Dole Philippines (DOLE-FIL) which began operations in 1963; 66% American equity – Standard Philippines Fruit Corporation (STANFILCO) which merged with Dole in May 1980
Location:	General Santos and Davao
Activities:	Growing and canning Dole pineapples, growing and exporting STANFILCO bananas
RP sales:[20]	DOLEFIL – ₱355,801,000; STANFILCO – ₱217,849,000 (both in 1979)

Nina's whole family is connected with Dole – her husband Alix and her three brothers. Her father used to work for Dole too, until he had to retire; he was given ₱3,000 ($405) severance pay.

The DOLEFIL hourly rates are as follows: cannery workers – ₱1.12, probationary; ₱1.36, under one year; ₱1.68, after one year; agricultural workers – ₱0.87, probationary; ₱1.11, under one year; ₱1.34, after one year.

Alix's first job was loading fruit. Now he loads fertilizer. His wage is ₱1.31 an hour (approximately 18 cents). Monthly take-home pay is ₱450. All Nina can buy out of his pay is rice and fish, a little milk for the four children, ages 2 to 6, occasionally some household items and clothing. 'I have debts at all the grocery stores in Polomok.' Her husband's pay is simply not enough, being far below the estimated monthly ₱1,555 that agricultural workers need to meet their basic requirements.[21] Besides, things are more expensive at the work site than in General Santos some 15 kilometres away. To get to General Santos, workers have to pay ₱2.50 in fares – but lower- and middle-level executives pay half-fare while top management personnel are given free rides.

There are also differences in the kinds of housing they get. The superintendents are housed in a country-club estate called Kalsangi and they live in style: huge modern houses with lawns, a 9-hole golf course, tennis courts, a swimming pool, and restaurant. It costs them less than $4 a month to send their children to a company school with top-notch teachers. Unlike the workers, they are provided with water and electricity. All these bounties are subsidized by DOLEFIL. Here it is a case of social welfare for the rich!

Other victims: Dolly is Nina's neighbour. She has been working in the cannery for nine years, preparing pineapples for canning and shipping. The machines rotate so fast that Dolly has had several accidents. Work is particularly difficult during the night shift from 6 p.m. to 6 a.m.

Dolly and the other women workers feel frustrated about their condition. The union is weak and the people unorganized. And there are very important matters that concern the entire community: pineapple monoculture produces soil which cannot hold water and therefore erodes; and the chemicals used for the bananas have harmful effects on the workers' health – skin rashes, respiratory ailments – and cause ecological degradation.

Tess is a packer at TADECO, Tagum Agricultural Development Corporation, a contract-grower for United Brands (United Fruit) which exports RP 'Chiquita' bananas to Japan through the Far East Fruit Co., Tokyo, and United Fruit, Japan.

Tess works in one of the ten packing houses of TADECO. She stands on her feet the whole working day, and gets P7 a day plus P110 per month living allowance, so that she can make about P300 a month. A third of this is sent to her family in the Visayas.

On Tess's leg is a large reddish, raw area, about 6'' by 2''. The chemicals sprayed on bananas accidentally fell on her leg. There are many such accidents and allergic reactions.

Tess sleeps in a bunkhouse where 100 other women are packed like sardines. Unbelievably, 24 of them share one small room, sleeping in eight sets of three-tiered bunks.[22]

Wives of Loggers

Crucial in every strike is the support the workers get not only from outside allies but above all from their own spouses. A beautiful example of such support is the story of the Palanan women.

Across the Sierra Madre by the Pacific Ocean is the logging pond of one of Bueno's enterprises, a log exporting company. The loggers established their families in the vicinity.

Having been denied wages for two years, the loggers decided to go on strike in 1978. It was important for their wives to understand the cause and co-operate as the struggle became harsher and rougher. And they did! The women resorted to making salt by boiling water from the Pacific. They carried the heavy load of salt on their heads and traversed the mountains, a three-hour trek to Palanan. There, they bartered the salt for rice which they once again carried on their heads back to the logging area. After months of trials, the loggers and their wives tasted victory.

Brave Kalinga Women
The controversial Chico River Dam, an infrastructure project backed by foreign loans and meant to benefit TNCs with hydroelectric power, gave rise to the formation of very militant women among the Kalinga-Apayao tribes. When the National Power Corporation (NPC) sent men to survey the area, the women confronted the surveyors without fear of the military present. The women did not budge even when the military started firing, shooting the ground near their feet.

Another dramatic incident took place. An inter-*barrio* (village or settlement) mass action was organized by the women. They went to Tomiangan to dismantle the NPC camps there. Carrying the tent posts, canvas, and other materials, they walked 10 kilometres to the Philippine Constabulary Camp in Bulanao, Tabuk, and laid all these at the Commander's feet as a sign of their adamant opposition to the dam.

Conclusion
In the countryside, there are the beginnings of women peasants' associations. Of primary importance are the eradication of exploitative landlord–tenant relationships and an effective solution to the land problem. Through organized action, women's groups have tasted some success.

Meanwhile, the penetration of TNCs into agri-business, mineral exploitation, logging, and other sources of raw materials has worsened the plight of the people. Rural folk and tribal groups are threatened with ejection, loss of livelihood and cultural displacement as a result of the encroachment of corporate farms and big business.

Enlightened rural women see the importance of joining the men in fighting for their God-given rights. The men more and more realize and respect the value and capability of women in the struggle for a brighter tomorrow.

Women in the Service Sector

The vast array of secretaries, accountants, bank tellers and promotional people in the air-conditioned offices of Makati have something in common with the ladies-in-waiting in the bars and beerhouses, motels and hotels in Ermita. Wittingly or unwittingly, they are all at the service of the dollar/yen/deutschmark crowd.

Let us take two issues: promotion and prostitution, not necessarily faces of the same coin.
Promotion: It is amazing how advertising firms believe in a woman's ability to sell. For almost everything under the sun, they use a woman's body – her face, her lips, her hair, her hand, her legs, her contours, whatever part of this Eve appeals . . . and next to it, a TNC product, commodity or service.

Just leaf through any newspaper or magazine or turn on the TV and you will see: Moments of Hope; Kent – fresh, cool, and mild; Indian beauties – fashionable and sensible on Bajaj scooters; that Asian smile on Singapore airlines; Maidenform bras; Longine watches; Corega for false teeth; Love without Fear cream; sunblocking Coppertone; Happy Baby food grinders; and Oh, the women love Technegas technique . . . Indeed, impact advertising has overused women to create false wants, to feed on vanity, warped tastes and preferences, to alienate culture from Third World roots and realities.

Prostitution: Society has a way of producing prostitutes out of certain objective conditions: first, a shaky economic system that makes it very difficult to eke out a living and, second, through undue government emphasis on tourism as a dollar-earning industry.

Most often naïve young ladies from the provinces are recruited to promote the industry and win profits for the vertical integration of airlines, hotels, tour agencies, etc. – a living for the joiner, the pimp, and some foreign exchange for a dollar-starved economy.

Two other forces that aggravate the situation are American militarism and Japanese imperialism. Subic Naval Base and Clark Air Base, the largest American bases outside the United States, have made whores out of thousands of Filipino women. The 503 Rest and Recreation Centers in Olongapo employ 9,053 Filipinos and about 7,000 more are found in some 500 R & R spots in Angeles City.[23]

These R & R entertainers and the rest of the 300,000 hospitality girls, massage and bath attendants, performers in sex shows, hostesses and waitresses in clubs and cocktail lounges have been legalized by Article 138 of the Philippine Labour Code as 'professionals', in line with the 'adoption of a tourism-investment incentive programme', as part of the five-year development programme of the RP government for 1978–82. Without those 'hospitality girls', the millionth tourist mark would never have been reached in 1980.

The upsurge of tourists is mainly due to the Asian phenomenon of organized sex tours from Japan. Like a second Japanese invasion, plane-loads of some 200 men each arrive for a package deal: a three-day holiday whose main attraction is 'sexploitation' of a woman of their choice. From the airport, they are whisked to a house where they can call out the number of their bedmate for the night. The women are treated shabbily – no courtesies, not even a decent meal. They are not offered supper or breakfast. Hotel personnel who clean the rooms testify to the bestiality of these nocturnal encounters.

Case Study V: World Safari Club[24]

Corporation: World Safari Club, a Japanese transnational tourism corporation with headquarters in Tokyo (Mori Building, 7–5 Ginza, Chuo-ku). The WSC president is

Raoichi Sasagawa (who fought in Leyte during World War II), a personal friend of President Marcos. At the initiative and invitation of Marcos, Sasagawa was asked to promote tourism in the Philippines; and the WSC – 'to promote international friendship and to provide unlimited hunting, fishing, and diving' – was formed in October 1980.

RP location: The entirety of Lubang Island in Mindoro; later, Bicol and Northern Mindoro areas will be opened.

WSC privileges: WSC was granted the right to develop any kind of tourism wherever it operates in the Philippines. There is no need for the WSC tourist to purchase a fishing licence or to have a license to use a gun (even if he doesn't know how to use it), nor to observe any limits in hunting wild boar, deer, etc. (But WSC tours are exclusively for Japanese citizens – no other nationals are accepted.)

Sex tourism: WSC advertising makes it quite clear that urban sex, rather than big game, is the object of the tour: 'Safari is a romantic enterprise . . . Many WSC private companions will be presented . . . Private companions are offered after your arrival in Manila. They will accompany you to the areas and take care of you personally . . . They will accompany you in meals, parties, recreations on beaches (no tipping, please) . . . hot hospitality of the beautiful Filipinas . . . WSC has a plan to develop nudist areas, resort areas. Casinos for the members in the future.'

This commercialized sex tourism, which many view as a new form of Japanese imperialism, is currently taking place in Thailand as well as the Philippines.

Women on the Warpath

Although Spanish and American colonialism projected a stereotyped image of 'Maria Clara', quiet, gentle and docile, the Filipino women have come of age, strengthened by suffering, sharp and unbreakable like steel. They have joined the men and stood their ground on equal footing, taking seriously the deeper and broader problems of the country. Because of the particularities of the Philippine situation, the semi-feudal and semi-capitalist modes of exploitation and oppression, militant women have primarily directed their attention to educating the rural women and forming the Women's Organizing Group in the countryside.

Banded together according to a common line of work (e.g. those who prepare the sugar cane for planting in one group; those who weed in another group, and so on), the different groups go about recruiting members among the rest of the rural women workers until almost 100% of the women in a community belong somewhere. Unity stems from their common economic problems and their desire to alleviate their condition. Meetings are regularly held to discuss and resolve problems. The members help one another to understand the local sitution and its relation to the problem of the entire Filipino people. Members also launch self-help projects to earn additional income. There is much genuine caring and sharing in the women's groups throughout the country.

Tribal women are organized along similar lines. When an important issue springs up, it is not difficult to mobilize these women for concerted action as in the case of the Kalinga-Apayao women.

In the industrial areas, more and more women belong to genuine trade unions. They take the study sessions seriously and, knowing the whys and wherefores of how things came to be, they take up the fight, go on strike, and remain undaunted in the face of threats and harassment.

For both peasants and workers, getting to know the facts and figures and understanding the implications are important steps towards changing their lot. Therefore, a publication such as *IBON*[25] is an effective way of tackling the problems posed by TNCs. Nothing convinces as strongly as indisputable data. And teaching people to become critical and analytical gives them the skill with which they can handle the present and map out the future.

Most militant in the cities are the student groups. They are ever on the alert to pick up nationalist and anti-imperialist issues.

As for sex tours, a new movement has spontaneously emerged not only on a national but even on an international level: the Third World Movement Against the Exploitation of Women (TW-MAE-W).[26] Early in 1981 a synchronized protest against Japanese sex tours took place in the ASEAN cities visited by Prime Minister Zenko Suzuki.

The supra-national network of transnational corporations is so strong and far-reaching that it can only be toppled by Third World peoples in solidarity among themselves and with their allies in the First World.

One such endeavour is BALAI (Building Asian Links Against Imperialism).[27] This fellowship, through its Asian journal, works towards a responsible stewardship of God's bountiful resources in Asia.

If the women in the Philippines and the world over can unite for the cause of the oppressed and the deprived, then we can look forward to a promising dawn.

Notes

1. *Time* (29 September 1980).
2. 'Political and Administrative Bases for Economic Policy in the Philippines', World Bank (November 1980).
3. E. P. Patanne, 'EPZ Spells Opportunity', *Mabuhay*.
4. *Bulletin Today* (13 February 1981).
5. *Daily Express* (10 May 1980).
6. Edberto Villegas, 'Foreign Investments and the Multinational Corporations', 1978.
7. 'The Impact of Transnational Corporations in the Philippines', University of the Philippines Law Centre (1978).
8. W. Bredo, *Industrial Estates: A Tool for Industrialization*.
9. 'Free Trade Zones', *IBON*, 24 (July 1979).
10. 'Primer on Industrial Estates', *IBON* (1980).
11. 'Electronics', *IBON*, 47 (31 July 1980).
12. *Business Day* (30 January 1981).
13. *Times Journal* (3 February 1981).
14. *Business Day* (21 July 1980).
15. 'Bonded Villages', *IBON*, 29 (30 October 1979).
16. 'Women Workers', *IBON*, 54 (15 November 1980).
17. President Ferdinand Marcos, Address on the Silver Anniversary of the Central Bank of the Republic of the Philippines (14 January 1974).
18. Ben and Nile Langaan, 'Squatters in Their Own Land' (May 1980).
19. *Forbes* (26 May 1980).
20. *SEC-Business Day*, *1000 Top Corporations in the Philippines* (1980).
21. 'Wages', *IBON*, 40 (15 April 1980).
22. ICL Research Team, *The Human Cost of Bananas*.
23. Belen A. Tabuas, 'Olongapo's R & R Industry'.
24. Notes on the World Safari Club (1981).
25. IBON was founded in 1977 as a non-profit research and educational resource to meet the needs of community organizers and seminar facilitators in the Philippines. Sister Mary Soledad Perpiñan, the author of this chapter, is the contact person for the organization.
26. *TW-MAE-W Action Bulletin* (January 1980, and March 1980).
27. *BALAI Asian Journal* (December 1980, and March 1981).

19. Boycott

Abraham F. Sarmiento

The United Democratic Opposition (UNIDO) urged a boycott of the presidential election held in the Philippines on 16 June 1981. The effectiveness of the boycott is evident in the data which show that the votes obtained by President Marcos were less than the combined total of boycott and non-Marcos votes. UNIDO meant active non-voting – staying at home – in its call for a boycott; but for those who felt pressured to go to the polls on election day, UNIDO suggested that they write in the name of an opponent of Marcos or cast a blank or deliberately defaced ballot. Major newspapers abroad called the election a 'sham election' because of the UNIDO boycott.

Genuine democracy is founded on free, honest and orderly elections which allow the people to choose their leaders freely. Without such elections, those in power can become tyrants and impose their will on the nation by force. Through rigged elections, plebiscites and referendums, they then perpetuate themselves in office.

Boycott is a proper weapon which the people can wield to fight oppression and strive for the restoration of their rights. Boycott can take many forms. When workers strive to protect their rights, that is a form of boycott. Consumers can refuse to patronize greedy, dishonest and corrupt shops and business establishments. Students may boycott classes to force educational institutions to reduce tuition fees, restore academic freedom, or respect faculty and student rights. Newspapers may be boycotted if they abet the suppression of press freedom. Non-payment of taxes to protest against excessive taxation or the extravagant misuse of taxes is a variation of boycott.

The boycott weapon is thus available to citizens in a wide variety of circumstances: to fight abuse, injustice or tyranny by government officials, and to express public indignation in the hope of bringing about redress and needed change.

Boycott has been accepted as a legitimate practice around the world. Many countries, member-states of the United Nations (including the United States and the Soviet Union), have resorted to the boycott of meetings to protest against an injustice done to them or to other members of the UN. The United States, as well as other nations, boycotted the

Moscow Olympics in 1980 in protest against the Soviet invasion of Afghanistan. Lawmakers in many countries have boycotted sessions of the legislature or its committees in protest against injustices done to minority parties or for other justifiable causes. The boycott movement led by UNIDO during the 1981 presidential elections in the Philippines – like other boycotts cited above – is akin to a practice known as civil disobedience.

In his essay, 'Civil Disobedience and the Rule of Law' (1969), Francisco I. Chavez defined civil disobedience as

> the voluntary or willful disregard or violation of a plainly valid law, ordinance, court order, rule, regulation or the manner of implementation and execution thereof, usually in a non-violent manner, considered by the civil 'disobedient' as indifferent or unjust and for which violation the 'disobedient' is more than willing to accept and take the concomitant penalty the law attaches therefor.

Civil disobedience does not violate the rule of law because

> while one violates a law which one considers unjust in fulfillment of his moral duty, yet he vindicates it when he takes the penalty in fulfillment of his legal obligation. The object of the civil disobedience does not end upon the violation of the law protested against but rather his goal is to sear or awaken the attention of the community to the unjustness of such law and to the superior morality of his acts to justify it.

In fact, civil disobedience assumes the nature of a constitutional right. Thus, Chavez argues in his essay as follows:

> If in the history of labor, strikes were considered unlawful, in the course of time the law has not only tolerated but more importantly has recognized the right to strike without damage to the rule of law. This is because the law on its part had set down definite regulations, limitations and modes in the conduct of strikes. By analogy, applying similar regulations and restrictions in the conduct of strikes and by the observance of laid down criteria, the law could allow room for the recognition of the constitutional right of civil disobedience.

The righteousness of civil disobedience was preached and practised by Henry David Thoreau, who influenced Leo Tolstoy and Mahatma Gandhi. In his celebrated essay, 'Civil Disobedience', Thoreau held that it is not enough to be law-abiding. A citizen has a right to demand of the law that it be just, and to break it if it is not.

> . . . when the state does wrong, it is the duty of the individual to resist it – to withhold his tax, go to jail if necessary, make a protest, and refuse by all

means to cooperate in an unjust action. There will never be a really free and enlightened State until the State comes to recognize the individual as a higher and independent power, from which all of its power and authority are derived, and treats him accordingly.

Thoreau regarded civil disobedience as 'a higher form of obedience to the truth that lies within the self, out of which all social virtues must in the end be built.' He reasoned that 'whoever can discern the truth has received his commission from a higher source than the chiefest justice in the world who can discern only law.' According to Thoreau: 'The law will never make men free; it is men who have got to make the law free. They are the lovers of law and order who serve the law when the government breaks it.' Consequently, 'violent opposition to a government which enforced laws clearly opposed to basic human rights was not only excusable but the moral duty of concerned citizens.' As Thoreau said, 'individual man must resist evil, whether it appears as discrimination or in the law itself.' He believed, however, that 'force can be used justly only to make men free.'

The great Russian writer, Leo Tolstoy, advocated a means of ending a repugnant government similar to that suggested by Thoreau. In Tolstoy's essay, 'Civil Disobedience and Non-Violence', he described this as

> the simple, quiet, truthful carrying out of what you consider good and needful, quite independently of government, and whether it likes it or not. In other words, standing up for your right as a rational and free man without any concessions and compromises is the only way in which moral and human dignity can be defended.

Tolstoy's remedy included refusing to join the government 'because enlightened, good and honest people by entering the government give it moral authority which but for them it would not possess.' Moreover, 'if the government were made up entirely of that coarse element – the violators, self-seekers, and flatterers – who form its core, it would not continue to exist.'

According to Tolstoy, the attitude citizens should adopt towards the government was the following:

● If the government seeks to create an office which is a tool of oppression, the correct attitude for the citizen is: 'That is your business but we will not go to law before your instrument of oppression and we will not ourselves accept appointment to such an office.'

● If the government wishes to make court trial a mere formality in which judgement as desired by the rulers is certain, the citizen's attitude should be: 'That is your business but we will not serve as judges, or as advocates, or as jurymen.'

● If the government wishes to establish a 'state of siege' or lawlessness in which capital punishment is a natural condition of things, the citizen's attitude should be: 'That is your business but we will not participate in it and will plainly call it despotism, and capital punishment inflicted murder.'

● If the government wishes to organize cadet corps or schools in which military training is taught to strengthen repression, the citizen's attitude should be: 'That is your business but we will not teach in such schools, or send our children to them, but will educate our children as seems to us right.'

● If the government desires to reduce local government to impotence or sustain absolute rule, the citizen's attitude should be: 'We will not take part in it.'

● If the government prohibits the publication of literature that displeases the authorities, the citizen's attitude should be: 'You may seize books and punish the printers but you cannot prevent our speaking and writing, and we shall continue to do so.'

● If the government demands an oath of allegiance to the autocrat ruler, the citizen's attitude should be: 'We will not accede to what is so stupid, false and degrading.'

● If the government orders service in the army, the citizen's attitude should be: 'We will not do so because wholesale murder is as opposed to our conscience as individual murder, and above all, because the promise to murder whomsoever a commander may tell us to murder is the meanest act a man can commit.'

● If the government professes and erects a culture of idolatry, the citizen's attitude should be: 'That is your affair but we do not acknowledge idolatry and superstition, and we try to keep our people from them.'

Tolstoy believed that, if a person adopted such an attitude and was prosecuted for it, 'the government secures for him general sympathy, making him a martyr, and it undermines the foundations on which it is itself built, for in so acting, instead of protecting human rights, it itself infringes them.' He, therefore, concluded that:

> . . . it is only necessary for all those good, enlightened and moral people to act thus, and a nucleus of honest, enlightened, and moral people would form around them, united in the same thoughts and the same feelings, and to this nucleus the ever wavering crowds of average people would at once gravitate, and public opinion – the only power which subdues governments – would become evident, demanding freedom of speech, freedom of conscience, justice and humanity.

The biography of Mahatma Gandhi, released by the Indian government on the occasion of the Gandhi centennial celebration, gives an account of how non-violence was taught and carried out by this great man. It was the Rowlatt Bill, with its denial of civil liberties, which finally brought Gandhi actively into Indian politics; and, inasmuch as the Rowlatt Bill was a national issue, the struggle was to be launched on an all-India scale. Gandhi pondered what shape the struggle would take. He finally decided on the idea of *hartal* which called for a national observance of mourning or protest effected through the closing of shops and places of business. On Gandhi's call, the *hartal* was observed all over India, by Hindus and Muslims alike, and with an enthusiasm that surprised everyone.

The Indian leader roused the nation to non-cooperation. Many Indians renounced their titles and honours; lawyers gave up their practices; students left their schools and colleges; and thousands of city-born people went into the villages to spread the message of non-violent non-cooperation with the 'satanic' government to the masses, to prepare them to defy the (martial) law. The somnolent people awoke to a frenzy of courage and self-sacrifice. Women, secluded for centuries, marched in the streets with the men, thereby freeing themselves from their age-long shackles. In the wake of the massive popular reaction to Gandhi's call for non-cooperation, thousands were put in prison. Many more thousands were prepared to court arrest. And, in the end, the non-violence and non-cooperation brought liberation to the Indian people.

It is in this tradition that the UNIDO boycott of the 1981 presidential elections in the Philippines must be viewed.

20. Developing the Power of Communities to Defend Themselves: Towards a People's Security

Randolph S. David

I wish to begin this paper by asking you to listen to two songs that have recently become popular in organizing work among Filipino communities. The first one, 'Halina', is an original composition in Filipino by a young poet from the University of the Philippines, while the second, 'Tumindig Ka', is a translation by the same poet (into Tagalog, the major indigenous language in the Philippines) from the original Spanish song written by the martyred Chilean poet, Victor Jara.[1] Both songs are sung on this tape by a radical cultural group also based in the university.

Let us first listen to 'Halina'. The song consists of three short sections, each one dealing with a form of oppression in this country. Three images of oppression are projected: that of the factory worker in the person of Lina, that of Pedro the peasant, and that of Aling Maria's family exemplifying the urban poor who make their home in a garbage dump. Let me attempt a crude translation of this song, for the benefit of our non-Filipino friends here.

> Lina is a pretty young woman
> Works in the night shift of a textile factory
> Becomes a union member, joins a strike
> Suddenly there is disorder, Lina disappears
> When finally found, she is naked and dead.
>
>> Come, come everyone: let's clothe her body
>> And in our hearts, make room where Lina can rest.
>
> Pedro Pilapil is a peasant
> With no one to constantly commune with but his farm
> One day some people come to see him
> To claim his land
> Pedro resists and he is killed.
>
>> Come, come everyone, and in our hearts
>> Allow Pedro Pilapil to sow his seeds.

Aling Maria and her family live
Near a mountain of garbage
One day a bulldozer comes to demolish their home
Because tourists are coming
One more family loses its home.

> Come, come everyone, and in our hearts
> Build a new home for Aling Maria.
> Come, come everyone,
> Come, come.

What, to me, is striking about this song is not so much the way it speaks of the different forms of oppression in this country, but what it enjoins its listeners to do about it. There is absolutely no talk of redressing injustice before some court of law; no talk of bringing the oppressors before the authorities. Rather, there is a subtle hint that, since the oppressors are in authority, we are enjoined to create some space in our hearts for these victims of power, and somehow allow them to complete what they set out to do before their lives were interrupted by the oppressors.

The song does not mourn the victims of oppression; it asks the community rather to draw strength from their fate. There is no talk of seeking access to justice here; yet there is no resignation either. There is quiet rage, and an implied resolve to do something about all this when the time comes. The song leaves this question open. To some extent, an answer is provided by the Filipino translation of Victor Jara's 'Plegiara a un Labrador' (Prayer to a Worker'). This is how it goes in English:

> Stand up, look at the mountain
> Source of the wind, the sun and the water
> You who changed the course of rivers
> You who sow the flight of your soul.

> Stand up, look at your hand
> Take your brother's hand so you can grow
> We'll go together united by blood
> The future can begin today.

> Deliver us from the master who keeps us in misery
> Thy kingdom of justice and equality come
> Blow like the wind blows the wild flower of the mountain paths
> Clean the barrel of my gun like fire.

> Thy will be done at last on earth
> Give us your strength and courage to struggle
> Blow like the wind blows the wild flower of the mountain paths
> Clean the barrel of my gun like fire.

> Stand up, look at your hand
> Take your brother's hand so you can grow
> We'll go together united by blood
> Now and at the hour of our victory.
> Amen.

There is no quibbling in this song, no equivocation whatsoever about the course that justice should take. The singer tells the worker that it is to him that we all look to secure justice and equality in this world, reminding him that he has the strength to achieve this, but that he can only do so if he links up with his brother.

I am sorry if I go to great lengths to make a point, but what I have tried to bring out here is this: that the victims of power in our kind of societies today are increasingly turning to each other in their own communities to protect themselves from their oppressors. The abuses of those in power have taught them one lesson: that you cannot turn to the authorities if it is authority that oppresses you.

We are talking of access to justice in this conference, but our people have long understood that it is not access to the existing judicial system that they desire. What they desire is nothing less than to have enough power and strength of their own as communities to defend their interests against those who seek to violate them – typically through the use of 'legal', meaning official, instruments and processes.

The cause of justice is greatly enhanced by access to legal assistance: about this there can be no doubt. For justice to have any chance, however, there are some basic conditions. Firstly, one must have people who know – not just feel – that their human rights – not just their rights under the law – are being violated. Secondly, they must have both the will and the organizational capacity to bring these violations to the attention of a larger community, and to protect themselves against those who trample on their rights while their case is being heard. It is people and groups who meet these conditions who are able to make full use of legal assistance. Legal assistance does not and cannot create these conditions. The development of these basic pre-conditions for justice is the essential task that community organizers have assigned to themselves.

At no other time has this been more urgent than now, when the majority of our people confront not only private oppressors but the forces of the state itself. In the kind of societies we live in today in the Third World, we confront a state that has found common cause with the agencies of the world capitalist system. Under this arrangement, the state plays the role of foreman of its people to facilitate their exploitation and the plunder of the country's resources by world capitalism. In exchange, regimes that have long lost whatever shred of legitimacy they might have started with are kept in power.

If the oppressor is government itself, what meaning can legal recourse possibly have? When people cannot confidently turn to their own courts to press their grievances against government, then they seek alternative routes to justice. Two important routes have been opened in the Philippine case. The first involves strengthening the resolve of local communities to fight for their interests by assisting them in the collection and analysis of data to support their position, as well as providing them with forums in schools and in other organizations so that their plight may be known by a wider circle of people. In these forums, representatives of government and of corporations are typically invited to answer the charges of communities. The second route which has recently been opened is the concept of international tribunals to hear the case against dictatorships and fascist governments. Last year (1981), such a tribunal dealing with the crimes of the US-Marcos dictatorship was held in Antwerp.[2] While I doubt very much that such tribunals have any effective means for carrying out their judgements, I believe that their value lies not only in their contribution to the de-legitimization of oppressive regimes, but also in their offering some degree of protection to those communities which have been brave enough to bring their case to the attention of an international community.

The effectiveness or value of these tribunals is, however, also very much dependent on the ability and willingness of communities to unite and collectively articulate their common complaints. This, however, is a function of how well organized a community is. Two instances of displacement from lands illustrate this point very well – the first dealing with the determined struggle of the Kalingas, an organized community; and the second dealing with the plight of Christian settlers in Mindanao who are now being pushed out of their lands by agri-business.

In the remote highland communities in Northern Philippines, where Tribal Filipinos like the Kalinga and the Bontoc live, a 'peace pact' system has evolved which extends security to travellers from other villages. Under this system, a village enters into an agreement with a neighbouring village, under which the elders, speaking for their entire communities, mutually pledge to secure the lives and properties of both villages. In recent years, these bilateral peace pacts have become the model for broader multilateral peace pacts – in which several villages come together for a *bodong* to express their solidarity with one another against a perceived common threat. For the Kalinga and the Bontoc, that threat was the hydroelectric dam that the Philippine government is now building on the Chico River, using loans from the World Bank.

The government has made a very clear attempt to break an emerging united front of Igorot communities (the generic term used to refer to the Tribal Filipinos living on the Cordillera Ridge, such as the Kalinga, Bontoc, Kankanai, Ibaloi, etc.). Two tactics at least have been used, posing considerable difficulties to the beleaguered communities. First, the military contingent, sent to protect the surveyors and engineers of the construction project, included many draftees from the Bontoc villages. This meant that Bontoc Igorots were placed in a position where they had

185

to fight against Kalinga Igorots. This tactic viciously capitalizes on old inter-tribal enmities and aims to reopen ancient wounds that may have been partly healed by the peace pact system. Second, the government announced that of the four dams which have been planned for different points on the powerful Chico River, the first two – on Bontoc territory – were to be permanently shelved, leaving only the two dams to be built further downstream on Kalinga land. Such a move aimed to provide fertile ground in which to breed opportunism among the Bontoc who would now find little reason to join the concerted struggle against the dams.

Clearly, in this situation communities must now confront the forces of the state in an effort to save themselves from what they perceive to be their certain dissolution and death as coherent villages as a consequence of dislocation or resettlement. For these highland Filipinos who, in any event, have never been dependent on government institutions either to obtain their material requirements or to regulate their relationships with one another, there are no ideological dilemmas posed by the fact that the enemy here is the government itself. The Bontoc and the Kalinga have always perceived themselves to be self-reliant, autonomous and self-sustaining communities. They have asked nothing from government, except to be left alone, in peace. As one Kalinga elder eloquently put it to a high Philippine government official in a dialogue: 'God gave us our lands in Kalinga. God gave you yours in Manila. Keep to yours!'

Government, of course, will certainly not confine itself to Manila. Under its laws, all lands that have not been properly titled as private property belong to the public domain – meaning *not* that it belongs to the public, but that it belongs to the government to use and dispose of as it pleases. And these lands include all those that have been cleared, cultivated, made productive and settled by ordinary folk who, either out of ignorance or – more likely – out of a belief that people can only be stewards over the land but never its owners and possessors, did not bother to secure official titles to these lands.

Today, the plight of the Kalinga – the situation of a people who took the trouble to make land yield its bounty but now find themselves being ejected from it by a self-righteous state that has worked out its own concept of rightful property – is being repeated all over the country. But few, if any, among the Filipino lowland communities have had the solid sense of community and spontaneous outrage that the Kalinga in the North have displayed before what they perceive to be unjust encroachment by government into their lives. These lowland communities have not been as strong, in my view, primarily because the genuine ties of community have not yet really been formed. Most of these are migrant communities, peopled by settlers who left the villages of their birth to occupy lands that were just being opened up by a Philippine government that was uneasily testing the limits of its territory across virgin lands in the southern portions of the country. Thus, from the very beginning, these settlers were, in a sense, creatures of government, not only law-abiding, but also tracing their identity to the national government.

These migrant settlers came to Mindanao in 1913 and 1917, under the auspices of the American Insular Government in the Philippines, and again in the late 1930s under the sponsorship of the Philippine Commonwealth Government. Coming from the densely populated provinces of Luzon, these pioneering settlers constituted the civilian complement of a sustained 'pacification' campaign of the Muslim-populated parts of the country. In a very large sense, therefore, they were used as artefacts or instruments of the Manila-based central government. Today, they have outlived their former usefulness. The lands they have cleared have become attractive sites for corporate cash-crop plantations. A few of these lands were applied for as original homesteads, and therefore are properly titled. But the great majority consisted of raw land that was cleared but remained in the account books as public domain or, worse, had already been claimed by enterprising individuals who had access to the land-titling system.

In any event, such communities have not managed to develop the requisite sense of community that could allow them to put up a sustained and concerted defence against the systematic violation of their rights as human beings by agencies of the state itself. They have become so used to regarding the state as the exclusive protector of their rights as citizens that they crumble now that they have to face the same state as their oppressor.

A concept of the people's security must provide a way out of this dilemma.

Political scientists often tell us that our basic problem in the former colonies is that we have not completed the task of nation building. The concept of citizenship, they say, is underdeveloped. People still see themselves primarily as members of families, of clans, of tribes, of ethnic or linguistic communities, never as citizens of one nation. To a certain extent this is probably true in a country like the Philippines. But it is understandable that ethnic and tribal identities continue to be vibrant, for our people's progress into nationhood was interrupted at different points by colonialism. The nation under central government, therefore, could not properly be seen as the embodiment of our people's aspirations and interests. Today, under an authoritarian regime, manned by leaders who seem to owe their power to foreign governments and corporate interests, Filipinos are more than ever undecided as to whether their state is their defender and spokesman or the foreman of some foreign interest. In the context of such uncertainty, communities are beginning to fortify themselves, and are discovering or rediscovering that true security must begin from very strong communities, and that a unified nation can only be formed from solid and strong communities which are in a position to hold national leaders who make decisions in their name accountable.

In other words, the concept of a people's security must include provisions for communities which have to defend themselves against an unjust and oppressive state. This has become especially urgent in the face of the proliferation of repressive governments which, in the name of development, habitually set aside the rights of their own people to accommodate big corporate interests and ambitious development schemes.

Notes

1. Victor Jara, as folklorist and popular guitarist, became a symbol of the Popular Unity Government of Salvador Allende (1970–73). When the military coup occurred on 11 September 1973, Victor Jara was trapped with professors and students at the Technical University in Santiago (where Jara was scheduled to sing that day at the opening of an exhibition on the horrors of civil war and fascism). Taken with other prisoners to the main soccer stadium in Santiago, Jara insisted on singing to maintain the morale of his fellow detainees. Soldiers thereupon broke the fingers of both of Jara's hands and, two days later, machine-gunned him to death.
2. On the same model as the earlier international non-governmental inquiries of the Bertrand Russell Tribunal, the Lelio Basso Foundation and the International League for the Rights and Liberation of Peoples (both in Rome) organized the Permanent Peoples' Tribunal in 1979. In 1981, this tribunal held hearings at Antwerp on the Marcos dictatorship and United States involvement therein. A copy of the proceedings is available at the Human Rights Internet in Washington, DC.

21. The Work of CGRS in Developing People's Resources

Wanee Bangprapha

The Co-ordinating Group for Religion in Society (CGRS) is composed of priests and laymen from the Buddhist, Catholic and Protestant religions who share a belief in non-violence, and feel that religion and spiritual values have a central role to play in the development of Thai society.

CGRS was founded early in 1976, and during the first nine months of its existence worked on an *ad hoc* basis, co-ordinating the development activities of different religious groups in Thai society.

After the bloody events and coup on 6 October 1976, many members of CGRS became extremely concerned about the conflicts that seemed to be tearing Thai society apart, conflicts inconsistent with any religious principles. Extreme repression and oppression were occurring at that time, yet virtually no organization had the courage to stand up for its belief in basic human justice, even though more than 10,000 people had been arrested and languished in jail without trial, the press was muzzled, and other rights were suppressed.

We thus felt that it was our responsibility and duty to stand up for what we believed in, to help those who were suffering because of the conflicts in the society, and to struggle for greater justice and human rights.

For more than two years of its existence, therefore, emergency human rights activities became the central function of CGRS; it struggled openly and publicly at many levels, despite the insecurity of the political situation and the harassment and arrest of committee members and staff. In addition to providing material and human assistance to prisoners and their families, CGRS carried on a campaign for the release of all political prisoners and for the abolition of unjust laws.

Since the middle of 1979, as most of those who had been arrested in 1976 were freed, and many of the more severe laws or decrees rescinded, CGRS has expanded its activities from human rights work to development work in the rural and urban areas in order to fight against the root causes of human rights violations and oppression.

Developing People's Resources and Grassroots Work in Rural Areas

In 1979, CGRS started grassroots work by supporting indigenous rural development groups in a nutrition programme for children (called the 'To Our Little Brothers Programme'). In 1980 it began setting up rice co-operatives, producing micro media for the grassroots level, and organizing slum people for their own development. In 1981, CGRS started its work on child labour, which is a serious problem ignored by the public. Throughout, the Co-ordinating Group has carried on its co-ordinating work between religious organizations, enabling them to work together for the reduction of suffering in society, in accordance with the basic principles of all religions.

In all these activities, CGRS plays a catalytic and co-ordinating role, encouraging and educating people to realize their own rights and to join hands in the struggle and solve their own problems for a better and more just society.

Most Thai people are farmers and most farmers face serious problems of subsistence. These problems include: lack of knowledge, technology and funds to improve their production; the high price of fertilizers (they often have to devote 15 to 17% of their low annual income[1] to fertilizers); and an inadequate irrigation system (in 1975 it was estimated that, of potential agricultural land, only 4% was adequately irrigated), resulting in droughts and floods every two to three years which cause great loss of production. All these problems result in Thai farmers being heavily in debt, and facing the loss of their rights to their own land, and even starvation. Added to this, farmers and those who live in rural areas do not receive enough governmental services, whether social services (e.g. education or public health) or economic services (e.g. marketing information, appropriate technology, and government-set crop prices at a level to bring a decent return). Most important of all, farmers are denied the rights to organize and bargain collectively. For example, during the 'democracy period' (October 1973 to October 1976) 27 farmer leaders were assassinated and nine more were arrested or detained. Three years later, another two farmer leaders were assassinated as well.

While investigating the seriousness of these problems, CGRS members realized that the promotion of rural development provided another way of adapting basic religious principles to strengthen the people economically and politically, while promoting non-violent action. Thus in 1979 CGRS started supporting dedicated individuals and groups who struggled to improve their lives. We work with these individuals and groups according to the following principles: 1) supporting religious or community-based development groups that are currently receiving no assistance from any organization yet which have a clear long-term objective which emphasizes the active participation of local people, full utilization of local resources, and the aim of being self-reliant in the future; and 2) providing urban-based support services for the rural groups involved. Such services include: contacting government officials; arranging for 'experts' from the towns to help the groups tackle particular problems; providing books, documents and other educational materials; helping the groups if they face problems from officials or other influential people (through legal assistance, publicity in the mass media, etc.); helping the groups obtain support from other Thai organizations; and, finally, by providing small amounts of money to the groups if this is absolutely essential. But we do not believe that development is produced by money.

Along with activities in the rural areas, CGRS tries to conscientize town dwellers concerning the problems the rural population faces and encourage them to help both directly and indirectly.

Thus, CGRS grassroots work in the rural areas has operated in the following activities: 1) a nutrition programme for children; 2) establishing rice co-operatives (including reinstituting a traditional Buddhist ceremony) for the benefit of the local people; and 3) producing and disseminating micro media for education among Thai villagers.

The Nutrition Programme for Children

Since 1979, the Co-ordinating Group has focused on the problem of malnutrition as the main emphasis of its rural development work, because malnutrition is currently one of the most serious problems in Thailand and a concrete problem facing rural people every day.

Thailand traditionally has been called 'The Rice Bowl of the East' because it has always exported a large amount of rice and other food products. None the less Thai people suffer from malnutrition. Malnutrition is especially severe among pre-school children, and causes the death of approximately 50,000 each year. Yet in 1977, 2.9 million metric tons – which could feed 17.6 million Thais – were exported. And in March 1979, the director of the Nutrition Research Institute of Mahidol University disclosed that, of 7 million Thai children (up to 5 years of age), 4 million – approximately 60% – suffered from malnutrition of the first or second degree, while another 200,000 suffered more acute malnutrition and needed immediate medical care.

This malnutrition problem is undoubtedly closely related to the political and economic structure of the country and to the Thai government's development policy, which for the last two decades has stressed industrial development in urban and suburban areas, neglecting the rural population.

In working to solve this problem, CGRS hopes that villagers will come to understand these root causes of their poverty, and thus gain clearer direction for other activities towards self-reliance.

At the village level, after identifying villages facing severe malnutrition problems, CGRS seeks out village leaders who will carry out the anti-malnutrition project in the schools (run by the teachers), in the village's children's centres, or in the temples (run by monks). A local committee, made up of village leaders working with teachers or monks, then organizes groups of villagers who voluntarily prepare food for children free of charge with support from CGRS. CGRS also organizes a public information campaign, with the co-operation of village organizations and students' clubs, focused on children. This campaign, through exhibitions, pamphlets, poster sets and a slide show, is aimed at educating the public on malnutrition problems and gaining their participation in helping to solve them, including wherever possible small financial contributions. At the same time, the CGRS campaign is directed at the urban people, seeking financial donations from them as well, once they realize the magnitude of this rural problem and their responsibility for it (since they are among the causes of malnutrition).

CGRS provides other supports, such as seminars for the exchange of experiences, etc. And, while the lunch/nutrition programme is being established, the Co-ordinating Group encourages and provides support for the villagers to undertake other activities such as an agricultural programme (e.g. to set up a rice bank or co-operative). After two to three years of financial and these other supports, CGRS hopes that the villagers can be self-reliant in their nutrition programme and that the well-being of the people has been improved.

By the end of 1980, CGRS had helped set up and support lunch and nutrition programmes in eight villages in the poverty-stricken North-east and in the South of Thailand. Approximately 1,500 undernourished children are affected by these programmes.

Setting up a Rice Co-operative and Reinstituting a Traditional Buddhist Ceremony

In December 1980, CGRS helped set up a rice co-operative in Ban Tha Mafaiwan, located on Phu Lan Ca (a small mountain range) in Kaengkhro District, Chaiyaphoom Province, in the north-east region of the country. The rice co-operative was formally initiated by the Buddhist Abbot of the village. The co-operative's purpose is twofold; to solve the problem of finding sufficient rice for consumption, especially during the rainy season when transportation is very difficult; and to provide it cheaply, thereby lessening the villagers' burden of debts. The interest on a loan runs from 50 to 80% from the time of borrowing until the following harvest (i.e. between two and eight months). Therefore, farmers have very little chance of being free from debt. On the contrary, debts continue to increase and, finally, many farmers have to sell their lands in order to retire or lessen their debts.

Mafaiwan village is a big village, accommodating some 300 families, with a population of 1,800 persons. It is inaccessible by motor vehicles during the rainy season; the only way to reach it then is by walking uphill from Kaengkhro District, a difficult climb which takes an hour or more. Originally, the villagers concentrated on dry-field rice production, but the yield was rather poor. They therefore switched several years ago to growing tapioca and maize. As a result, all rice – the dietary staple – has to be brought in from down the hill. Yet, during the rainy season, travel is especially difficult. Furthermore, if Mafaiwan villagers purchase their rice from Kaengkhro District trading centre down below, they have to pay a lot more (some 700 baht per sack, on credit); this puts those who are already poor further into debt.

The villagers planned to set up a co-operative, pooling their capital so that they could again grow rice, and in sufficient amounts to last all year round. A committee of 11 village leaders was elected to manage the new co-operative but it still lacked sufficient capital to meet the needs of the community. At this point, the Co-ordinating Group for Religion in Society agreed to support the new rice co-operative. CGRS provides its support through a campaign based on the *Phapa* ceremony, a traditional Buddhist ceremony still widely appreciated among the Thai population. Originally, the *Phapa* ceremony was somewhat similar to society-wide tithing; it stemmed from the Buddhist laymen's desire to provide the monks and their novices with their daily material needs and thus enable them to spend their lives in a manner becoming their status and perform their religious duties smoothly. This would not only preserve the good religious traditions of the people but also benefit the surrounding communities, since in olden times the Buddhist temple was both the spiritual and social centre of the community. In recent years, however, although the *Phapa* ceremony remains a popular tradition among the Buddhists, its original purpose has become corrupted or distorted – to one of erecting permanent edifices asserting the dominance and arrogance of the temple, while the surrounding communities are left in absolute poverty.

CGRS's campaign has sought to restore the ceremony to its previous function of benefiting the whole community. The campaign for *Phapa Koa* (or Rice *Phapa*) has been addressed to the urban population, asking them to donate rice, rice seed and/or money for the Mafaiwan rice co-operative. Other religious organizations and student Buddhist clubs in various Bangkok universities have warmly co-operated in CGRS's campaign; the press has also given it wide publicity, stressing the *Phapa Koa* 'ceremony' as a revitalized and functional religious approach to social needs.

Apart from raising needed capital for the rice co-operative, we also have invited 'experts' from other villages of the region which have already developed successful local co-operatives to share their ideas and experiences with the Mafaiwan people. Through such local-expert exchanges and seminars, we are encouraging the local villagers to build their own community-development grassroots network among themselves.

Producing and Disseminating Micro Media for Education among Villagers
Micro media, an alternative form of media, involve slide shows, poster

series, puppet shows, various kinds of street and community theatre, 8 and 16mm film, articles, pamphlets, leaflets, etc.

CGRS began its micro media work in 1980, to educate poor and illiterate villagers on their various problems and the possible solutions: community health and nutrition, the exploitation of the rural areas, appropriate technology, co-operatives, and so on.

The Co-ordinating Group's micro media projects are also directed to the urban population:

> 1) organizing street theatre on relevant social problems (such as the rights of women, political repression in Korea);
> 2) setting up a slides and materials centre, where micro media on different topics such as transnational co-operation, refugees, women, malnutrition problems, the labour movement, etc., can be bought, rented or borrowed for educational purposes. This centre stocks not only CGRS materials but also those produced by other organizations in Thailand and other countries;
> 3) providing training in drama, slide and materials production for groups in various universities both in Bangkok and up-country; and
> 4) supporting, by advice, technical support, or small sums of money if absolutely needed, other groups committed to producing micro media for informing and conscientizing people.

The Committee also plans soon to provide training courses for concerned villagers and rural-development workers on simplified street theatre performances and adaptations of other versions of micro media that can be used in their own educational programmes.

Grassroots Work for People in the Urban Areas

The number of slums and squatters in Bangkok is increasing, due to rural poverty and the deceleration of the city's development. (Its expansion started nearly two decades ago and enabled Bangkok to become the national focus of investment, industry, commercial activities, education, etc.) It is estimated that at least 800,000 people – some 15% of the city's population – live in some 410 slum neighbourhoods in Bangkok. Apart from poverty, unemployment, narcotics and the lack of education, one of the most important problems they face is the threat of eviction. In spite of evictions for slum clearance, however, the slums are growing rapidly in size and number and have become a big social problem.

From the 1981 survey of the National Housing Authority, it was disclosed that among the 410 slum areas there, people were already being evicted from 39 and were under eviction orders from 90 others, involving in all some 200,000 low-income people or about 25% of the slum population. The evictions were directly caused by the city development programme: construction of highways, government buildings, industrial and commercial complexes, new residential housing for middle- and upper-income families. However, even where the slum dweller rents the land under legal contract, or even owns it, and has built upon it, the highest level of compensation is between 10,000 and 20,000 baht (at 23 baht to $1, between $435 and $870).

CGRS's slum activities concentrated on the evicted and the slums under eviction orders. To help reduce or solve the problems, it is important for the slum people to understand why they are in such a situation, for them to see how their problems relate to the political and economic structure of the society, and for them to see that they all have the power to change their lives for the better and to develop their community.

The Rama IV Slum
The CGRS's slum work was launched in 1980 by aiding the Rama IV slum dwellers in Bangkok during their long struggle against eviction.

The Rama IV slum is located between Rama IV Street and the Klong-Toey Tobacco Plant. There are more than 600 families (a total of approximately 4,000 families) living in this area of 102,500 square metres. The families have lived there from 20 to 80 years. They rented the land from the Royal Crown Property Bureau. Later they faced eviction by a private construction company named Saha Krung Thep Pattana Company, Limited.

In 1965–66, nine fires suspected of being arson occurred in the Rama IV slum. Following the fires, the Royal Crown Property Bureau (RCPB) turned down the requests of the owners of the burnt houses to rebuild – with the explanation that it wanted to rent the land to the Bangkok Metropolitan Authority (BMA) which would renew the community. However, on the same day (3 January 1967) that RCPB signed the contract to rent BMA the land, the BMA immediately subleased this land without any bids to the Saha Krung Thep Pattana Company, despite the fact that the former leases of the slum dwellers were still valid. The slum dwellers were then faced with the threat of being forced to leave the land, but no definite action was taken. Then, in 1974, the Royal Crown Property Bureau directly signed a rental contract with the Company permitting it to undertake an urban renewal project on the Rama IV slum land. Because of the resistance of the slum dwellers, the private company moved slowly, mainly (like the BMA before it) issuing threats. But in 1979 the RCPB insisted that the Company move ahead with the renewal.

Thus, the Co-ordinating Group for Religion in Society together with the Credit Union Co-operatives Centre helped set up the Klong-Toey Community Development Credit Union Co-operative Ltd, as a legal body representing the Rama IV community and its demands that new leases be granted for the people's land and the entire development of the project be registered with the municipal authorities and developed in the name of this Community Co-operative. The Rama IV people also elected the members of the Community Co-operative Committee. Through such organizations, the people have learned that their problems were not merely individual problems, but the problems of the whole community; and only through unity would there be a chance of winning the struggle.

CGRS also helped the Rama IV people to hold a press conference and stage a direct action in front of the national Parliament, urging the MPs and Senators to give them justice and investigate corruption in the leasing of the land. The people themselves made five appeals to the King and Princess.

Finally, at the end of 1981, an agreement was reached whereby the Rama IV slum dwellers would not be forced to leave the land involuntarily and the company would construct new housing units for all dwellers. However, the company has since tried to avoid the high cost of constructing housing units, by giving small sums of money to individual families in order to get rid of them because it intends to build a large commercial complex and earn more money. The struggle of the Rama IV people, therefore, continues and still needs support from all concerned parties to see that the agreement is implemented.

Meanwhile, CGRS also worked with the people to improve conditions for the Rama IV community. In addition to organizing informal education for children and adults, CGRS played a catalytic role among the slum dwellers in their development activities, such as the construction of pavements and the installation of water facilities.

In order to strengthen the struggle and development work of the Rama IV slum dwellers, CGRS arranged a network among groups of slum dwellers in other communities and a group of concerned community organizers. This did a great deal to encourage people's participation in the community.

In the future, CGRS's slum work will include: 1) providing legal assistance for evicted people and those threatened; 2) informing slum people on the methods and the tactics used in evictions through various micro media programmes; 3) development work according to the people's needs as determined by them; and 4) building a network among successful and experienced slum leaders and slum people threatened by eviction.

Child Labour Activities

The Co-ordinating Group for Religion in Society is extremely concerned about the growing problem of child labour. In 1978, for example, 44% of all children aged 11–14 (which includes school age) were employed in various sectors. Due to poverty and drought in the rural areas, 200,000 child workers migrated to Bangkok, mainly from the north-east. The children were taken by their parents to the 'broker agent for labour' or the private 'job centre' which pays parents about 1,500–2,500 baht ($65–$109) per year per child. In many cases, the brokers went into the countryside themselves to search for children. These children would then be placed by the agents at various factories. (There are about 5,000 small factories located in Bangkok.) Even though it is illegal to employ children under 12 years old, many factory owners still prefer the risk since child labour is both very cheap and very easy to control. In most cases, children are not allowed to contact or correspond with their parents.

Even though there are certain kinds of work which do no harm to children, and even though child labour is inevitable in a country like Thailand, given the present socio-economic conditions, it still obstructs their personal and social development. We can discover, from newspaper reports alone, that many children in small-size factories suffer from overwork: usually ten or more hours a day, seven days a week with no holiday. They have no bargaining power against the employers who usually use violence to force them to comply. They can never bargain for better conditions of work, food and shelter, or any welfare and security. Therefore, in most factories that employ child labour, working and living conditions are very poor and unhygienic. Children usually work in a room where the temperature is very high and air circulation insufficient. The Division of Women and Children of the Labour Department reported in 1977 that each child worker has to sleep in an area averaging only 1 square metre. Most children examined were found to be physically toil-worn, ill-looking, and many had become crippled. Newspapers reported in 1978 that some had died after only three months of work.

CGRS seeks to restrict itself to a co-ordinating and catalytic role, rather than tackling problems directly itself. And on an issue like child labour, the Co-ordinating Group engages in even wider collaboration because it is a problem which concerns governmental, as well as non-governmental, organizations.

CGRS, therefore, started its work on child labour in 1981 with strong emphasis on establishing the Centre of Concern for Child Labour (CCCL) with the collaboration of another seven non-governmental organizations, including human rights, social welfare, and lawyers' groups. We also invited government members (e.g. from the Division of Women and Children) to sit on the advisory board of the CCCL.

The new centre will receive direct information from anyone who comes across illegal employment or maltreatment of children. The centre will also act as a co-ordinator with each governmental agency involved in a particular case and will take immediate action in rescuing the children, giving them physical and legal aid, finally returning them to their parents if possible or relocating them where they can develop physically and mentally. The routine services of the centre, moreover, include visiting those factories where children are legally employed and registered, to give them medical help and recreation and to provide temporary foster care in cases of need.

As a member agency of CCCL, CGRS also launched a campaign in November 1981 to mark the 32nd anniversary of the Universal Declaration of the Rights of the Child. Through radio broadcasts, press conferences, posters, mini-exhibitions, and so on, the public has been informed of the child labour situation and requested to give information on the maltreatment of child workers in neighbourhood factories.

In all the above activities, it should be stressed, the CGRS does not plan to operate alone, but, instead, to help form as many different groups as possible to take on the various functions. If any group is fully prepared to take on an activity, CGRS will drop that activity and take on others. Basically, CGRS does not want to claim credit for any achievement but would like others to feel that they have achieved the target so that they will be motivated for further struggle.

All in all, CGRS tries to ensure that there is the widest possible participation in the achievement of its objectives: reducing the suffering caused by the conflicts and the increasing polarization that exist in Thai society, and in the longer run applying the basic principles of all religions for the non-violent development of society, a development rooted in spiritual, more than materialistic, principles.

It is our deeply rooted belief that ultimately people's quality of life can only be improved if they struggle themselves for its improvement. You cannot give people freedom, satisfaction of their basic spiritual and material needs and happiness; they must take them themselves.

Note

1. Per capita annual income of agricultural workers averages 7,113 baht ($309) but in the north-east, which is the poorest region of Thailand, the World Bank reports that rural people earn only 241 baht ($10) monthly – which is one-third the national average wage.

Part IV:
Conclusions

22. Conclusions

Among the ASEAN participants in the Access to Justice Conference, the main issues of concern were the following: the powerful versus the powerless; protection of detainees; freedom of the press; the right to freedom of association; the rights of indigenous peoples and minorities; economic rights; and, lastly, the relevance of international norms on – and of intergovernmental institutions and procedures concerning – human rights.

Within the framework of these broad issues, a consensus emerged which embraced seven points.

First, repression, particularly political repression, and other violations of human rights in these five nations reflect larger (i.e. than simply national-level) structures, institutions, whole systems. And the central problem, in both politics and economics, is to find effective means for shifting power from the powerful to the powerless.

Second, political action, mass participation, and democratization are essential tools for the promotion and protection of human rights, because legal and procedural protections are by definition and in fact absent from non-democratic political systems.

Third, the economic and political dominance of the First World inhibits genuine development within the Third World. However, at the same time it is equally true that international and/or First World pressures (from both governments and non-governmental organizations based there) can prove effective in focusing attention on and then alleviating human rights abuses.

Fourth, the national situations of the five ASEAN nations (and, indeed, of most of non-Communist Asia – and Africa and Latin America as well) have much in common. The major commonalities are: a centralizing executive power; a military establishment readily tempted to displace civilian politicians, especially popularly elected legislatures; easy reliance on states of exception (i.e. martial law, state of emergency, of siege); weak civilian judiciaries and bar associations; criminal code legislation permitting harsh punishment of dissidents as 'subversives'; maldistribution of income, reflecting (and in turn causing) large inequalities in power and wealth; exploitation of the rural poor, by both the national government and foreign multinational corporations (particularly with respect to land rights); repression of indigenous minorities, and often of non-national minorities as well; and the need for basic structural reforms.

Fifth, the myths propagated by national governments – propagated by the national executive powers, really – to maintain the total political élite in power must be exposed and destroyed. Of these myths, two in particular are common: the claim that there is a conflict between, and that a trade-off is thus necessitated between, economic development and political rights; and the equally destructive myth that human rights are merely a Western liberal-democratic ('bourgeois') cultural artifact that is utterly irrelevant to the Third World.

Sixth, the linkages between human rights, development, governmental power, and participation in decision-making need to be subjected to more rigorous analysis and directed research.

Seventh, greater regional co-operation among existing non-governmental organizations on human rights issues of mutual concern is both feasible and desirable. (In fact, as a result of the ASEAN workshop, one movement has successfully established regional co-operation and another is on the way to doing so.)

Finally, on the separate issue of the relevance of international standards, institutions, and procedures to the prevailing abuses of human rights within the ASEAN nations, a problem arises which is common to much of the Third World. Initially, even among lawyers and other human rights activists within the Third World, one encounters either simple unfamiliarity or basic doubt and scepticism concerning the potential effectiveness of any resort to existing intergovernmental mechanisms. And clearly there are difficult problems of access to such institutions, arising from physical (and financial) distance from the United Nations organs, from cultural-linguistic distance from the official languages of these institutions, perhaps even from alleged 'national character' traits which inhibit disclosure of domestic violations to international scrutiny and possible condemnation. However, many of these same problems exist, albeit on a smaller scale, within their own societies. Moreover, these same human rights advocates will agree that much of what they are already doing within their own societies – whether it is legal assistance to the imprisoned, humanitarian aid to the families of victims, or research and publication on the condition of the rural poor – is directed toward forming and shaping a public opinion that will hold their own political élites to the promises laid out in the constitutions that the latter themselves have written. In a broad sense, these are all efforts to create a domestic public opinion effectively demanding that 'the law' does in fact mean something, and in particular that rulers are bound by their own rules. In the same vein, international human rights law is not a self-executing solution to the problem of abuses of human rights in the ASEAN region *or anywhere else*; it does, however, create one more arena, provide one more set of techniques, which can be employed by domestic advocates and their transnational allies for attempting what has been termed 'the mobilization of shame' in the building of a world public opinion which effectively constrains the actions of national leaderships.

It is within the above context that the ASEAN conference participants agreed that campaigns for the ratification – by their governments – of international instruments such as the new International Covenants would be useful for increasing public awareness of human rights within their own countries. Similarly, judicious appeals to the relatively less visible and controversial intergovernmental forums, such as the International Labour Organization and UNESCO, provide an alternate human rights strategy not yet sufficiently explored and exploited by the non-governmental organizations of the ASEAN region. Furthermore, the participants emphatically agreed on the importance of increasing their own domestic organizational capabilities for: fact-finding and policy-related social science research; documentation, organizational outreach, and networking; on-site inquiry, prison inspections, and trial observation; and transnational communication and publicity.

Finally, the ASEAN participants gained appreciation of the fact that, in approaching distant inter-governmental arenas, the Third World organizations do not have to do all the work themselves. Other international NGOs already exist – the International Committee of the Red Cross, the Federation Internationale des Droits de l'Homme, the International League for Human Rights, Amnesty International, and the International Commission of Jurists, to cite only the better-known ones – with both effective access to such international human rights institutions and a genuine need for the reliable information that only the intra-national groups can provide. In short, for promoting and protecting human rights internationally, a division of labour – in terms of functional specialization, co-ordination, and co-operation – is both necessary and quite feasible.

Appendix
Declaration of the Basic Duties of ASEAN Peoples and Governments

The Regional Council on Human Rights in Asia, a non-governmental organization founded in Manila on 18 February 1982, by jurists and other human rights advocates of the ASEAN countries (see *HRI Reporter*, Vol. 7, No. 3, pp. 570–1) met on the eve of Human Rights Day 1983 in Jakarta, Indonesia, 'to assess the changes that have taken place in the human rights situation since it was established, and to chart the course it should take in the coming year.' The Council issued a Statement on the Promotion of Human Rights in the ASEAN Region and a Declaration of the Basic Duties of ASEAN Peoples and Governments. We excerpt from the documents.

Statement

The Council notes with regret that the state of human rights in the ASEAN region leaves much to be desired. Some limited advances appear to have been made in some countries in the region. For example, in Malaysia, the Philippines and Thailand, the press appears to exercise more freedom and to be more balanced in its reporting of news and views. In the Philippines, there also appears to be more room for peaceful assembly and protest. But these gains are the result more of government tolerance, sometimes under pressure of foreign governments or world public opinion or of actions by people's organizations, than of a sincere recognition by the authorities concerned of the rights of the people. And the gains have been outweighed by shocking examples in some countries of the region, for example: in Indonesia, the summary extrajudicial executions of persons suspected of being common criminals; in the Philippines, the assassination of the opposition leader, former Senator Benigno S. Aquino; in Singapore, the relentless persecution of the sole opposition Member of Parliament; and in Thailand, the murder of members of the press.

Apart from these shocking events, other violations of basic individual and collective rights continue throughout the region, and the structures that breed them abide and have been strengthened. Unexplained disappearances, extra-legal executions of political dissenters, prolonged or indefinite detentions, exploitation of women, children and migrant workers, denial of workers' rights, eviction of poor communities, evacuations of villagers, oppression of minorities, denial of civil trials and judicial review, and abuses of authority – all these practices unfortunately persist. And so do the poverty, inequality, injustice, militarism, and dependent underdevelopment that foster these violations.

Laws have been enacted that legalize and institutionalize impairments or abridgements of basic rights. Lack of independence, or innovativeness or of social awareness has led the judiciary to accept these laws as valid. And human rights organizations are apprehensive that the limited gains so far attained may be lost soon, because the economic difficulties confronting the governments of the region may induce them to become even more repressive.

In this situation, the Council finds it imperative to reaffirm certain basic principles:

1. Human rights are not merely ideals or aspirations. They are claims that inhere in all persons and all peoples by virtue of their human dignity, claims that all other persons, peoples and governments have the duty to honor. The concept of human rights is universal and dynamic. It is not the exclusive property of any one people, place, or region of the world. Its content enlarges as the needs of human beings and communities expand. But at its core is always the deep recognition of the inalienable human dignity inherent in every man, woman and child.
2. Every person and every people have the right to self-directed development. The primary goal of development must be both to wipe out poverty . . . and to provide an improving quality of life in all its aspects, material and spiritual, for all the people. Consequently, authentic development cannot be attained without respect for basic individual and collective human rights.
3. Human rights are violated not only by unjust acts but also by unjust national and international structures. To work for human rights then is not only to combat instances of injustice. it is also to seek to change structures that exploit not merely individuals and peoples but nature itself. One such structure is authoritarian government that denies the right of peoples to participate in making decisions that affect their life and the future of their children.

In elaboration of these principles, the Council has adopted the 'Declaration of the Basic Duties of ASEAN Peoples and Governments'. It has furnished copies to the ASEAN Secretariat and urged all governments of the region to adopt and implement its principles . . . In the coming years, it will disseminate, and propagate and explain the Declaration to the peoples of the region.

Out of the many tasks it faces, the Council has chosen to concentrate during the coming year on a campaign to seek the release of political prisoners, particularly those detained without trial.

Declaration of the Basic Duties of ASEAN Peoples and Governments

Inspired by Asian reverence for human life and dignity which recognizes in all persons basic individual and collective rights, rights that it is the duty of other persons and governments to respect;

Moved by the wretchedness, the hunger, the pain, the suffering and the despair which engulf untold millions of Asians;

Aware that these inhuman conditions are neither predestined, inevitable nor irremediable, but mainly caused by the failure to recognize, or the refusal to respect, the individual and collective rights of Asian peoples;

Convinced that these conditions prevent or retard the transformation of social, cultural, economic and political institutions that denigrate human life and dignity, and retard the development of Asian peoples; and

Deploring the failure of most Asian governments to ratify the International Covenants on Human Rights and their protocols, and to provide effective machinery for their implementation;

The Regional Council on Human Rights in Asia adopts this declaration . . .

Article I. Basic Principles

1. It is the duty of every government to insure and protect the basic rights of all persons to life, a decent standard of living, security, identity, freedom, truth, due process of law, and justice; and of its people to existence, sovereignty, independence, self-determination, and autonomous cultural, social, economic and political development.

2. In particular, it is the duty of every government to respect, implement, enforce, guarantee, preserve and protect, at all times, the following fundamental liberties and rights of the people and ensure that such rights and liberties are incorporated in its national constitution beyond impairment or abridgement by statute or executive action:

2.01 The right to life, liberty and security of person;

2.02 The right to freedom from torture, cruel, inhuman and degrading treatment or punishment;

2.03 The right to equal protection before the law, equality before the law, and to an independent and impartial judiciary;

2.04 The right to freedom from arbitrary arrest, detention, exile, search or seizure;

2.05 The right to freedom of movement and residence;

2.06 The right to freedom of thought, conscience and religion;

2.07 The right to freedom of opinion and association;

2.08 The right to freedom of assembly and association;

and the other rights and freedoms of individuals and of peoples set forth in

● the Universal Declaration of Human Rights, International Covenant on Civil and Political Rights, and the International Covenant on Social, Economic and Cultural Rights;

● All Declarations of the General Assembly of the United Nations on particular human rights, such as, for example, the rights of peoples to self-determination, the rights of women, of children, of the disabled, and of refugees, freedom from genocide, freedom from racial discrimination, and freedom from torture;

● The Declaration and Action Program for the Establishment of a New International Economic Order and the Charter of Economic Rights and Duties of States;

● International humanitarian law, including the protocols to the Geneva Conventions of 1949;

● ILO Conventions, particularly those on the rights of workers to self organization and collective bargaining;

● The bill of rights of its own national constitution and laws, including customary law, when said rights are broader in scope than the basic rights recognized in international instruments; and

● This Declaration.

Appendix

It is likewise the duty of every government to ratify the International Covenant on Human Rights and their protocols, of the United Nations.

It is the duty of all individuals and peoples to exercise their rights and freedoms in the spirit of human solidarity, respecting and defending the rights and freedoms of others. It is likewise the duty of all individuals and peoples to assert, defend and protect their sovereignty, to preserve and enhance their culture and identity, to develop and use their native talents, abilities and resources for the betterment of society, to respect and obey the laws which accord with this Declaration, and to denounce and resist persistent violations of their basic rights and freedoms.

[The Declaration then sets out the duties of states, in detail, in the following articles:]

Article II	Peace
Article III	Independent Development
Article IV	People's Participation
Article V	Social Justice
Article VI	Education
Article VII	Mass Communications Media
Article VIII	Cultural Communities
Article IX	The Military
Article X	Torture and Similar Practices
Article XI	Public Emergencies

Human Rights Internet

HRI is an international communications network and clearinghouse on human rights, with universal coverage. Over 2,000 individuals and organizations contribute to the network.

Since accurate information is a precondition to effective action, the HRI furthers the defense of human rights through the dissemination of information; networking and outreach; and promotion of teaching and research. Internet publishes the *HRI Reporter*, the most current, comprehensive reference work in the human rights field. HRI is building a computerized data base to continually update bibliographical and organizational indexes and to facilitate information retrieval. It collects syllabi, bibliographies and other teaching resources; conducts seminars; maintains a unique library of fugitive materials (newsletters, reports, unpublished papers, pamphlets, tracts, and public documents difficult to obtain through conventional outlets); and edits an annual series of this documentation on microfiche. In addition to compiling regional directories of human rights organizations, HRI develops guides for teaching and research.

Founded in 1976 and based in Washington, D.C., HRI is a non-partisan, non-profit organization open to all who subscribe to the Universal Declaration of Human Rights.